Between Cultures

Developing Self-Identity in a World of Diversity

H. Ned Seelye AND Jacqueline Howell Wasilewski

Printed on recyclable paper

NTC Publishing Group
Lincolnwood, Illinois

To our multicultural paleolithic ancestors who still talk to us
through their inventions and through their genes.

Cover illustration by Steve Johnson and Lou Fancher.

Library of Congress Cataloging-in-Publication Data

Seelye, H. Ned.
  Between cultures : developing self-identity in a world of
diversity / H. Ned Seelye and Jacqueline Howell Wasilewski.
    p.   cm.
  ISBN 0-8442-3305-6
  1. Pluralism (Social sciences)—Psychological aspects.
2. Multiculturalism—Psychological aspects.   3. Identity
(Psychology).   4. Socialization.   I. Wasilewski, Jacqueline Howell.
II. Title.
HM276.S44   1996
306—dc20   95-38407
                                                              CIP

Published by NTC Publishing Group
4255 West Touhy Avenue
Lincolnwood (Chicago), Illinois 60646-1975, U.S.A.
© 1996 by H. Ned Seelye and Jacqueline Howell Wasilewski.

6 7 8 9 0 BC 9 8 7 6 5 4 3 2 1

Contents

Foreword *by LaDonna Harris*   xi

Acknowledgments   xv

Introduction: Multiple Roots   xvii

Part 1

Shifting Boundaries   1

CHAPTER 1

Identity Drift   3

Shipwrecks: A Parable   3

    The Pull of the Sea   4

    The Pull of the Anchors   6

      Value of "Obscure" Languages   8

Notes to Myself   10

CHAPTER 2

Boundaries of Blood   11

The Ribbons That Bind   11
  The Mix   11
  The Clan, Band, or Family   13
    What's in a Name?   14
Surviving through Diversity   15
  Biological Diversity   15
  Cultural Diversity   16
Valuing Multiculturalism   17
  The Generational Hurdle   17
  The Conformity Hurdle   18
  Diversity, A Global Resource   19
    The Limited View of the Monocultural   20
Notes to Myself   21

CHAPTER 3

Boundaries on the Map, Boundaries on the Mind   25

The Elusive Search for an Appropriate Boundary   25
  Nationality   26
  Ethnicity   30
  The Village or City   32
    **Don't Bother Me, I'm Having a Slow Century
    of It   33**
Notes to Myself   35

CHAPTER 4

Boundaries on the Body   37

Body Image   37
"Race"   38
  Race: A Social Construct   38
  The "Selective" Nature of Race   39
    Are You Full-Blooded?   41
  Race: A Biological Construct   42
Notes to Myself   44

CHAPTER 5

Boundaries on the Tongue 45

Silent Language Boundaries   45
  Blinks and Winks   *45*
  The Sound of Culture in a Sneeze   *46*
Spoken Language Boundaries   46
  Vous Parlez?   *46*
  Bilingualism, Asset or Deficit?   *49*
  Advantages of Switching between Two Languages   *51*
    Some Advantages of Being Bilingual   **51**
  Advantages of Thinking in Different Languages   *52*
  Advantages of Discussing Different Topics   *53*
  Officially Speaking   *54*
  Language and Identity   *55*
    Hyphenation as a Form of Identity   **56**
Notes to Myself   58

CHAPTER 6

Culture, The Mother of All Boundaries 61

Boundaries That Define   61
Who Knows Air? Who Knows Water?   62
  Comparing Societies   *63*
    Borrowing Cultural Innovations   **63**
    Cultures' Common Denominators   **64**
  Multiple Socialization   *66*
Culture: Invisible Tyrant or Liberating Savior?   67
Notes to Myself   71

CHAPTER 7

Boundary Strain 73

Are You Sick?   73
  Close to Madness   *73*
  Is a Rose a Rose?   *75*
Is Multiple Socialization Inherently Stressful?   75
    **The Stress of "Progress," the Strain
      of Migration**   **76**

The Distressed Cultural Refugee   77
The "You Tonto, Me Lone Ranger" Metaphor   78
Cobblers See Shoddy Shoes, Psychiatrists See Psychos:
    The Disease Metaphors   80
. . . And Educators See Dunces   81
The Marginal Man   83
Different Latitudes, Different Attitudes   84
Unusual Behavior   84
Functions of "Dysfunctional" Behavior   85
Hysteria   85
Would YOU Follow a Half-Blind Guide?   **86**
Schizoids "R" Us   86
Notes to Myself   88

CHAPTER 8

The Authentic Actor 93

Authenticity and the Theater of the Self   93
Surrounded by a Stage   93
The Idea of Consistent Personality and Role   **94**
What Do Actors Do?   95
Many Roles, Many Plays   95
What's in a Role?   96
Role Switching, A Talent We All Possess   96
The Jekyll-Hyde Phenomenon   97
Learning Role Subtleties   97
Victim! Assigned versus Assumed Roles   99
Am I Simply My Role?   101
Split Asunder   101
Is There a Me?   102
Is There a Self?   103
The Three Faces of Me   105
The Biological Me   105
The Conscious Me   105
The Me in Society   105
Notes to Myself   107

CHAPTER 9

Who Are We between Roles?   109

Authentic In-Betweenness   109
Orchestrating a Functional Self across Roles   110
  Eliciting Changes in Behavior   111
Role as Coat or as Core?   112
  Kejime   113
  Tatemae and Honne   113
  Role Redefinition and Negotiation   114
  Three Other Kinds of Selves   114
Can't Be a Cowboy in a Noh Show? But You Can Create Your
  Own Role in Your Own Show   115
  Altering Old Roles, Creating New Roles   115
  Personae   116
  Set Design   117
Many Theatrical Traditions   118
  From Bunraku to Improv   118
  Emerging Theatrical Traditions   118
  Recognizing Complex Selves   120
Notes to Myself   122

Part 2

Beyond "Fixed" Boundaries   123

CHAPTER 10

From Rat Deva to Pure Energy   125

Cosmologies of the Spirit and of the Mind   125
  The Power of Mythology   125
  Spiritual and Religious Cosmologies   126
  Finding Flexibility in Set Systems of Spirituality   127
  The Case of the Kitchen Rats   128
Classical Science Cosmologies   130
  Mechanical/Structural Metaphors   130
  Organic Systems   131

Metaphors of Pure Process   133
   So, How Do You Imagine Yourself? *134*
Notes to Myself   136

CHAPTER 11

I Am Like a Diamond   137

Metaphors That Sparkle in the Light   137
   Personal Uniqueness *137*
   Multifaceted Individuals *138*
   Teeter-Tottering between Expressiveness and Being Seen
     But Not Heard *138*
   Multifaceted Cultures *139*
Between Facets   140
   Intercultural Space *140*
   Are You Liminal? *141*
   Multiple Belongingness: The Sunflower Self *142*
Notes to Myself   145

CHAPTER 12

Imaginary Creatures, Questers, Games and Circuses   149

Exotic Visions   149
   The Dangerous *149*
   The Mysterious *150*
   The Merely Curious *150*
Metaphors of Pure Imagination   151
   The Trickster Coyote *151*
   Cognitive Complexity *151*
   The Dream Machine *152*
   The Scroobious Pip *152*
I Am a Traveler and a Tinker, Therefore I Guess   153
   The Good Guessing Way *153*
   I, Pathfinder *154*
   Don't Be a Wimp—Be Dynamic! *154*
Games and Circuses   155
   The Clown *155*
   Virtual Reality *155*
Notes to Myself   157

CHAPTER 13

Perception, Perspective, and Polyphony — 159

Kaleidoscopic Visions   159
  Perception and Multiplicity   *159*
  A Matter of Perspective   *161*
The Truth or the Beauty Quest?   161
  Truth, A Cyclops's View   *162*
  Objective Truth   *162*
  Subjective Truth   *164*
  The Beauty Way   *164*
  Do We Have to Choose Truth or Beauty?   *166*
Polyphony: A Blending of the Beauty and Truth Ways   167
  A Sunday Afternoon in Tokyo   **167**
Notes to Myself   172

CHAPTER 14

Another Metaphor, Anyone? — 175

I Ching, Therefore I Am   175
  This Century's Major Categories of Metaphors   **176**
Generating Your Metaphor of Identity: Who Am I?   177
  Check that Assumption   **182**
Some Metaphors from Japan   183

CHAPTER 15

Final Thoughts — 191

Set on a Multicultural Path   191
Afterword   194

Appendix: Why Metaphors   197
References and Further Reading   201
Index   225
About the Authors   233

Foreword

Between Cultures: Developing Self-Identity in a World of Diversity is both timely and desperately needed. The struggle for power is no longer between East and West, democracy and communism. The peoples of the world are now struggling for cultural and political autonomy. As people cry out for recognition and cultural identity, they want their place in the sun.

The lessons taught in *Between Cultures* will bring us closer to the realization of that dream. Many multicultural people are plagued by a nagging insecurity that diminishes their remarkable potential. *Between Cultures* provides an excellent means for sorting out how the stories from diverse traditions come together in our own personal lives.

How can cultural and political autonomy coexist in a larger society? At the heart of this issue is how people identify themselves and how their identity affects their opportunities to survive with dignity. Too often we yield to the labels others put on us. The reality is that each of us comes from a long line of ancestors who were raised in many different cultures. This can complicate the search for our identity. *Between Cultures* is important because it provides a peaceful and healthy way to coexist with individuals from diverse cultural backgrounds.

As cultural groups throughout the world struggle for autonomy, and as tribal and ethnic strife become the focus of unrest on nearly every continent, I believe that multicultural people—certainly tribal peoples—have a unique opportunity to make a positive contribution to our global society. This book takes a long and pioneering step toward enabling the resolution of identity conflicts.

It is not always easy to have your voice heard, because we all speak and hear through our own cultural values. Raised by my Comanche grandparents in rural Oklahoma, words and tones of voices were important and the only form of discipline we experienced. In raising my own children, I found that their Scots-Irish American father and his family used words and tones of voice very different from my Comanche relatives. I had to learn how to interpret his tones in a non-Comanche manner. Our children learned both types of communication.

During my career, I have met many people (mostly tribal people) who will literally shut off all communication when they encounter this clash of values. Instead of learning to interpret or deal with this clash, they retreat.

I identify with this book on many levels. The daughter of a Comanche mother and an Irish father, I was raised in Comanche culture by my Christian grandmother and my Eagle Medicine Man grandfather. Both of my Comanche grandparents were born to intermarriages between Comanche and Spanish or Mexican Indian captives. I married my high school sweetheart, Fred Harris, whom my family called, with some concern mitigated by amusement and affection, "poor white trash." We had three children. My youngest daughter married a lawyer whose father is Eskimo and mother is German. Their child calls me *Kaqu,* Comanche for grandmother. He calls his German grandmother *Oma.* From the age of five, my grandson has said that he belongs to "five tribes: cowboy, Comanche, Irish, Eskimo, and German." I want to help create a world where he can live comfortably in all "his tribes." I want him—and everybody's grandchildren—to find their place in the sun.

I have known both authors of *Between Cultures* for a long time. For years, Jackie Wasilewski and I have had fun while we worked and learned together; we still collaborate on many issues and I always enjoy our time together. I have also, over the years, collaborated from time to time with Ned Seelye. I know them both to be personally and professionally committed to the great promise accorded us by our multicultural heritages. They are both respected scholars and doers, and both possess an in-depth knowledge of how culture influences our lives. They have shown an extraordinary ability to work productively in multicultural situations around the globe. Their views merit a thoughtful hearing.

I recommend this marvelous book to all who want to free their own potential to live in harmony with themselves and with their brothers and sisters from other backgrounds, whatever their tribal origins. We must all confront the wonderful complexity of our multicultural heritages, just as my grandson is doing. *Between Cultures* speaks in many tones. Some are humorous, others metaphorical. Some tones inspire us to think, others to feel. But all of the tones convey respect for the reader and a commitment to insight.

LaDonna Harris
President
Americans for Indian Opportunity
Bernalillo, New Mexico, USA

Acknowledgments

It is a lot easier to read a finished book than it is to read a manuscript on its way to becoming a book. The reading is even more difficult when you are expected by the authors to critique it so that they can improve it. Because it is hard to get strangers to perform this demanding and largely thankless task, friends are pressed into service. But how can they do this without hurting the authors' feelings, they wonder? How can they let their friends, the authors, know that this or that passage or chapter left them confused or irritated? We asked our readers to be brutal. They responded bravely and candidly, and we are most grateful for this.

Theodore Fuller, Ph.D., school psychologist at the Tyler Vision Program, District of Columbia, read the very first, very rough, draft of this book. David S. Hoopes, Toby Frank, and Margaret D. Pusch, friends from Intercultural Press, read the second draft. Three people read the third draft: María Medina Seidner, of the Bilingual Education Division of the Texas Education Agency; Louise Anne Slavcoff Baird, member and secretary of the Board of Trustees of Grove City College, Pennsylvania; and Elizabeth Akiya Chestnut, research associate at the Laboratory of Anthropology (Santa Fe, New Mexico) and project director at the Indian Pueblo Cultural Center (Albuquerque, New Mexico). Elizabeth edited the manuscript with an active and discerning hand; she stalked our thoughts and expressions with Sherlock Holmes-like resolve, and commented extensively, eruditely, and helpfully. The final set of manuscript readers examined the fourth draft: Anne Knudsen, an executive editor at NTC Publishing Group, and her colleagues Richard Hagle and Paula Dempsey.

Participants in our SIETAR International workshop, Washington, D.C., June 1993, on "Authenticity and the Theater of the Self," contributed several metaphors that we have used.

Beryl Hammonds graciously allowed us to quote her poem, "I Am Not a Dark-Skinned White-Girl" (Vancouver, WA: Distinct Production, P.O. Box 1764, 1993).

LaDonna Harris, an internationally respected advocate for better opportunities for indigenous peoples, herself a member of the Comanche Tribe (and a candidate for Vice President of the United States in 1980), graciously consented to write the Foreword. As founder and president of Americans for Indian Opportunity, Harris has been on the cutting edge of initiatives to enhance the cultural, social, political, and economic self-sufficiency of Indian tribes. She works with tribal governments and peoples to develop leadership, institutions, and structures—based on traditional tribal values—that can deal with ongoing change. She has built many joint coalitions of indigenous peoples and non-Indians to address pressing issues such as how to reincorporate traditional tribal dispute-resolution methodologies into contemporary systems of government.

Introduction: Multiple Roots

Many millions of people have roots in two or more distinct cultures. These people often develop a view of the world and their place in it that has been enriched by contrasting systems of thought and affect. This enables them to see many things from fresh perspectives.

If you find yourself with each foot in a different culture, this book is for you. You may feel, sometimes, the disorientation of the shipwrecked, pulled by churning cultural currents. This book gives you an energizing approach to unraveling your own sense of self in a multicultural world.

Perhaps you came by your multicultural credentials by being raised in a home where the language or culture differed from those of the "mainstream" society. Maybe each of your parents came from a distinct culture, or you yourself are married to someone from another culture. Perhaps you are living in a culture other than your "home" culture, maybe as an immigrant or refugee, or you have lived abroad for years, maybe as part of the family of a transnational businessperson, sales rep, educator, technical aid specialist, or missionary. Perhaps you are a teacher or student in a multicultural education program, such as bilingual education, English as a second language, or foreign language programs. Perhaps you are a global nomad, a diplomat, international civil servant (UN, World Bank), or church representative. Perhaps you are the spouse or child of a global nomad, a "third-culture" or "Euro-kid," or a "military brat."

Perhaps you don't consider yourself multicultural but work or live in an atmosphere of cultural diversity. You may be a health or social service professional serving multicultural clients, a foreign student adviser, or a specialist in intercultural communication. As an educator of people of mixed national, ethnic, or racial backgrounds, or as a student who plans to go abroad for study or who is already participating in a student exchange program, you nonetheless may feel the currents of culture in your daily life.

Some people experience other cultures as a "bubble traveler," protected by their institutional support network from having to adapt to local norms. An example of "bubble travelers" are U.S. military personnel and their dependents stationed at Guantánamo Bay Naval Station in Cuba, a piece of real estate totally fenced off and isolated from the rest of the island. If you want to burst out of the bubble and enjoy the riches other cultures offer, this book may provide some ideas on how to do it. (You are *not* a "bubble traveler" if you have been in a country long enough to learn its language.)

Like many readers, you may defy categorization. Perhaps you are one of that rare breed who is moved simply by curiosity to pick up this book. Welcome to the diverse world of multicultural happenings, where things are almost always not as they seem.

Between Cultures: Developing Self-Identity in a World of Diversity attempts two things. The first is to dispel the confusion and clarify the stresses and anxieties common to those who cross or live on cultural boundaries. Even those who have lived for years in different cultures fall victim to clashes in cultural values. Things are done differently, and people think differently, but it's hard to pinpoint exactly what the differences are, and what they mean. Discerning cultural patterns can seem an unending and at times frustrating endeavor. But when a pattern emerges, it's like turning on a light in a dark room. This book will help throw that light switch on.

The second objective of the book is to help those caught between cultures craft an identity that will help them live life to the full and enjoy the riches of multiculturalism. The big drawback to being multicultural is that you do not fit into most people's pre-set categories. You are neither fish nor fowl, but both. The challenge is to be fully aware of your own complexity, and the task is to be able to articulate that complex reality to other people who do not share your same background.

Between Cultures breaks new ground. It not only captures how it feels to be adrift in a multicultural sea, but also it helps those blessed with a life of cultural diversity to find and maintain a strong sense of personal identity while rafting the whitewaters of culture.

Part 1

Shifting Boundaries

We don't have to worry much about having our world view, and especially our sense of identity, challenged by people of other cultural persuasions as long as we limit our interactions to people who think exactly like us. A dull prospect.

Living on a cultural border or crossing cultural boundaries changes that. The borders may be those of kinship, nationality, ethnicity, race, or language. As we move across a cultural border, we change our language, costumes, food preferences, and the priority of our values—and sometimes the values themselves—depending with whom we are interacting. Once we cross a border, we lose the single norm against which to judge behavior, but we gain fresh perspectives.

If you are a wealthy jet-setter, your fluency in several languages and your ability to function in different societies will be admired by many. If, on the other hand, you are a migrant farm laborer, you may discover that *your* multilingualism and *your* multiculturalism are not valued. You aren't fluent in the "right" dialects. You don't move in the "right" circles. You are often treated as if you had *no* language (only a "dialect") and *no* culture (just substandard customs).

How can we get a better grasp of the slippery things that affect the sense of self of a person who routinely lives on or crosses cultural boundaries?

Each society offers us a range of roles, and with each role a set of idealized behaviors. We are child, adolescent, adult, parent, grandparent; we are third-string football player on the high school team, winner of an essay on acid rain, college graduate; we are carpenter, Scout leader, high-rolling member of the bowling team, church volunteer. We change these roles seamlessly, even though each calls for different behavior.

1

The role switching we do in everyday life, the actors' ability to play many roles, and the ability of multicultural people to play many roles in many cultural settings are three variations on a common theme—adjusting our behavior to meet social expectations.

Who is the real person behind the various roles? How do we maintain a sense of core authenticity while we perform multiple roles? How are social truths formed? No man is an island, John Donne tells us from his early 17th-century perch on a British Isle. As we develop in complexity we are notably affected by the feedback we get from others. It is this need for social affirmation that generates the entire issue of authenticity for multicultural people.

1

Identity Drift

Shipwrecks: A Parable

Homo sapiens does get around. Our species has been perambulating about the planet since its emergence. Moved by chance, misfortune, or intent, generations upon generations have traversed the globe. Humans are found even where rattlesnakes choose not to abide.

Germans have their *Wanderjahren*. Australian Aborigines have their "walkabouts." Scots hike their northern mountains. Americans drive, hitch, or bus the "open road" cross-country at least once before settling down. The Oneida have chronicled 10,000 years of wandering about the planet (Underwood, 1993a).

Rivers and seas have powerfully channeled this wanderlust. Irish clan lands were always bordered by rivers, so each clan had access to the sea. In the 6th century, the Irish monk St. Brendan voyaged in a bowl-shaped leather boat to what is now Canada.

The Pull of the Sea

Prior to the European discovery of New Spain (modern-day Mexico), Caribbean currents in a whimsical change of mood washed a handful of shipwrecked sailors ashore. It was like a mighty baptism: they went under as Castillian sailors and emerged as neophyte Mayans.

All but two perished in their first few years of life as slaves to the Mayans. One of the survivors, Jerónimo de Aguilar, was soon slated to star in a ritual of human sacrifice. This inspired him to escape to a village where he found a leader who was content to keep him in slavery, but—and this was important to Jerónimo—alive. The other survivor, Gonzalo Guerrero, as we shall see, fared differently. These events, recounted by one of Cortés's soldiers 50 years after they took place (Díaz del Castillo, [1570], 1955), transpired not too far from what was to become—in another five centuries—the popular resort island of Cancún. This is just off the Yucatán Peninsula, that part of Mexico where immense limestone formations give rise to a flat, hot jungle land mass that juts out into the Gulf of Mexico.

Eight years after the shipwreck, Hernando Cortés made several brief landings on Yucatán and got wind of his countrymen's existence. The first clue was that the inhabitants of the peninsula, upon seeing the Europeans, called them *castila*. This sounded suspiciously like a corruption of the Spanish word *Castilla,* the kingdom of Queen Isabella. Where could the Mayans have heard that word?

Whatever other reasons he might have had for contacting his displaced countrymen (Mexico's first undocumented aliens?), Cortés was soon to realize that their linguistic skills would prove invaluable to his plans for Gold, God, and Glory. The beginning of the conquest of Mexico was just around the bend, in 1519. Cortés was told by Mayan merchants that because the shipwrecked Spaniards were slaves, it was appropriate to provide their owners with a payment. Cortés sent letters and ransoms with the merchants, and within a few days contact was made with Jerónimo's owner. After so many years as a slave, Jerónimo was looking the worse for wear. Delighted at achieving his freedom and at the prospect of reuniting himself with his countrymen, Jerónimo walked the five leagues to the village where the other living survivor of the shipwreck resided. But as much as Jerónimo de Aguilar pleaded with Gonzalo Guerrero to return with him, Gonzalo refused.

Although Gonzalo also had begun his tenure in the Yucatán as a slave, his conditions (unlike those of Jerónimo) had improved. Gonzalo had married a local woman, and they were raising their three children in a family that expressed itself in Maya, *Nan caxilok jun a lej, maltiox che la* (Mama, please pass a tortilla). When his group went to war, Gonzalo Guerrero was drafted from the reserves with the equivalent rank of captain and was appointed to a position of village leader (*cacique*). He was content where he was and had no desire to reestablish contact with his former countrymen.

Besides, he explained, he was somewhat embarrassed. "What will those Spaniards say of me when they see me going around like this!" (He had, among other accouterments, stylish Mayan facial tattoos and holes in his ears for ornaments.) Then he turned to his children and said, "Look at my children, aren't they really good looking!" He had forgotten much of his Spanish in the eight years he lived as a Mayan, and sensed—correctly—that his *paisanos* would regard him most curiously. His Mayan wife spoke up to Jerónimo: "Look, why does this slave come to get my husband? Get out and don't talk any more." Jerónimo took Gonzalo aside but couldn't budge him.

Jerónimo returned alone to join the expedition. His knowledge of Mayan language and customs, combined with his fluency in Spanish, provided the Spaniards with one of the two keys they needed for their impending conquest of Mexico.

The other key was in the bilingual head of a bright Aztec woman who was one of 20 women given to the Spaniards as an appeasing gift by Yucatán Mayans.

Malinche, as she is often called (although the Spaniards preferred to call her Doña Marina), was a Nahuatl-speaking Aztec, the product, as we would say today, of a troubled home. Born to a wealthy and politically influential family in or near Coatzacoalcos, Malinche's father died while she was a child. Her mother remarried and had a son by her second husband. The son was greatly favored over the daughter. To get rid of the daughter (there were inheritance issues), they sold her from her home into slavery to Mayans a little to the east (who in turn sold her to another Maya-speaking family in a nearby village). Little Malinche, the mother and stepfather told the neighbors, had died.

Malinche (a.k.a. Malintzin or Malinalli) was swept, metaphorically, from her Aztec moorings to land on a Mayan beachhead. She shared much with the shipwrecked Castillians. Shifting tides and changing seas inexorably pull some things into murky depths and throw others onto uncharted shores. Things and people from different realms are thrown together and mixed into recombinant forms. The pull of the sea stirs the crucible of change and creation.

By the time Cortés arrived, Malinche, grown to womanhood, spoke the languages of the two most politically powerful empires in the northern half of the Western hemisphere, the Aztec and the Mayan (empires that were ruled by councils of leaders, not by the omnipotent kings that the Spaniards imagined).

As Cortés's intrusion into Mexico progressed, Malinche would translate from Nahuatl into Maya, and Jerónimo would translate from Maya into Spanish. In due course, Malinche learned Spanish. She bore Cortés a son.

Without the multicultural gifts provided by one shipwrecked sailor and one slave girl, things might have turned out very differently for the Spaniards, and many Mexicans today wish that they had.

Prompted by the invasion of the Spaniards, Mexican Indians would have their identities challenged by a new language, a new religion, and new ways of doing many things. How is the sense of self molded in people who learn to accommodate two different sets of cultural expectations? What does it mean to function within the ground rules of new cultures? How do you act "normally" under these conditions? The two shipwrecked sailors from similar backgrounds and thrust into the same strange society made very different decisions. One was only too glad to renounce his adopted Mayan ways; the other became a contented family man and village leader among the Mayans. One felt more strongly the pull of his first culture; the other had settled into the rhythms of a second. Malinche, alienated through no fault of her own from her natal Aztec culture, as well as from the Mayan culture she was forced to adopt, threw her hat in with the newcomers.

The multicultural perspectives of Jerónimo, Gonzalo, and Malinche were put to the service of opposing cultures on the eve of a historic cataclysm. Their multicultural skills altered the course of world history.

The Pull of the Anchors

The pull exerted by each culture, sometimes stronger in one direction, sometimes in another, affects all who have to manage—consciously or unconsciously—the codes of two or more distinct cultures. You are stretched between cultures when you have been raised in a multicultural household or when you have lived for years in a second (or third) culture where you are dependent on doing things the local way if you are going to accomplish anything. This requires following the local code—truth, justice and, when in the United States, the American way (to borrow a line from Superman).

Spending a couple of weeks at the international Hotel La Campement on the outskirts of Timbuktu may not prove much of a stretch, because most of the people you meet there are doing their best to accommodate you.

Located in the middle of Mali in West Africa, Timbuktu has a population of about 20,000, three-quarters of whom are Islamic. Most inhabitants speak Bambara and/or French, but Senoufo, Sarakolle, Tuareg, and Arabic are also spoken. No red-blooded Timbuktuan expects short-term visitors to know much about them, their culture, or their language. But if your mind, as well as your body, regularly crosses cultural boundaries, and if you care about behaving more or less appropriately in each cultural setting (different latitudes, different attitudes), then you feel the pull.

Millions of people worldwide experience this pull of two or more dissimilar ways of thinking and acting as a sense of being different. Neither beast nor fowl nor fish. Kindred spirits are hard to find. In neighborhoods where provincial feelings run strong, perhaps you feel you are on a tightrope swaying between two cultures. You try not to look down, just ahead, and hope you can anticipate the pull of contradictory gravitational forces and maintain your balance.

Writing on the aftereffects of immigration, William A. Henry III, the late essayist for *Time,* characterized the feelings of some segments of U.S. society: "To study anyone's culture but one's own . . . is to commit an act of identity suicide." In a contemporary example of this fear in action, the Associated Press reports that the school board of Tavares, Florida, voted 3–2 to require schools to teach that "American culture is superior to all others."

The illusion of maintaining a superior, pristine identity begins to crack, however, when you live for some years in another culture or on a cultural boundary. In societies that are strange to you, if you want to avoid being miserable and if you want to succeed in any venture (mercantile or otherwise), you have to observe some local norms to get along. At this point, when you are enriched by profound familiarity with a second (or third) culture, getting a handle on your sense of self can become a slippery business, because your "community" of important others now includes people of quite different views of how the world works.

Travel broadens one's "neighborhood" in mind-boggling ways. A student at International Christian University in Tokyo, the daughter of a fashion designer in Paris, was raised as a small child by her grandmother in a village in Cameroon. She later continued her education in France, Brazil, and Germany, as well as in Yellow Springs, Ohio. She completed her university education in Tokyo. During this educational odyssey she lived in the *favella* of Rio de Janeiro and in housing projects in New Orleans, and she worked with autistic children in Toledo, Ohio. During her year in Tokyo she had a Dutch boyfriend.

This young woman's task of accommodating many different cultures generates a common complaint in people who find themselves living multicultural lives—they may experience difficulty feeling "authentic." People who move repeatedly across cultural boundaries often question the validity of their "self" or, alternatively, of their "selves." Who are they, they wonder. Ronnie C. Chan, a Hong Kong business tycoon who was born and raised in China and educated in the United States where he lived for 16 years, says he can "unscrew my [Chinese] head, put it in my briefcase, and screw on my American head" when the occasion warrants. One Japanese student refers to her "double personality" when she reminisces about her several years' study in the United Kingdom.

An old African-American song to which boundary crossers might resonate expresses the weariness born of a sense of distance and stateless roving: "Sometimes I feel like a motherless child / A long way from home." Where is home? If "home" is various places, if we feel a different kind of "at-homeness" in each place, and if we act differently in each place, are we the same person in each place? One European editor says that a migrant needs more than "the place of origin and the place of arrival," the boundary crosser needs a metaphor "for the processes of journeying" (Papastergiadis, 1991).

How do multicultural individuals get, and hold onto, a satisfying sense of continuity and character during their journey as they continually adjust their values and actions to accommodate people in two or more distinct societies? Some people find that link to both continuity and character through a sense of family.

Each generation is strongly influenced by the previous; we would not be who we are today without the evolving cultures to which we are heir. As we look back at our own family across one generation or many, we discover many differences in lifestyle: our ancestors thought differently, talked differently, acted differently, and lived under different cultural rules. If we look back far enough, and sometimes we do not have to go back so far, our ancestors lived in other parts of the world and survived within other cultural systems.

The next chapter explores in more detail the kinship ties that link us to the past, ties bequeathed us by our families.

Value of "Obscure" Languages

Geopolitical conditions, in a flash of gunpowder, catapult "obscure" languages to life-and-death relevancy. Aztec and Mayan were not the only strategic languages. At one point in the conquest of Mexico, conversations with Cortés traveled through four languages (Totonac to Nahuatl to Maya to Spanish, and back again). People who speak *any* second language, the languages of the former Soviet Union—Lithuanian and Georgian, to name but two—of Yugoslav Bosnia, Serbia, Slovenia, or Croatia, of Nigeria's Yoruba or Ibo or Hausa, have needed skills in global economies. There is no language too "exotic." In a recent instance, some government managers of U.S. foreign relations were looking for a speaker of Macedonian; their only speaker had recently retired.

Notes to Myself

1. One example of when I felt two cultures pulling me in different directions was when . . .: _____

_____

_____

_____

_____

_____

2. One time when a skill that I had learned in one culture helped me in another culture was when . . .: _____

_____

_____

_____

_____

_____

Boundaries of Blood

The Ribbons That Bind

Our families throughout history have separated and merged, combined and recombined in many different ways.

The Mix

For as long as Homo sapiens has been hanging around rivers and springs, men and women have lived with "significant others" from different cultural backgrounds. For most of our species' history—painted in caves or carved on rocks and mostly forgotten by us all—our ancestors lived multicultural lives. Typically, our mothers came from one part of the forest, our fathers from another. They often spoke different languages. Many groups only allowed marriage to take place with people from outside their own group, a sound genetic policy. Some tribes routinely raided other communities for women and children, often to replace their own lost in war. The Comanche of the southwestern United States and Mexico, who often captured children as well as adults and then integrated them into their communities, joke about their many-faceted ancestry. Alexander the Great paired 20,000 of his soldiers with Persian brides to consolidate a major military conquest in 324 BC. There has been enough interbreeding for as long as there have been humans to ensure that people from even the most isolated communities can successfully procreate with individuals from any other human population.

Examples of mixed communities are everywhere. V. G. Kiernan (1978) describes the British as "among the most composite Europeans," a mixture of indigenous people and invading Celts, Germanic Saxons, Danes, Flemings, Vikings, and Normans. Kotkin (1992) observes that other entrepreneurial tribes (besides the British) prominent in the emerging global economy have long histories of living in diaspora. As early as 500 BC, Jewish colonies stretched from Persia to North Africa, and the movement of Chinese traders into Southeast Asia had begun even before Jews were forced from their homelands by the Romans. People from the Indian subcontinent have been trading in southern China and much of Southeast Asia since the 4th century AD. Victor Pereda (1995) traces his Sephardic Jewish ancestry into 15th-century Spain, where coercive Christian "conversions" mixed hundreds of thousands of Arabic, Jewish, and Christian families.

The challenge of functionally integrating the multicultural issues of co-herence and identity at both the personal and community levels is ancient. This challenge reaches as far back into the past as our double-stranded deoxyribonucleic ribbons tie us to our multicultural ancestors. And they challenge us in the present as well.

Most of us in today's world find ourselves in multicultural surroundings. Some of us enter a multicultural environment every time we open our front door and step out onto our block and cruise around the neighborhood. Our own families, when parents or grandparents come from different cultural backgrounds, are increasingly multicultural. A third of U.S. residents listed at least two nationalities for their ancestry on the 1990 Census. The actual numbers of mixed ancestry undoubtedly are much higher.

Although in many parts of the world couples of obviously diverse back-ground were common enough, in the United States, a nation of immigrants, up until the end of World War II it was rare to see couples of mixed "race" or faith. As recently as the 1960s, in smaller towns, people would stare at the few mixed couples they encountered, or avoid looking at them altogether. Today few extended families in the United States do not contain someone from another culture and, not infrequently, from another race. A 1993 survey by *Time* magazine reported that 72 percent of those polled knew married couples who were of different races (*Time. Special Issue: The New Face of*

America, Fall 1993, 64). Over a recent 20-year period, the number of U.S. mixed-race marriages had increased from 310,000 (65,000 of which were black-white combinations) to more than 1.1 million by 1990. *Time* reports that "[t]he incidence of births of mixed-race babies has multiplied 26 times as fast as that of any other group." By 1993, 52 percent of Jews were marrying gentiles, 65 percent of Japanese-Americans married people with no Japanese heritage, and 70 percent of Native Americans married other races.

These marriages produce children of mixed heritage. Five hundred years ago the pull of the sea impelled people to move in search of wealth and power. Today, over half of the earth's inhabitants are linked to people thousands of miles away through the force of the global economy. Our lives are intertwined, and even John Doe and Joe Blow are becoming aware of the multicultural dynamics operating in their lives and histories.

But what to do as human cultures, some with little if any prior contact with each other for many centuries, increasingly converge upon one another and rearrange themselves into new patterns? These "rearrangements" can be expected to occur over very long periods of transition. More and more people will experience a multicultural milieu in which they will meet their needs and realize their dreams. Instead of being a marginal experience (if it ever was), growing up multicultural will be increasingly recognized as the ordinary, everyday experience of most of humankind.

The Clan, Band, or Family

Kinship, however defined, often has provided vital identities. Scots continue to identify themselves as Campbells or McGregors or Burns. Present-day economic activities of "overseas Chinese" (*hua qiao*) are organized along family lines. For Comanches, the band was the largest political unit. These old identities continue to be accessible to many of us.

Since prehistoric days in North America, one could belong to the Turtle Clan. Recently, a Mohawk woman sang at a wedding in a small Anglo community in upstate New York. After the service, the woman excitedly told the father of the groom that she had met a Seneca woman at the wedding, and that she, too, was from the Turtle Clan. In the Iroquois Confederacy, of which the Mohawks and Seneca are a part, clans cut across tribal boundaries, and, therefore, are one of the social institutions that help knit together the Confederacy, just as kin ties helped orchestrate diplomatic relations during the era of European hegemony. One Bulgarian family has been in the business of diplomacy for more than 200 years, and has family "branches" in England, Italy, France, Mexico, and the United States. A member from the titular U.S. branch was born in Brazil, grew up in China, and married in England.

In many parts of the world, kinship remains an important ingredient of self-identity. The trick is to integrate kin ties that embrace two or more distinct groups. European royal houses seemed to have little trouble integrating diverse family backgrounds, even when they were at war with some branches of the family. Peasants and serfs also did their share of intermarriage but were less motivated to record the details. As with other identity markers, kinship boundaries can be a wall used to exclude others or a line used to relate to others. This is the paradoxical nature of all boundaries. They both separate and connect (Flemons, 1991).

What's in a Name?

Words can make you feel glad or bad. The social order can even deprive people of their dignity—or personhood—if they do not fit into existing socially acceptable verbally labeled categories. An example of this is that in France, *everyone,* irrespective of religion or national origin, has to choose first names for their French-born children that are taken from a government list of French names of Catholic saints; it is against the law to do otherwise!

In present-day Japan, Korean-Japanese, many of whose families have been in Japan for three generations, cannot become citizens without changing their family names to Japanese family names—Japan's version of "you are welcome to join us only if you completely assimilate."

Another example of being name-conscious comes from the U.S. city of San Francisco, before direct dialing became possible. There, the telephone operators servicing Chinatown had to connect lines on the basis of people's names, not their numbers. Substituting numbers for names was seen by the Cantonese immigrants of the day to be degrading; it deprived them of their personhood. The operators had to know all of their customers by name! This same deprivation of personhood can be accomplished by forcing people to enter into coercive environments such as concentration camps, prisons, military service, hospitals, or even government bureaucracies. In these environments, too, numbers often substitute for names. ("Wait till your number's called.")

Surviving through Diversity

Besides luck, survival requires appropriate genes and a nurturing culture. The more varied each is across the human population, the better our chances as a species.

Biological Diversity

There is a difference in the way human and nonhuman life forms tend to make the adjustments needed to survive. It is not a difference in kind, but rather in the degree to which instinct rather than learning accounts for the ability to adjust to a changing ecology. Behavioral change occurs in nonhuman life forms largely through genetic selection (i.e., Darwin's natural selection) and other biological forces such as genetic mutations, genetic drift, and migration. This selection is brought about through the interaction of life forms with forces that favor the propagation of certain genes—the ability of a moth to blend into its surroundings, for instance, or the propensity for life forms low on the food chain to have large broods. In nonhuman life forms, behavioral characteristics seem more influenced by inborn instinct than by learning, although both occur even in single-celled creatures.

We humans, too, are biological creatures whose physical properties are evolving through the interaction of genetic selection and mutating genes, along with other biological forces, and we are ultimately dependent upon our genes for survival. Although less than 2 percent of the 100,000 genes each human possesses differs from those of chimpanzees and gorillas (1.7 percent and 1.8 percent, respectively), the difference is critical. Try as we may, we can't sire offspring with nonhuman primates. With chumps, yes; chimps, no.

In modern Homo sapiens there are no subspecies to evolve different genetic directions as there are in birds and bees and cinnamon trees—and as there may have been in ancient hominids. In spite of much 19th-century Western scholarship that argued that different "races" signified different species, all of the wonderful varieties of modern Homo sapiens belong to one interbreeding species, a species with surprisingly little genetic difference individual to individual, holding "at least 99.9% of our DNA sequences in common" (Sagan and Druyan, 1992, 415). This is strong evidence that there has been recurring interbreeding across human populations since time immemorial. This is not surprising, given the ancient mobility of humans (Bentley, 1993; Gamble, 1993; Mascie-Taylor and Lasker, 1988; Rouse, 1986). There is no reason to doubt that the trend of the last few centuries toward even greater genetic similarity will continue to accelerate.

We still have mostly the same genes that our Cro-Magnon and Neanderthal ancestors had, jazzed up by a few random mutations, and most of the nonlethal mutations are—in the short run at least—irrelevant. In fact, most (97 percent) of the nucleotide molecules in our DNA are inactive sequences of amino acids that lack activating codes (Sagan and Druyan, 1992). (If "irrelevant," nonworking genes are excluded from the comparison, humans and chimps share 99.6 percent of their active genes.) Mutations increase the genetic diversity of the species, and this may give our descendants a better shot at survival as physical conditions on earth change. Perhaps there are genes in the population that confer resistance to increased radiation caused by falling ozone levels.

Genetically speaking, healthy populations are diverse, heterogeneous populations. A current innovation in breeding programs for modern zoos underscores this reality. Zoologists track down wild individuals of endangered species, tranquilize them, extract semen, freeze the samples, then artificially inseminate captive individuals. This increases the genetic variation of the zoo specimens and makes them healthier. Species that are forced to breed within a small community increase their risk of inheriting the same deleterious recessive genes from both parents. Overall, 25 percent of purebred dogs in the United States, for instance, have serious genetic problems. Some breeds of dogs do considerably worse than the average. Seventy percent of collies suffer from genetic eye trouble, 30 percent of Dalmatians inherit deafness, 60 percent of golden retrievers suffer from hip dysplasia, as do an even higher percentage of German shepherds. When left alone to interbreed randomly, dogs tend to grow up medium sized and yellow coated. These genetically diverse mongrels may not look as cute as purebreds, but they are healthier. In humans, "mongrels" tend to look better than either of their parents.

Occasionally, animal species are identified that have hardly any genetic variation, individual to individual, even in the wild. Cheetahs are an example. These species are in deep trouble. One new disease could wipe them all out. Because of these dynamics, human intermarriage with people from different areas of the world is, from the perspective of the biological survival of the species, a good thing. It increases the variety of shared genes.

Cultural Diversity

Intermarriage is also good from a cultural vantage point. Cultural diversity enriches our ability to survive. Just as "irrelevant" genetic mutations may be on call within our DNA, individuals with different cultural viewpoints are on call within our societies to aid the group in adjusting to life's changing conditions. Diverse, multiple perspectives—even unpopular ones—offer humans an important mechanism for survival.

Skill in developing multiple perspectives is present abundantly among individuals who have been raised with roots in different cultural traditions. Perhaps your parents spoke a language at home that was other than the "mainstream" one, or you observed ethnic or religious traditions that differed from those of your neighbors. Maybe you just looked different, were treated differently, and therefore saw things differently.

In short, the odds of our species' survival are improved to the extent to which each society contains multicultural individuals. In fact, because our species relies on cultural adaptations more than on biological change for its survival, it is this *cultural* diversity that provides the *best* chance for the survival of humans. In spite of a long history of global mixing, serious examination of what happens inside the mind of an individual who has lived extensively in two or more different cultures is a recent event, and honoring this experience an even more recent occurrence.

Valuing Multiculturalism

Many of society's institutions discourage multiculturalism. Consider the Chicano first-grader, suffering through reading in a language he does not yet know so that in high school he can suffer through classes in beginning Spanish, a language he was forced to forget. Extinction of minority cultures is an ill-thought-out wish of many "mainstream" peoples worldwide. In areas where pressures to conform to mainstream values have won out, society has sown bitter seeds of repression that often bear toxic fruit.

The Generational Hurdle

It is not just "society" that resists cultural pluralism—parents, too, can pose a "generational" hurdle. To the extent that parents want Juanito to be a little replica of themselves, talking, acting, and thinking as they do, they are consigned to disappointment. Each generation gets to modify the rules of the game. The culture of the children cannot be precisely that of the parents. If it were so, the children's ability to adapt to a changing world would be sacrificed for the expediency of the status quo. When this kind of rigidity is widespread in a society it eventually results in that society's cultural death by asphyxiation.

Inheriting plural traditions and integrating them into our lives are two separate issues, for the multicultural credentials we inherit from our family ties are not always recognized or appreciated.

The Conformity Hurdle

In a suburb of Chicago, a preschool boy asked his Hispanic mother to stop talking to him in Spanish when they were out in public. He did not want to be "different." She ignored this plea for cultural anonymity. A short time later, the boy's father was awarded a senior Fulbright lectureship at a university in Ecuador and the whole family journeyed south.

Both parents began socializing the child into "appropriate" values. "You are really going to enjoy going to kindergarten in that pretty school down the street." "It'll be fun meeting all the new kids in that nice school down the street." The markedly introspective child just listened. Finally, the first day of school approached. "Well, tomorrow is your first day at the new school down the street. You'll really like it." For the first time since the indoctrination began weeks earlier, the child spoke.

"Is the teacher going to talk to me in Spanish?"

The father explained that in the United States where most people speak English, the schools use English, and in Ecuador, where most people speak Spanish, the schools use Spanish, but that he would do all right because he was bilingual.

"If the teacher talks to me in Spanish, I won't answer," announced the child. His decision was made. And for a month, he did not speak a word to anyone at school.

Then one day he came home for lunch and announced that he had had a conversation with his teacher. You could have heard a pin drop. The parents looked at each other, then the mother asked what they had talked about.

"She said '¿Cómo te llamas?' [What is your name?] and I said 'Mikey.' " That was it, a humble beginning, but great oaks from little acorns . . .

On the plane back to the United States, Michael sat in the row in front of his parents. The woman in the seat beside him asked him who he was.

"I'm Mikey, and I'm bilingual," was the unequivocal response.

Labels do make a difference in how you see yourself. They certainly make a difference in how others see you. It helps for parents to tell their children—explicitly and redundantly—that is it wonderful to be multilingual and multicultural.

While, without exception, we all count multicultural ancestors on our family tree, pressures to conform exclusively to the norms of one society or another have pushed many individuals to allow their gifts of multicultural skills and perspectives to atrophy. In spite of a multicultural endowment, many people have returned to the dark part of the cave, where tunnel vision prevents them from a broader view of the world. Not all who have a multicultural past, lamentably, are card-carrying, practicing multicultural individuals, complete with broadened perspectives and a larger cache of thinking skills and alternative ways of doing things. You have to value the skills of the boundary crosser to acquire his or her uniquely creative views on human conditions.

Mikey, the reluctant speaker of Spanish in public, grew up to be a mechanical engineer. His U.S. company regularly flies him to Puerto Rico to troubleshoot mechanical systems in a factory whose workforce is Spanish-speaking. His bilinguality is a distinct asset and that (along with engineering competence) is why he gets the assignments.

Diversity, A Global Resource

The great challenge of our time is to view diversity as a resource rather than as a problem. "All people need to develop and enhance their ability to deal with diversity in a positive way," says Alvino Fantini (1991), a professor at the School for International Training in Brattleboro, Vermont. "Virtually every country is facing intensified cultural diversity, contradicting and challenging earlier traditions of nationalism and homogeneity." Simply challenging a potentially stagnant intellectual status quo makes a contribution to our species's collective survival.

"The primary reason youngsters need to study multiple cultures is to learn how to develop multiple perspectives," Edmund Gordon (1991), a Yale professor of psychology, states. "This capacity," he continues, "is essential to developing intelligence." Gordon sees the central issue to be one of enabling students to use "broad, often conflicting bodies of information to arrive at sound judgments," a critical skill where the lines on the map are never the same, century to century.

An exceptionally creative artist, F. Hundertwasser, penned a sign displayed in his permanent exhibit in Vienna that says, "If we do not honor our past, we lose our future. If we destroy our roots, we cannot grow." If past is prologue, the existence of other cultures everywhere on the globe provides a source of many useful innovations and adaptations that will benefit everyone.

One thing we learn as we trace our own family ties back across time is that we all share ancestors. We can can take great pride in these multicultural roots and in the heritage and accomplishments they imply. While family ties establish our multicultural credentials, they do not solidly anchor our sense of identity. The next chapter explores national and ethnic boundaries and their relevance to self-identity.

The Limited View of the Monocultural

One persuasive reason to travel is to overcome the cost of cultural isolation: the easy chair prevents us from understanding the extent to which culture—rather than objective reasoning or other lofty conceits—programs us to behave the way we do. Culture is like air; it is hard to see. We've got to get outside our culture to see it. One way to do this is to take an interest in how things are done in other cultures. People who grow up in a multicultural home or community routinely develop multicultural perspectives.

A. J. Liebline (1970) asserts:

It's the outsider who avoids getting lost in the trees, he sees the forest. Yeats, Joyce, Shaw, from Ireland; Eliot, from Missouri; Pound, from Idaho, were the innovators of twentieth century English literature. Beaverbrook from the Maritimes; Luce, from a missionary family in China; Thomson, from the Ontario bush, became the giants of twentieth century publishing. Detachment and perspective permit pattern recognition.

Multicultural people, so often labeled "marginal" or "outsiders," would seem essential to the well-being of any society. Besides enriching the collective wisdom with other perspectives of reality, often their language skills and their personal contacts with people who live in other societies contribute meaningfully to national social and economic life.

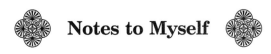

Notes to Myself

1. As much as I can reconstruct, after talking with my relatives, the family I was born or adopted into consists of the following people across the last five generations. (Try your hand at filling out Exhibit 2.1.)

_____

_____

_____

_____

_____

Need help? There is a lot available for doing genealogical research. A computer search of one university library listed 661 books on 351 different geneologically related topics, from the Acoma Indians of New Mexico through the Zapotec Indians of Mexico. Robert Reed (1979) published five, 28-page booklets on how to research one's ethnic-American heritage; they are aimed at Americans of Black, Chinese, Irish, Japanese, and Native American descent. Smith's (1983) *Ethnic Genealogy: A Research Guide* is helpful. Two books for helping Jews establish their genealogy were prepared by Rottenberg (1977) and Kurzweil (1980). The world's most complete genealogical archives are kept by the Church of Jesus Christ of Latter Day Saints (Mormons) and are made available to the public. Contact any Mormon church for details.

22

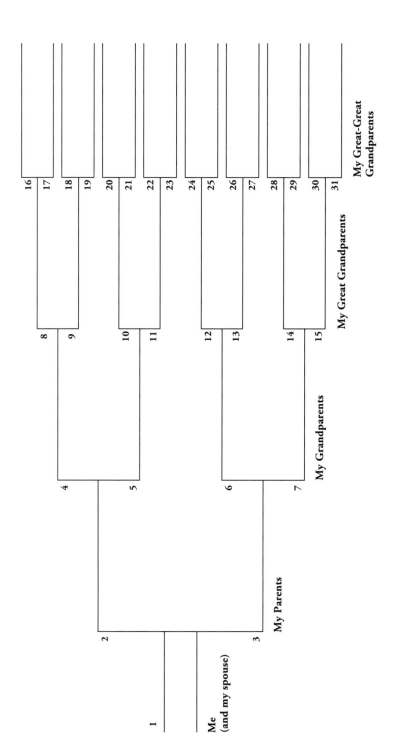

Exhibit 2.1. Family Tree

2. As far as I can tell, they were born in the following places in the world:

_____

_____

_____

_____

3. Of my 30 most recent ancestors or at least all of them I could identify (many people, especially Americans, can only go back two generations), the following is a list of their cultural backgrounds:

_____

_____

_____

_____

4. My family name has undergone the following changes across the generations:

_____

_____

_____

_____

5. I remember a time when my multicultural perspective gave me an insight that did not occur to my monocultural friends:

_____

_____

_____

_____

Boundaries on the Map, Boundaries on the Mind*

The Elusive Search for an Appropriate Boundary

It is said that a person without a category is a most wretched creature. People seem to need to place other people into recognizable slots. This is one reason why stereotypes are so reassuring.

It is far more difficult to deal with someone without the decipherable markings of the socially relevant "facts" of place of origin, race or ethnicity, language, religion, social class, age, and gender. Besides, as gregarious animals, humans seem to do better when they feel a part of an identifiable group.

---

* This chapter heading is adapted from the title of a wonderful book by C. Douglas Lummis, *Boundaries on the Land, Boundaries in the Mind.* Lummis was a U.S. Marine in Okinawa when Okinawa was returned to Japan in the 1970s. When he mustered out of the Marine Corps, like Gonzalo, the Castillian sailor in the time of Cortés, Lummis never went home again.

Group identity affords a sense of belonging, of roots, a feeling of continuity across time, and an identifiable source of allies in times of crisis. Many people connect to a larger community through a sense of shared nationality or ethnicity. Others connect through race, the subject of the next chapter, or through language or religion, subjects touched on in later chapters.

How sufficient are the categories of nationality and ethnicity as organizing and anchoring metaphors for the multicultural person?

Nationality

Until the 19th century there were no nation-states. That's just a gnat's blink ago. For most of human history—some four million years, according to the fossil record—people were born and died in small groups of 20-30 individuals, finding their food by hunting mammoths and gathering acorns while looking out for saber-toothed tigers. These people—our direct ancestors—leaned on family or clan ties for their group identity. Typically, the larger collective of our ancestors who spoke the same language called themselves simply "the People."

For the past 6,000 years (about the extent of our awareness of written history, beginning in Southwest Asia and Egypt)—and until very recently—the most common form of political organization has been the dynasty (Anderson, 1991). This political form was organized around a "high center" that did not pay much attention to its peripheries or boundaries, but rather to lines of loyalty and obedience. Empires were not contiguous; they transcended language, ethnicity, and geography. Belgium and the Low Countries, for example, were part of the Spanish Empire, but separated from Spain by France.

Nor did the subjects of the Empire share a sense of common ancestry. Columbus was "Genovese," from the city of Genoa, sailing under the Castillian flag. (He was not "Italian," because Roman city-states did not coalesce as a nation until 1870.) The dynasty continued to be the prevalent political form right up to 1914. Cortés bowed before the Queen of Castilla, and when he planted a flag on a Caribbean beachhead it was the flag of Castilla, for "Spain" was not yet a political entity. Other dynasties were similarly diverse. The ancestors of Archduke Ferdinand, who was assassinated in Sarajevo in 1914 (the spark that set off World War I), certainly did not belong to one narrowly defined people. His ancestors, members of the Austro-Hungarian imperial house, the House of Hapsburg, included 1,486 Germans, 196 Italians, 147 Danes, 124 French, 89 Spaniards, 52 Poles, and 20 English (Anderson, 1991).

Anderson goes on to say that at the time of the English-speaking American colonies' struggle for political independence from England in 1776, there were no nation-states. The early U.S. idea was of a confederation of smaller political units, rather than a nation. This confederation, incidentally, was based on the model provided by the Iroquois League, the first such confederation in recorded history (Johansen, 1982), and founded somewhere between the 14th and late 16th century by Hiawatha and Deganawidah (Josephy, 1993; Weatherford, 1991). For the founders of the United States of America, there was no mention of Christopher Columbus, the Pilgrim Fathers, the "American" nation, or the "historical antiquity" of the "American" people.

It wasn't until after the French Revolution (begun in 1789) and the Napoleonic Wars (1800–1815) in Europe that the modern idea of a nation-state and its trappings (republican institutions, common citizenship rather than subject-hood, popular sovereignty, national flag and anthem) gained strength in the popular consciousness. Johansen says that the first three concepts of this mix were based on European observations of political organizations among North American indigenous peoples of the eastern woodlands and northern plains. (These tribes mostly included the Iroquois Confederacy with its five nations—Seneca, Cayuga, Onondaga, Oneida, Mohawk, and later, in 1715, a sixth nation, the Tuscarora—along with the Huron, Neutral, Tobacco, Erie, Honniasont, Conestoga, Susquehannock, Ojibwa [Chippewa], Potawatomi, Miami, Illinois, and Cree.) These observations contributed mightily to Enlightenment ideas about "natural man" and "the pursuit of happiness" as a valid political goal for all members of society.

Although as late as 1914 dynastic states still made up the majority of the membership of the world political system, by the late 19th century the idea of nationhood had solidified. This notion typically assumes that a nation consists of one people, indivisible, with shared values, speaking one common language, and occupying one clearly bounded and mostly contiguous piece of real estate.

In encounters in international space we almost invariably identify ourselves nowadays as Swedish or Indonesian or Brazilian or Japanese or according to whichever nation-state issued our passport. "I'm from Nigeria." Or the ubiquitous, "Ahm Amurikin." These collective, nation-state identities are attached to us like baggage stickers advertising Niagara Falls or the Shrine at Lourdes. This political reality suggests a less-than-satisfying identity metaphor: *I am who my passport says I am.*

The Czech historian Dušan Třeštik (1995) reminds us that a nation is nothing natural that grew up like a tree. Nationalism is primarily subjective.

It is an act of collective will. It has no objective markers. It is an ideology, the result of willful, purposeful thinking.

Nationality is, to use Anderson's words, an "imagined community," socially constructed by humans, as, we shall see, are all identities. Nationalities, like other identities of multiple communities, are "historical constructs perpetually undergoing reconstruction" (Balibar and Wallerstein, 1991; see also Gellner, 1987; and Gellner, Hall, and Jarvie, 1992). Imagined or not, nation-state identities are now endemic. Perhaps this is a tribute to the power of the state, with its control of military forces and public education, its economic viability, and its influence—and, in most countries, control—over the mass media. Perhaps it is because "national defense," with its martially stirring parades and its righteous indignation and outrage directed toward the despised outsiders, is so comforting as we huddle together in mutual fortification.

Nationality is a convenient, simplistic way of identifying ourselves, and it does give us the illusion of having roots, although the nation-state is too infant a concept for the roots to go very deep. We only identify ourselves as French or American or Liberian on specific occasions such as Independence Day, national election season, during war, Inauguration Day, upon the death of a famous politician, or when we meet people in an international setting where nationality assists a first-tier attempt to get to know a stranger.

Since it is only relevant in limited circumstances, it is curious that the nation-state entity has so shanghaied the issue of our identity. It is rather like knowing one's astrological sign. Or, in a Japanese setting, knowing one's blood type.

Within many countries on the domestic front—not in international space—we often ask others about their historic group identity. If an American asks this of another American, she does not expect "American" to be the response. Rather, she expects the other to respond that his background is German and English, or whatever. Many people are rather selective about which of their nationalities they list. Nationality can be used as a protective shield in multiethnic societies where one's patriotism can be put in question by impolitic responses. A resident of a western U.S. state is of Hispanic and Native American heritage and fluent in English and Spanish. He assures his English-speaking neighbors that he is "first and foremost an American," and only secondarily Hispanic and Indian.

Nationality, often justified by the political priorities of a vested few, sometimes attempts to unify peoples of diverse ethnicity who live within its boundaries by transcending ethnic or tribal allegiances. Our ethnicity may be Norman or Frank or Burgundian or Gaul, but if we unite under the nation-state banner of France, we have come to see ourselves as French.

However, setting aside ancient identities in favor of modern national ones seems to serve as a stop-gap measure rather than as a long-lived solution to individual and collective identity issues, as we have seen in Bosnia, Rwanda, Myanmar, and Ireland, and among the Kurds in Iran, Iraq, and Turkey, and so on around the globe.

Within these national borders fealty is demanded by the state from diverse ethnic groups, groups which formerly might never have felt any sense of community. At the same time, nation-state borders cleave former ethnic communities. The Kurds in Turkey are to show allegiance to Turkey, while their relatives in Iraq bow to that state's claim of allegiance; their relatives across the border are now to be considered "foreigners." The recently invented nation-state, on the other hand, has geographically fixed the lines of primary loyalty. Nation-states impose borders on the map and matching borders on the mind. Yet the 20th-century political nation-state is not the end of humanity's search for ways to organize a just society—it is a way station along a long road.

The usefulness of nationality in the formation of our sense of self is narrow. One family has children who possess passports issued by two nations, Guatemala and the United States. They are descended from at least three major racial groupings—Celtic-Anglo-Hispanic Caucasian, West African Black, Mayan Indian. They are fluent in three languages: Spanish, English, Russian. Obviously, to see their identity principally in terms of one nationality is not very informative. Doing so would define an identity devoid of personal interests and life decisions. It would rob them of their history.

Simple nation-state affiliation does not suggest the complexity of someone who has been socialized into several cultural systems. Writing in *Time* magazine, Pico Iyer ruminates:

> Who am I, I sometimes wonder, the son of Indian parents and a British citizen who spends much of his time in Japan (and is therefore—what else?—an American permanent resident)? And where am I?

As influences impacting on our sense of self, nation-states are less than 200 years old. Although this youthfulness does not defuse nationality issues, the relative recency of nationality as a category of identity does allow us to see more clearly that we are the result of a three- or four-million-year succession of multicultural ancestors who have gone through many political transmutations. Such a transmutational identity is far more realistic and should not totally surrender its sense of self to the infant, transitory idea of the nation-state. As humans, we are more than citizens of a nation-state, although—recently—we are that, too.

It takes more than our passports to give us a persuasive sense of self. Perhaps we should not let current boundaries on the political map unduly influence the dynamic boundaries in our minds.

Two other, more ancient, identities are those associated with ethnicity and with village or city.

Ethnicity

Although usage varies, ethnic identities do not generally refer to nation-states. Rather, ethnic groups are either smaller groupings within a population, or a population that these days spills across several nation-state boundaries. Sometimes they are identified by the language they speak (the Quechua Indians of South America identify themselves according to their historical empire—*Inga simi* or "Inca people"), sometimes by their religion (Jews), sometimes by a cultural collective that cuts across many ethnic groups (Chinese), and sometimes by someone else's term for them. Most of the world calls one upper-Amazon tribe the Auca, which means "savage" in Quechua; they call themselves the Huaorani.

Ethnic identities are older than nation-state identities and often transcend modern political divisions ("the Arab states"). Jerónimo de Aguilar, the shipwrecked sailor discussed in the first chapter, identified with people who spoke Spanish (*españoles*) and with the Kingdom of Castilla, not with the yet-to-be-formed nation-state of Spain. In some cases, these older descriptions of who we are (Hessian) have been replaced by nation-state monikers (Germans).

Ethnic identities, like national identities, are mutable. The same individual is descended from many ethnic groups and often changes his or her "preferred" identity at different times depending on the circumstances. Ethnic identities are also of largely contemporary relevance. They were not generally accepted by our ancestors as legitimate lines of demarcation, inasmuch as they fought their "ethnic brothers" as bitterly as they subsequently fought "foreign devils." The Japanese before the Tokugawa Shogunate illustrate this well.

Within the confines of our modern nation-states, most of us still identify simultaneously with older ethnic lines: we are Breton or Aymara or Ibo or Jew. People choose and select their nationality and ethnic labels from among the many represented on their family tree, and simplifications are common. That is, many nation-state and ethnic labels of our ancestors are selectively ignored, even if we are aware of them. Older people, at least in the United States, tend to identify with a greater number (Waters, 1990).

While not all identities are officially recognized, in the United States—a nation that for a long time tried to construct for itself a homogeneous, "melted" identity—the proportion of citizens claiming minority roots is growing swiftly. The 1980 Census reported that one of every five Americans belonged to a minority group, but by 1990 the proportion asserting Native American, Hispanic, Asian, or African roots had jumped to one of every four! When you add to these four identities first-generation Americans of European ancestry, the proportion of "ethnic" people becomes even more startling. This phenomenon is not confined to the United States. "Ignored" identities don't seem to remain ignored; they often reemerge in startling ways, as the contemporary politics of identity and nationalism demonstrate on all continents.

Is ethnic conflict inevitable? Many people fear the divisive effects of multiculturalism and multilingualism that numerous countries experience. Unrest among ethnically identifiable sectors of the population can certainly disrupt national life (Horowitz, 1985; Boucher, Landis, and Clark, 1987). Developments in the 1990s in what used to be Yugoslavia, and in Rwanda and a score of other nations, do nothing to allay these fears. (Contrary examples, such as peaceful Switzerland, go largely ignored.)

A number of concepts have been rallying cries for ethnic struggles in the 20th century: political self-rule, economic opportunity, cultural identity, and religious freedom (Nash, 1989). What are the conditions that make ethnic identity foment riot and rebellion? Most often, this occurs when individuals feel that they are being denied society's scarce resources—money, prestige, power—*because* of their ethnic, racial, or religious membership. Both the way society is structured ("old boys' network") and the psychocultural dispositions of its social segments (who would be a suitable marriage partner?) contribute to conflict (Ross, 1993a, 1993b).

A cynical result of exploiting one group or another by denying them society's rewards is that this makes life for the privileged set more comfortable, freer. It frees them from a certain amount of repressive, stultifying labor and at the same time increases their share of money, prestige, and power. The 200-year history of slavery in the United States (plus another hundred years of second-class status for descendants of the former slaves) dramatically illustrates how the assumed importance of skin color made life easier for whites (Steinberg, 1989).

Equal opportunity societies would have little to fear from ethnic diversity, because multiculturalism does not pose any *intrinsic* threat to national viability—*if* opportunity is not skewed in favor of privileged ethnicities. It is when certain sectors of society have—or want—a disproportionately large piece of the pie that trouble looms on the horizon. The ingredients of ethnic conflict are social, economic, or political dominance by a cultural elite, and, concomitantly, the limited availability of options for future growth because one is born into the "wrong" social identity. Nobody wants to be treated unfairly.

Almost any observable feature can serve to distinguish sectors that enjoy privilege from sectors that are disadvantaged. Physical features (whether a male is circumcised, for example), dress (including whether a male wears an earring in the right or left ear lobe), ancestry, social class, posture, behavior, linguistic nuances (even tiny ones such as whether you say *ain't* or *isn't,* and whether you pronounce *aunt* to rhyme with *ant* or *font*). In such settings of exploitation, if a mother speaks Nahuatl to her son on a crowded elevator in Mexico City, he may feel uncomfortable at having been given a linguistic marker of lower social standing.

It does not have to be this way. Even high-status individuals can be magnanimous, and even dominant cultures profit from learning from others. At an international conference on Women for Mutual Security (January 1991) held in Vanuatu in the South Pacific, Fanaura Kingstone, a Cook Island Maori woman, shared her vision for the new global order: "A system where the voice of the hummingbird is heard with as much respect as the voice of an eagle."

Ethnicity is but one alias among many. The village or city of origin offer an additional source of identity.

The Village or City

The village is, of course, a smaller, but often a more cohesive identity within our larger ethnic or tribal divisions. Before the arrival of European invaders, for many Native American tribes such as the Pueblos and many of the Arctic peoples, the village was the largest political identity. Even contemporary people identify themselves according to their "village." An attractive white woman visiting a remote village in Kenya identified herself this way: "I'm from Turin. You know, where they make Fiats."

Another example of identifying oneself in terms of a city of origin rather than a country of origin occurred in France. A couple, magnificently attired in the dazzling color of Mayan Indian dress, was waiting in line to attend a production of the Paris Opéra. Curious, a fellow-in-queue asked where they were from. "Quetzaltenango," was the proud response. After all, doesn't everyone know the name of Guatemala's second city? A visitor from the United States to Peru was asked where he was from. "Chicago," he replied. "Ah," the Peruvian's eyes lit up, "bang-bang-bang-bang-bang!" The 1920's crime connection lingers still.

Having one's most consistently inclusive identity reside at the village, town, or city level is not so different from the identity conventions in Europe in the 14th century, which saw the emergence of the Hanseatic League, a political and commercial league of northern Germanic towns. In the present era, many nation-state provinces and large cities maintain commercial representatives stationed all over the world, keeping alive in an international mercantile context the ancient entity of village or city-state.

Vestiges of earlier city-states linger on. Several Italian city-states provide modern examples (San Marino and the Vatican, to cite two), as does the city-state Singapore in Southeast Asia, and the 19 Pueblo Indian towns in New Mexico (USA).

The usefulness of place of residence as a meaningful marker of identity is inversely proportional to the degree of geographic mobility in the community. Multicultural individuals customarily travel from place to place, and this obscures the relevance of any one village or city.

Don't Bother Me, I'm Having a Slow Century of It

Liebline says that in the histories of most peoples, there are eras of long lapses during which they lie "creatively fallow." He goes on to observe that Western European man did not add anything to ancient culture for a thousand years or more; the Jews between the Diaspora and their emergence from the ghettos in the 19th century did nothing that a historian could not cover "in a long footnote." Liebline explains:

> When they reentered the world, the Jews, as though seeing for the first time the structure to whose piecemeal growth they had contributed almost nothing, produced within a century a series of epic innovators—Karl Marx, Sigmund Freud, Albert Einstein, and scores of hardly less original luminaries such as Kafka. The reemergence of the Islamic peoples, when complete, may give us the same kind of constellation.

Are *you* having a slow time of it? Contrary to the opinions of vociferous monocultural fanatics, it hardly seems appropriate to call a trait of our species—multiculturalism—a fad. Individuals who have been socialized in two or more cultures have existed for as long as Homo sapiens has pondered survival from the jaws of death. Being multicultural affords special perspectives. This is not to say that multicultural individuals develop the same views, as Jerónimo de Aguilar and Gonzalo Guerrero illustrate. In some fields—social sciences, education, tourism—being multicultural greatly increases employment opportunities. In other fields, it just helps one think more creatively.

More because of their mutually exclusive nature than because of their fickle mutability, identities spawned by nation-state or ethnic affiliations do not provide a good fit for most multicultural individuals. The next chapter examines the fit of race as an anchor of identity.

Notes to Myself

1. The "shortened" way I refer to my nationality is

   _____

   _____

2. The longer form of my nationality would be:

   _____

   _____

3. The shortened form of my ethnicity is

   _____

   _____

4. Trying to include all of the ethnicities on both sides of my family, for as far back as I can go, the longer form of my ethnic background would be:

   _____

   _____

5. Adding religious identities to my background would produce the following hyphenated identity:

   _____

   _____

6. My ancestors have been in the same town or city for _____ years.

4

Boundaries on the Body

Body Image

Our body shapes, as everybody knows, affect our self-image. What is not so well known is how culture shapes that image.

One of the authors was raised in Pennsylvania and by early adolescence had reached his full height of 5'6½" (every half-inch was important then). He realized he was short. Then at the age of 16 he moved to Mexico. To his surprise, he discovered that often he was the tallest one standing on the (second-class) bus. After several years of experiences like this he adjusted his earlier conclusion: he was now, it was apparent, of at least average height. In fact, he never again thought of himself as a short person. Now, had he reached, say, six feet by adolescence, but moved to Africa to live with Watusis, the story would have had a different ending: he might have regarded himself as a short six-footer among all those seven-footers.

Whether you consider yourself as beautiful or homely is largely a function of culture. A neighbor, born and raised in Italy, complains that men did not find her attractive in Italy because she was too skinny. Now that she has moved to the United States and put on weight, the same fate has befallen her. She's too fat for many American men.

In some countries, "race" provides the one overriding description of "body type" that is most pertinent to your future survival: socially, politically, and economically.

"Race"

Everyone belongs to a "race," or at least can be put into a racial category. This fact might not mean much, though, since there is no common definition of what "race" is.

For good reasons, the vocabulary we have available to discuss "race" often makes it difficult to get a clear bearing on the subject. In 19th- and early 20th-century England, as well as in many other areas of the world, race and nation were regarded as "virtually synonymous terms" (Shipman, 1994). In a symposium staged in the Czech Republic in 1995 and attended by Europeans from many countries, the participants experienced difficulty discussing the topic of nationhood because of the widely differing denotations of the terms *nation, race,* and *ethnicity.*

Race: A Social Construct

In Latin America, "race" is more cultural than physical. A person whose ancestors for centuries have been Aztec ceases to be Indian when he or she becomes fluent in Spanish, dresses in Western clothes, and otherwise acts in ways indistinguishable from his or her "non-Indian" neighbors. These persons do not lose their Indian background, but they lose their "Indian" label. The "cosmic race" (*la raza cósmica*) in Latin America is, as José Vasconcelos elaborates (1977), a mixed race of European, African, Indian, and Asian origin.

During colonial times in what is now Canada, the charter of the trading entity, the New French Company, issued by Cardinal Richelieu in 1628, provided that any Indians who converted to Catholicism "shall be held to be native Frenchmen" (Weatherford, 1991). In this instance, religion determined race. At the other end of the hemisphere, race was not infrequently determined by success. One baby born in Brazil to an Afro-Brazilian family had his race listed as *preto* (black) on his birth certificate. When he enrolled in college, his records showed him as *mulato* (of mixed black-white parents). After graduation from college, he went into business, and over the years he became quite wealthy. When he applied for a passport to visit Europe, his race was listed as *branco* (white). One of the points that this example illustrates is how social class distinctions can be more important than "racial" labels.

Everybody has multiracial antecedents if they go back far enough. Sometimes you don't have to go back very far. An African-American resident of Albuquerque, New Mexico, by chance ran into a Euro-American with the same Scottish surname. The ensuing discussion revealed that their great-great grandfathers were brothers who emigrated from Scotland to the United States in the 19th century. One went north and married a white American, the other went south and married (in a black Baptist church) a black American. Until this meeting in Albuquerque, neither family knew what had happened to the other branch.

The "Selective" Nature of Race

Changing social constraints affect which "race" we choose to identify with. People often feel certain social advantages in recognizing one racial background over another. Having ancestors from certain stock is seen as very positive, although the specifics of which stock is valued and which is not go in and out of fashion. Each region of the world applies its own ever changing opinions of the social significance of belonging—or being assigned—to one group or another. Several examples from the United States will illustrate these dynamics as they have been manipulated by government agencies, although most countries yield their own illustrations.

Intermarriage in the New World was commonplace, especially in the Hispanic, Luso-Brazilian, and French settlements where European women were not much encouraged to immigrate. For three centuries, Spaniards (and in Canada, Frenchmen and Scots, and in Brazil the Portuguese) married Indians so frequently that mixed-race children became the norm in many areas of the colonies (Mexico, the U.S. Southwest, and Manitoba, to cite a few examples). The European settlers, as well as the Indians, also intermarried with blacks. This was especially true in the Caribbean, Mexico, parts of Colombia, Brazil, and in the Spanish territory of Florida. In southern United States, Indian tribes (such as the Seminole and Lumbe) gave refuge to escaped slaves up through Lincoln's Emancipation Proclamation in 1863.

Intermarriage was not uncommon, although it was less frequent, in the British colonies where the settlers were encouraged to immigrate with their European wives, and where religious and Puritanical influences served to inhibit a practice common in French, Hispanic, and Portuguese settlements. Namely, living with an Indian woman (or a woman of African origin) in "unofficial," sometimes polygynous, marriages of either short-term or lifelong duration. One estimate of the extent of U.S. intermarriage with Indians places the number by mid 20th century at between 10 and 20 million U.S. citizens with some Indian ancestry (Taylor, 1984).

In one British colony in the New World—later to become the southern U.S. state of Virginia—intermarriage with Indians was especially common-place. During the 20th century, residents of the United States have been increasingly proud to note some Native American ancestor in their background, although this person rarely can be identified by name. When laws were passed after the Civil War (1861–1865) prohibiting intermarriage with people from other "races," Indians living in Virginia simply identified themselves as "white" in the next Census. Under these laws—the last anti-miscegenation law was struck down by the U.S. Supreme Court in 1967—Americans were constrained by many state governments to identify themselves as black if they had one African-American grandparent. The fact that these individuals would also be three-fourths white was not deemed socially relevant.

In some areas of the country the situation was even more absurd. Even "one drop of Negro blood" made you black in the eyes of many American bureaucrats. One woman in Louisiana could not get a U.S. court—including the Supreme Court in 1986—to reclassify her as white when her only black ancestor had been her great-great-great-great-grandmother!

In the United States, the "one-drop" rule was applied only in cases where black ancestry was involved. Its purpose, historically, was to increase the size of a slaveholder's "property" in the face of increasing numbers of mixed-race children being born on his plantation. In Mexico, the several hundred thousand blacks who had been imported as slaves have long since disappeared into the general population through intermarriage and a disinclination on the part of Mexicans to apply such curious "blood-quantum" criteria to racial classifications (Aguirre Beltrán, 1972).

This blood-quantum criteria for "racial" membership has been applied differently by U.S. government agencies, according to their vested interests. While in the case of blacks it was designed to keep numbers big so slave property would increase (one drop made you Negro), later, in an Act of Congress in 1898, the same concept was applied—with a twist—to keep Native American populations small. This was done by requiring an individual to have a relatively high amount (usually a minimum of 25 percent) of Indian "blood" to be classified as Indian. The purpose of this U.S. Bureau of Indian Affairs policy—later adopted by the majority of Indian tribes and written into their constitutions—was to *diminish* the number of Indians eligible for federal benefits, many of which had been negotiated through treaties during the Indian Wars of the 18th and 19th centuries.

While one drop of African "blood" made you black, it takes a lot of drops—one-fourth or more Indian "blood" from a specific tribe—to make you Indian. There is a current trend in many tribes to redefine their membership away from the Bureau of Indian Affairs' "blood-quantum" criterion back to the way Indians had traditionally defined themselves—according to an individual's cultural descendancy. As one Native American leader puts it, "What difference does it make how you look? The important thing is how you behave."

Are You Full-Blooded?

Perhaps we should say something about "blood." It comes in four inherited groups (A, B, AB, O) based on the presence or absence of antigens in the red blood cells or in the plasma that trigger immunological reactions to the red blood cells of other blood types. Most people also have an inherited antigen in the red blood cells called an Rh factor. If you have it, you're Rh positive, if you don't, you're Rh negative. The specific kind of antigens (if any) found in your blood plasma gives you your blood type—O positive, for instance.

None of the blood types, though, corresponds to any one "race," however "race" is defined by local people. The use of the term "blood" is a carryover from the recent past when the role of genes in heredity was not understood. In fact, physical anthropologists have not discovered any single genetic trait that exists exclusively in any one "race," although some rare blood antigens have been found solely among very small groups of isolated peoples. These small groups, however, do not correspond to any known "racial" groupings.

If "race" is defined so differently by different cultures, and if intermarriage over the centuries has occurred frequently, and if all genes exist in all major population groups, then is there really a physical category that can be called "race"? Nope. Race is a social concept; it does not exist in nature (Montagu, 1942; Tobias, 1972).

Race: A Biological Construct

This is not to say that there aren't genetically induced differences in human appearance from region to region, only that these differences do not enable even the most conscientious scientist to accurately categorize any given individual by racial categories.

People currently classified as "white" and people currently classified as "black" have about the same range of skin colors within their respective populations. A notable difference is the *frequency* of a given skin color in each group, but even this is not very helpful. The "typical" skin hue of Caucasian people from India is considerably darker than the "typical" Caucasian hue from Norway. Many African Americans are much lighter than the "typical" Caucasian from India.

How then does one explain the ease with which you can distinguish a black from an Asian from a northern European? The distribution of the few genes that reveal themselves in physically observable features (phenotypes), such as skin and eye color, or hair color or texture, do differ in general frequency from region to region. The genes for nappy hair exist in all the major populations but are most frequent among groups of African origin. It is easy to differentiate "typical" representatives of the different "races," but to do this, you have to ignore all of the gradations in between, and pretend that the "typical" representatives look like people of that "race" across the board. But they don't. The majority of a population probably does not look much like the "typical" models. Most of the world expects a "typical" Caucasian to be tall, fair-skinned, blue-eyed, blond, and thin-lipped. "Typical" blacks are tall, very dark skinned, brown-eyed, and thick-lipped. Does either description fit you? How dark are "typical" Africans? (A black poet [Hammonds, 1993] says "Shades of black women are as beautiful as the variant shades of roses.") With the Mbutu (Pygmy) and the Watusi in mind, how tall is the "typical" African? The genetic variations among people of the same "race" are greater than the differences between groups (Cavalli-Sforza, Menozzi, and Piazza, 1994).

Population geneticists, tracing blood antigens in hundreds of thousands of individuals from about 2,000 communities and tribes around the world, currently estimate that Europeans are a hybrid population, with 65 percent of their genes from Asian populations and 35 percent of their genes from African populations (Cavalli-Sforza, Menozzi, and Piazza, 1994).

The myth of race affords some people a metaphor that allows them a sense of cohesive identity. For although there is no genetic basis for racial classifications, there may well be some compelling social and historical commonalities in a particular enclave of that "race" that makes the term useful when defining oneself: "Black is beautiful." When one group has been under the thumb of another group, these circumstances elicit sympathy toward that group's sense of community in calling itself "black," for example. One is less sympathetic to a dominant group's use of the same device to express pride of community; the "Aryan race" of Nazi Germany comes quickly to mind (Shipman, 1994).

Most anthropologists, and even many geneticists, still use the vernacular term *race* when they talk about genetically induced varieties in human populations, even though they acknowledge the inadequacy of the term. It is wise, however, to beware of "racial" categories when *others* are defining *you*. It usually will not be to your advantage, as the "one-drop" rule in the United States demonstrates. One U.S. middle-school student of mixed-race parentage had white classmates who would ask, out of curiosity, how much African ancestry he had. The mathematically sophisticated student always responded, "one-third." At home he would relate these incidents for the amusement of his older brothers, for none of his classmates picked up on the fact that you can be one-fourth or one-half black, but you can't be one-third!

The mythical boundaries of "race," like the imagined boundaries of nationality and the elusive ties of ethnicity, are not as helpful in defining our diversely formed identity as they appear at first glance. Are language boundaries more helpful? Can language provide the basis for a sense of community and self-identity? The next chapter explores this issue.

Notes to Myself

1. On a scale of 1 to 10, with 10 being the stereotypical ideal, and 1 being far from the stereotype, I would rate myself _____ in terms of my "race."

2. There are many ingredients to my physical identity. Some of them emerge from within, other are imposed from without. Ingredients from within include:

   _____

   _____

   _____

   _____

   _____

   Ingredients from "outside" include:

   _____

   _____

   _____

   _____

   _____

Boundaries on the Tongue

Silent Language Boundaries

When the moon is in your eye, you don't have to know the language, advises an old song. Much effective communication—some experts say most—requires a language system that is nonverbal. A mother's smile across the room is enormously meaningful to her child. Both nonverbal and spoken language systems affect how we feel about ourselves.

Blinks and Winks

Singing sea chanteys does not make you a sailor. Our self-identity requires social validation. The need for social validation is one reason why nationality is a convenient, if misleading, label of identity. Even in those societies that perceive "the person in society" to be relatively independent of the social context, some degree of social validation of behavior is required for *meaningful* behavior to exist in society. There is no speaker without an audience. As the Zen masters ask, "What is the sound of one hand clapping?"

To illustrate the need for social validation of behavior, Clifford Geertz (1972) offers an example of the difference between mere actions and socially meaningful behavior by contrasting a blink with a wink. If you simply look at the physical movement of the eyelid, both behaviors are identical. For a blink to become a wink, however, the social context in which it occurs has to provide a mutually agreed upon meaning.

There are many commonplace examples of this differentiation. Sometimes scratching one's upper lip simply means it itches. In China, it is an invitation to sexual intimacy. In every society there exist conventions that distinguish mere actions from meaning-laden conduct. Latin Americans (and members of many other societies such as Native American and Chinese) often point by pursing their lips, a gesture that looks like a nervous tic or a kiss to those socialized differently.

The Sound of Culture in a Sneeze

Both sounds and actions get their meaning, if any, from social conventions, not from any intrinsic significance in the action or sound. Involuntary reflex actions are an exception—to a point. A sneeze is a sneeze in any culture, but sneezes often "sound" different from language to language. A Portuguese sneeze sounds like a nasal *achín,* while a Spanish sneeze sounds like a sibilant *achís,* quite distinct from the English sound of *achou.* In some cultures, such as the German and Hispanic, one is expected to "notice" a sneeze and to respond immediately with a courteous *gesundheit!* or *¡salud!.* Other cultures, such as the Japanese, ignore it.

Spoken Language Boundaries

Often, the most foreign thing about the foreign culture is the foreign language.

Vous Parlez?

Of all the reciprocal, mutually intelligible behaviors that make up a culture, *language* erects the biggest boundary between people of different cultures. If you can't speak the language, you are reduced to understanding a version of events that only roughly approximates a complete understanding. You are entirely shut out of most of the nuances that give interpersonal communication its spice. Language is the key to opening the culture's coffers of interrelationship and knowledge riches.

In the midst of our dynamically interactive turn-of-the-millennium world, suspicion still greets things "foreign." In some circles, even studying a foreign language can be subversive business.

"If English was good enough for Jesus Christ, it's good enough for me!" said an impassioned member of a school board in a rural town in southern Illinois, in the middle of United States. The board member had unwittingly repeated, word for word, H. L. Mencken's earlier parody of cultural ignorance. The board, after heated discussion, voted to discontinue its French courses.

This does not change the fact that the most important skill for entering deeply into another culture is fluency in the appropriate language(s). In the United States, to take one example, a country of immigrants who speak (in the aggregate) hundreds of languages from all corners of the world, the vast majority of primary and secondary schools offer only two foreign languages: Spanish and French. In the language instruction that is offered, there is lingering fear of cultural contamination. This fear is especially acute when the foreign language is spoken in a country with which international political relations are strained. U.S. students used to risk "becoming communists" by studying Russian.

In the United States, foreign language teachers are instructed by their methods professors to teach students to understand native speakers of a language but to reassure the students (and their parents and communities!) that they will not have to change any of their own beliefs in the process. Their patriotism, religion, family values, and sense of identity will remain unaffected, they are told.

We are born with a predisposition to speech. Unfortunately, we are not born fluent in even a single language, let alone several. Even though we descend from a long line of cunning linguists, each of us has to start from scratch. It is much easier to learn only one language, just as it is easier to learn either literature or mathematics, instead of both. Ignorance is easy (but costly!). When you add the difficulty of learning another language to social, lowest-common-denominator pressures to speak only the language of the tribe, many multicultural parents find it too easy to cease passing along their ancestral language(s). When you have loved ones residing in two different cultures with which you maintain contact, however, incentives are high to learn the languages you need to talk with them.

In too many countries to list, on all continents, people are reasserting cultural identities with increasing resolve. They may speak first languages other than the "official" ones. Many countries (e.g., India, Ghana) have always had hundreds of different languages. Papua New Guinea, for example, has 820 languages (at last count) in a population of 3,000,000. Some countries even have more than one "official" language: Canada has two, Switzerland has four, India (the world's most populous democracy) has 14.

The United States doesn't have an "official" language, although 98 percent of the respondents to the 1990 Census reported that they spoke English "well" or "very well"; 11 percent of U.S. households contained speakers of other languages. Concerns voiced since the early 1980s over minority language issues include language conflict, patriotism and "Americanization," minority language rights, the "endangered" status of English, bilingual education, and international needs (Crawford, 1992). Not all states react the same to these issues. In the face of intermittent popularity in neighboring states for an "official English" movement (read: English only) that would deny bilingual voting privileges and other public information services to non-English-speaking residents, one southwestern state (New Mexico) has declared nine languages to be official in that state (English, Spanish, Navajo, Apache, and the five Pueblo languages: Tiwa, Tewa, Towa, Keres, and Zuni). One might note that eight of the nine languages have deeper roots in America than those of English-speaking people.

Fluency in a common language provides a potential means to a shared identity. Jerónimo de Aguilar's predominant identity was with other speakers of Spanish; Gonzalo Guerrero's was not. Whether two people who speak variations (dialects) of the same language see each other as members of the same group varies from culture to culture (as well as from person to person). Some cultures (e.g., Chinese and Arabic) are more inclusive than others (e.g., French). That is, wide speech divergences—different accents, different vocabulary—may be seen as irrelevant or, conversely, as exclusionary. Does an American, for example, through the medium of a shared language, identify with people from India, Scotland, and Kenya? Much depends on the extent to which the general cultural milieu is perceived to be the same. Although a person from Kenya speaking English (the usual language in schools) may be more understandable to an American than a Scot from Glasgow, many white Americans may well identify with the latter more than the former because of other considerations. In the Spanish-speaking world, where Hispanic-Catholic mores predominate, national and regional accents are not seen as so exclusionary as in the English-speaking world where immense differences in culture prevail between English-speaking countries. Even so, once you are armed with the appropriate language—if not yet with the appropriate dialect—you are well on your way to forming a sense of cohesion with those with whom you interact.

Between Cultures

Bilingualism, Asset or Deficit?

Not surprisingly, fluency in two or more languages is highly associated with multiculturalism. That's the good news. The bad news we have already noted: learning a second language—at whatever age—is harder than just learning one language. It is instructive to look at how children learn a second language.

Children must recognize—and then separate—two distinct language systems, each signaling meaning in different ways. When Seelye asked two of his preschool children how many languages they spoke (their mother always spoke to them in Spanish, their father in English), there was a long pause while they considered the question. "Two," responded one child. After complimenting them on their mental acuity, the father then asked which two languages they spoke. After another pause, the other child said, "Mami and papi."

Learners of a second language must master many structural devices. Lado (1957) identifies some of signaling devices commonly shared across languages. They include word order (pocket watch, watch pocket), verb inflections (call, called), function words that do not themselves have meaning (of, that), pause (a red, wine keg; a red wine keg), intonation (he's cute, he's cute?), stress (óbject, objéct), correlation of forms (I read, he reads; a marriage promise, a marriage promises), tone (the word pitch that some languages such as Chinese use).

While most languages include most of these grammatical devices, a meaning that is signaled by one structural device in one language can be indicated by a different device in another. A question, for example, might be signaled by a function word in one language and by word order or intonation in another.

Another source of difficulty is that children have to learn different sound systems, thousands of new words, hundreds of new ways to say things, and the distinctive rhythms that each language uses. Take the issue of which syllable to stress. In Czech, the first syllable is always stressed, in Spanish the next to the last syllable is most often stressed, in French it is the last syllable, and in Japanese none of the syllables are stressed. Someone who speaks Spanish with an English intonation appears somewhat excited or agitated to the native speaker of Spanish. To an English ear, Spanish may sound much more monotone and staccato than English. To a Chinese ear, the non-tonal languages may appear undernourished.

Human babies make many sounds, some rather bizarre. Gradually, the child learns which sounds convey meaning. Often small phonetic differences make a big difference in meaning. An example of this from English is the *i* in pin and the *e* in pen. Linguists call the smallest unit of sound that makes a difference in meaning a phoneme. Sometimes rather large phonetic differences have little or no phonemic effect on meaning (you/yawl). Each language makes its own conventions about which sounds are meaningful and which are not. Your languages interfere with each other. Instead of saying *casa blanca* (Spanish for "white house"), inexperienced speakers might say, incorrectly, *blanca casa,* using the English word order.

Many researchers have looked at the struggling bilingual child and concluded that bilinguals are handicapped when compared to monolinguals. In fact, in the first third of the 20th century virtually all of the Western research into bilingualism concluded that bilingualism negatively affected intelligence! The studies themselves contained glaring intellectual deficiencies on the part of the investigators. They did not control for intervening variables such as age, sex, class, ethnicity, intelligence (and what any given test was really testing), social status of each language, conditions and age under which bilingualism began (e.g., began the second language in primary school, each parent spoke a different language, moved to another country at the age of 10), how different the first and second languages are (English/French versus English/Japanese), and the extent to which the social setting values communicative competence over grammatical accuracy.

In addition, these studies used analytical techniques (inferential statistics) that determine the degree to which bilingualism is *associated with* measures of intelligence. However, these research techniques *do not* determine causation, in spite of the researchers' naïve claims. If, in a sample of students, you discovered that blue-eyed children (or children with large ear lobes) were better readers than brown-eyed children, would you conclude that eye color (or ear lobes) *caused* the reading ability?

Bilingualism got a bad reputation, at least when it occurred among the poor and downtrodden. By contrast, in jet setters, fluency in many languages has always been a sign of meritorious achievement and prestige. The effects of coercion, subjugation, and poverty were not weighted heavily—if at all—by these earlier researchers. Multiculturalism was discouraged, and people raised in multicultural environments were pressured to "fit in" to the prevailing dominant cultural milieu. School officials discouraged the use of other languages at home and prohibited their use on school grounds. Should this be seen as just another example of "different latitudes, different attitudes"? Or is there intrinsic worth in maintaining multilingual communication skills? We believe that adding knowledge and skills is sound; subtracting hard-earned capabilities—especially one as intrinsically utilitarian as language fluency—is unsound.

One negative finding that has stood the test of improved research methodology is that bilingual children do tend to have a lower vocabulary in either of their languages than that possessed by their monolingual peers. The bilingual child might know more words *in total* than the monolingual child, but he or she knows fewer words in any one language. Different reasons are offered to explain this. For one, the child tends to hear each language less since time is shared between two (or more) languages. Whether bilingual adults also have more limited vocabularies has not been documented.

Can the very efforts we expended as children or adolescents to learn new languages lead to anything desirable—other than the valuable ability to communicate with many additional people? Some educators, linguists, and psychologists think so. There are at least two structural advantages and one informational advantage to speaking more than one language: gains emanating from switching between two language structures; gains from thinking in two different language systems; and information gains from listening to the differing culturally specific topics of discourse common to each language community.

Advantages of Switching between Two Languages

Sandra Ben-Zeev (1984, 1977a, 1977b, 1972) has demonstrated that children who are bilingual have greater cognitive flexibility in some areas than their monolingual cohorts. She compared Hebrew-speaking children to their monolingual peers in an affluent northwestern suburb of Chicago and in Tel Aviv. Several years later she replicated most of her findings in a study of Spanish-speaking bilingual children (compared to their monolingual peers) in lower socioeconomic neighborhoods of Chicago.

Some Advantages of Being Bilingual

Sandra Ben-Zeev, and others cited by her, have found that bilingual children:

- Analyze language more intensively than monolinguals
- Are capable at an earlier age than other children of separating the meaning of a word from its sound
- Are superior to their monolingual peers in ability to play with words

- Excel at symbol substitution, which depends on a grasp of the basic idea (and not on particular words) that "the structure of a language is different from the phonological representations and meaningful words in which it is embodied," and that linguistic structure is arbitrary and subject to change
- Are better able than monolinguals to classify items consistently and then to reclassify the same items using another type of classification, and then to switch to a third type of classification
- Have a greater tendency than monolinguals to elaborate without being asked
- Tend to approach some tasks "with a more analytic strategy"
- Tend to "root the stimulus word to a concrete situation," indicating awareness of the importance of social and linguistic context to deciphering the meaning of an utterance
- Are significantly better able to use teacher hints as cues to successful task completion
- Exhibit "unusual attention" to details in restructuring exercises
- Notice details that better integrate a narrative or picture sequence more often than monolinguals do
- Demonstrate greater social sensitivity than monolingual children

In her studies, bilingual children are seen to have developed a high ability to understand language as a system and to take different perspectives. Ben-Zeev sees these characteristics as resulting from the efforts of bilingual children to counteract structural interference from the two (or more) languages they juggle.

Advantages of Thinking in Different Languages

Another structural dimension of language comes about as it is fine tuned by its speakers to communicate in ways that integrate a worldview with the demands of local environmental conditions. Eskimo languages, for instance, with their hundreds of words to describe the nuances of snow and ice, are better equipped to promote understanding of conditions necessary for arctic survival than are languages that have grown out of needs imposed by arid conditions. To some extent, people talk about different things when speaking different languages, and the languages themselves may evolve to accommodate this. Sapir (1949) and Whorf (1964), two influential linguists, argue that the structure of a given language may even shape one's thinking, not simply facilitate an ecological accommodation. Yupik and Arabic facilitate different perspectives of the physical world and reflect different social conventions.

Advantages of Discussing Different Topics

"Mr. Wong's horse ran away." This allusion to a classical Chinese story conveys the rich context of folk wisdom. In this story, after Mr. Wong's horse ran away he cried and ranted. How was he going to till his fields, go to market without his horse? Woe to him, a miserable little farmer! Two weeks later his horse returned, leading a band of wild horses. Later Mr. Wong's son broke his leg. "Woe to me! Why am I the victim of the worst fate? Without my son I will not be able to get enough food to eat!" Several weeks later the local lord went to war. All the neighbors' sons were conscripted except for the disabled son of Mr. Wong.

Words and phrases only make sense if you know the context in which they are used. What does *of* mean? Or *get*? Or *poor,* or *old,* or *beautiful*? You need a context for most words to convey meaning. A highly important context is the culture in which the word is spoken (or signed).

If we go beyond the structural aspects of language acquisition and look at the social contexts within which language is used, the *content* of what is passed on by parents and peers, neighbors and cousins, comes into focus. The songs and adages, the norms and procedures, the topics of conversation—in short, the culture's knowledge and wisdom—is filtered and fed to each individual as she or he grows up. Multicultural persons not only have developed a keen ability to shift perspectives, they also have more perspectives.

A bilingual Irish poet, Nuala Ní Dhomhnaill (1995), chooses to express her poetry in a language that has a 1,500-year written tradition but that is spoken natively by only about 2 percent of the people in the Republic of Ireland. The Irish language, she says, is especially attentive to the rhyme and meter of sound and to certain types of relationships, such as our interface with the "otherworld." The Irish language enables her to enter a "reality" where one can jump back and forth with aplomb between the living and mythical beings.

Because different languages facilitate different perspectives of reality, knowing more than one language can confer distinct advantages to bilingual adults.

Fluency in shared communication systems is absolutely necessary to penetrate a culture, but it is not enough. To the extent an individual "speaks your language," literally and figuratively, he or she shares your group's distinctiveness. But here again, the lines are fuzzy. Within any one language, there are many gradations of speech. Some are regional, some are based on social class variations, and some originate in age or gender distinctions. Even when you succeed in finding someone who speaks just like you—maybe your next-door neighbor of the same age and gender—you might find that you have little else in common. Your neighbor might not be on your wavelength in spite of shared languages.

Officially Speaking

One way to plumb the acceptability of multicultural persons in a given social setting is to sample the categories available for describing them. The arbiter of meaning in highly literate modern societies is the dictionary—that compendium of usage blessed by scholarly recognition. Let us look up the meanings of three words closely associated with descriptions of multicultural people: authentic, identity, and diversity. A common dictionary in the United States is *Webster's New Collegiate Dictionary,* and well-worn copies occupy a place on the bookshelves of most middle-class households.

If we look at the formal Webster's (1967) dictionary definitions of *authentic,* we see the following traits listed:

Genuine: Being actually and exactly what the thing in question is

Veritable: True existence; actual identity; worthy of acceptance or belief

Bona fide: Accordance with an original of a type without counterfeiting, admixture or adulteration; no impurity or pollution; sincerity of intention

Trustworthy: According with fact or actuality; not imaginary, false, imitative

From these definitions we can see one factor that contributes to why multicultural people, at least in English-speaking United States among people who share these meanings, might run into difficulty getting their selves socially affirmed. The "thing" they are is not adequately encompassed by an existing category in their social environment, so people have difficulty labeling them. They are not without "impurity," and many monocultural folks regard multicultural folks as false, like a counterfeit bill. If you are not an English-speaking American, you might want to look up similar words in your own dictionary to become aware of the nuances associated with the multicultural experience in your own cultural—and linguistic—setting.

Even one of Webster's formal definitions of *identity* poses problems for the multicultural person:

Idem—the same: Sameness of essential or generic character in different instances; sameness in all that constitutes the objective reality of a thing

Oneness: Unity and persistence of personality; the condition of being the same with something described or asserted; identical equation

The terms *identity* and *identical* can be confused. Most dictionaries recognize that *identity* involves those characteristics that distinguish one individual from another, whereas *identical* involves *sameness.* Some of the obstacles encountered by multicultural people arise from this widely-shared confusion of *unity* or *coherence* with *sameness.*

Let us look at the other side of the coin—diversity. The concept of *diversity,* that is, "distinguished by various forms," is conventionally seen as antithetical to one's ability to have an identity. Diversity is perceived by conventional thinkers as inconsistency, something not stable or trustworthy. Definitions of diversity need to be widened, obviously, to accommodate virtuous folk who have been socialized in two or more cultures.

Popular as well as dictionary definitions of key concepts such as *authentic, identity,* and *diversity* can put multicultural people's status in jeopardy. In many societies, multicultural people have not been consecrated with an existing category within their social environment. Many people have difficulty labeling them. And, as we observed before, woe to the hapless "person without a category"—the individual without a socially acceptable label! They are seen to be homeless; they have no socially established category to inhabit.

Language and Identity

In some small language communities, language provides a distinguishing label that its speakers accept as central to their sense of identity. The upper-Amazon Cofán—all 500 of them—illustrate why this may be so. Here, as with most small, largely self-contained cultural systems, language is coterminous with tribe, culture, and even kinship. In larger societies, however, language is not as associated with other facets of socialization. English is a good example of a language where its speakers may share few cultural values in common, country to country (India, Kenya, and the United States, for instance).

If not the deceivingly fixed boundaries of nationality, ethnicity, "race," or language, then what other boundary can provide the grounding for our sense of self-identity? The next chapter explores the capability of *culture* as such a boundary.

Hyphenation as a Form of Identity

There is a language usage that triggers consternation among some multicultural people—dual or hyphenated identities: Korean- Japanese, Mexican-American, Italian-American, and so on. (In English, these identities are generally, but not always, hyphenated.) Some groups have loved their hyphens, and some have hated them. Some have fought to obtain a socially recognized hyphen, and others have fought to get rid of it.

The purpose of some hyphenated people has been to become socially visible, others to become, or remain, socially invisible. These choices depend on what is socially and politically strategic at the time. Figuring out which hyphenation—or lack thereof—is "politically correct" at any one time requires the willingness to continuously scan a constantly changing social environment.

Some groups have not cared what other groups have labeled them, taking whatever label society applies to them and converting it into a badge of pride. Even overtly derogatory terms can be defanged if those who are the objects of the term choose to do so. Two examples. In many parts of Latin America, especially in Mexico, citizens of the United States are referred to—denigratingly—as *gringos*. But so many Americans in their travels throughout the region have taken the term to describe themselves, that it has had its venom greatly diluted. The second example comes from Belize, a largely mixed black and white English-speaking country bordering on Mexico and Guatemala. There, many citizens call themselves, with pride, "niggers," a term that in most U.S. contexts is seen as highly derogatory. In Belize, people say things such as, "Those Guatemalans think they can come here and beat up on us. But we'll show them what these niggers can do."

In certain contexts, even highly nationalistic countries acknowledge the relevancy of compound national identities. We see these joint handles in the newspaper. "Among Catholic-Americans, birth control . . ." "Jewish-Americans support political efforts to . . ." Often, dual nationalities are recognized. "The educational level of Japanese-Americans . . ." "The Italian-American voting block . . ." This is obviously a simplification of religious or nation-state affiliations. The user does not ordinarily distinguish between practicing and nonpracticing Catholics, or between Hasidic and Reformed Jews. Nor does the user distinguish between first-, second-, or third-generation Japanese-Americans, or between assimilated and nonassimilated Italian-Americans.

In practice, hyphens are not applied with egalitarian resolve. One rarely hears an American referred to as Anglo-American or German-American—the two most common current American ancestries in the United States—except in the writings of American Indian organizations that use the collective term *Euro-American* to describe the European invaders and their descendants. The United States has been host to hordes of Welsh and Scots, but one does not hear these Celts called Welsh-American or Scots-American, although the Celtic Irish-Americans are everywhere. What's more, the Irish don't mind at all being called Irish-American, they just don't want to be mistaken for English.

Are some of us overly sensitive to being hyphenated? Yes. Is there something intrinsically degrading, something insulting, implied in being hyphenated? No. The overly touchy may be people who have not come to grips with their own multicultural past. Everyone, rightfully, is hyphenated. Even many pre-Columbian Indians had intermarried with people from other tribes; they were Dineh-Jemez, or perhaps Lakota-Cree. The real problem, as we see it, is not that there are hyphenated identities, but that there are not enough hyphens used. To acknowledge only *two* identities misses the reality. So, instead of grumbling about being relegated to hyphenated status, ask other people what their hyphens are. We are all "living on the hyphen," as one Cuban-American critic, Gustavo Pérez Firmat, puts it (quoted in *Newsweek,* July 10, 1995, 34). A slightly different formulation, "Life in the Hyphen," was coined by Mexican-born writer Ilan Stavans for the title of the opening chapter to his book on Hispanic identity (Stavans, 1995).

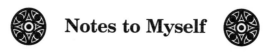 **Notes to Myself**

1. The language(s) I learned at home while I was growing up is (are):

_____

_____

Later, I learned the following languages:

_____

_____

Here's how I learned them (example: studied them in school; worked with people who spoke that language):

_____

_____

_____

_____

2. In my family tree, counting as many past generations as I can trace, the following languages were spoken:

_____

_____

_____

_____

3. With the language(s) I now speak, I would be able to talk with the following of my great-grandparents:

_____

_____

_____

_____

_____

4. When I looked up words like *authenticity, identity,* and *diversity* in dictionaries of my own language(s), they caused me the following problems:

_____

_____

_____

_____

_____

5. I remember some examples of how the older people in my family used words that I don't use anymore:

_____

_____

_____

_____

_____

Culture, The Mother of All Boundaries

Boundaries That Define

So, we return to our question: What boundaries, real or imagined, define us?

Familiar cultural demarcations—national, ethnic, and "racial" labels—are like lines drawn in shifting sands. There is no "pure" nationality, ethnicity, or race. Boundaries are drawn with bold and clear lines on parchment, but, as we have seen, in many instances they would be more accurate were the cartographer blind drunk. The mythical "race," the imagined nationality, and the mystically defined ethnicity are "pretend" boundaries. These "pretend" boundaries are politically functional only when they confer on the people with the given tag their fair share of the socioeconomic pie.

There are other group boundaries, boundaries that are more stable than the pretend boundaries of nationality, ethnicity, and "race." Foremost among these are the boundaries created by the collectively shared systems of affect and cognition that we call culture. Formidable divisions are formed by the way we are socialized into these systems. From the cradle we begin learning information that has been passed down over the generations. It lets us in on the rules by which "civilized" life will be played. For their indoctrinees, these systems feel "natural," and the rewards and punishments meted out for proper and improper behavior feel "right." Culture, this mother of all boundaries, does not obey the nation-state lines drawn (and redrawn) on the map, or the membership criteria of "race" or ethnicity, or language, or even the ties of family membership. It is a boundary that conditions its recipients into a reasonably cohesive system for viewing themselves and the world. It is, of course, invented and arbitrary, but it molds our worldview more so than political or ideological divisions. Sometimes this boundary seems invisible, anchored in air and water.

Who Knows Air? Who Knows Water?

Those of us who grow up with each foot in a different culture have a unique opportunity to view objectively what in most people is a conditioned reflex beyond easy scrutiny—the role culture plays in the formation of thought, feelings, and behavior.

"We don't know who discovered water, but we're certain it wasn't a fish," John Culkin wryly observed. It is not until the fish is removed from water that it becomes aware that water exists. Gregory Bateson (1972) reminds us that it is when we are in direct contact with contrasting ways of doing and thinking that the validity of each culture's "game" is called into question. We can be the fish who "discovers water."

It is useful to distinguish those values we hold because of the fickle finger of fate—because we grew up in certain families or in certain cultures and not in others—from those we have chosen as a result of intelligent reflection or compelling affect. How do we distance ourselves momentarily from the cultural conventions that have been ingrained in us since childhood? For if we don't distance ourselves from these mostly invisible influences, we cannot tell which of our values may represent more than mere reflex conditioning. Are we like trained dogs? Do we salivate when we hear the toll of the in-group?

There are several ways to achieve this distance, to view water from the perspective of air, and air from the perspective of water. We can compare the values and behavior of one society to those of another, or we can personally experience multiple socialization in more than one society.

Comparing Societies

When we compare the values and the behavior of humans in one society to those in another, we discover how each set of values makes *internal* sense. Values and behavior fit together (approximately rather than perfectly) in all societies to enable its members to survive. Moreover, we usually do more than merely survive, we live with some sense of style. We flourish. It is sobering to remember, though, that not all societies are served well by their beliefs and many of both, societies and beliefs, do not survive.

Borrowing Cultural Innovations

Just as everyone's chromosomes contain whole bands of genes that have survived intact from life forms now extinct (all life forms share some DNA), so does every culture incorporate social forms it has borrowed from other cultures.

Examples are everywhere. We borrow words from other languages (English, a Germanic language, dips heavily into Latin), we borrow technological innovations (gunpowder and spaghetti from the Chinese, the latter by way of Italy), we borrow dress (the ubiquitous American blue denim jeans), and music (an old Incan song, called *El Cóndor Pasa* in its later Spanish edition, became popular in the United States with words from the Simon and Garfunkel version, subtitled "I'd rather be a hammer than a nail").

Humans appear to thrive on multicultural cross-pollination. Imagine how different our life would be without the contributions of ideas and artifacts from all over the globe that we see in our everyday life.

It is from comparing one society to another that anthropologists have identified the universality of the belief that one's own society has the "truest" values. This is an ethnocentric conviction that cannot, of course, be true in any absolute sense. This collective sense of superiority may be an extension of an innate value wired into our individual heads through the dynamics of natural selection. As Robert Wright (1994, 380) puts it in his masterful review of evolutionary psychology:

Think of it: Zillions and zillions of organisms running around, each under the hypnotic spell of a single truth, all these truths identical, and all logically incompatible with one another: "My hereditary material is the most important material on earth; its survival justifies your frustration, pain, even death." And you are one of these organisms, living your life in the thrall of a logical absurdity.

Beyond a conviction of collective moral superiority, cultures share many similar categories of behavior, although they do not share the specific behaviors associated with any given category. While they share food taboos, for instance, people in some societies eat beef but not pork, while those in others eat no flesh at all.

Cultures' Common Denominators

The categories of experience shared by virtually all cultures, according to the anthropologist George Murdock, include age grouping, athletic sports, bodily adornment, calendar, cleanliness training, community organization, cooking, cooperative labor, cosmology, courtship, dancing, decorative art, divination, division of labor, dream interpretation, education, eschatology, ethics, ethnobotany, etiquette, faith healing, family, feasting, fire making, folklore, food taboos, funeral rites, games, gestures, gift giving, government greetings, hair styles, hospitality, housing, hygiene, incest taboos, inheritance rules, joking, kin-groups, kinship nomenclature, language, law, luck superstitions, functions, mourning, music, mythology, policy, postnatal care, pregnancy usages, property rights, propitiation of supernatural beings, puberty customs, religious ritual, residence rules, sexual restrictions, soul concepts, status differentiation, surgery, tool making, trade, visiting, weaning, and weather control (Murdock, 1965, 89; see also *Human Universals* by Brown, 1991).

Besides shared classifications (categories) of experience, societies share many social dynamics, not all of which are ennobling. For example, males invest, on the average, more time in the care and raising of children who carry their genes than in children in the family who do not, such as stepchildren. Each society provides behavioral options that enable its members to satisfy basic needs (maximize pleasure, minimize pain) in a socially acceptable way. To quote again from Wright (1994, 260):

> Human beings are designed to assess their social environment, and, having figured out what impresses people, do it; or, having found what people disfavor, avoid it. They're pretty open-minded about what "it" is. The main thing is that they be able to succeed at it; people everywhere want to feel pride, not shame; to inspire respect, not disdain.

The specific behaviors societies offer to satisfy these needs, however, differ widely from society to society. The contrast is often startling, from shrinking heads to getting a Ph.D. in Provençal literature, both of which are done to gain in personal wisdom and community stature. There is always enough cross-cultural inconsistency in how things "ought" to be done that it is easy to spot many instances where the codes of "appropriate" human behavior appear to differ arbitrarily from culture to culture.

When one young American set off as a teenager to seek his fortune in Mexico, he prided himself on his sense of honesty. Truthfulness and frankness are values much esteemed in the United States. He told it like he saw it: *pan pan, vino vino* (literally "[he calls] bread bread, [and] wine wine"). This value ran smack into a widely held dissimilar value in Mexico: that more important than being honest with people is being sensitive to their feelings. "White lies," then, were not only used to cover more social situations than was customary in the United States, but "lying" was essentially downgraded to "fibbing," and a fibber was noticeably preferred over someone who was either "too indiscreet" or "too frank." Sometimes even mischievous lying is adaptive to trying circumstances. A Dutch specialist in intercultural communication, Mieke Janssen-Matthes, relates how during the Nazi occupation of Holland her parents would tell her that she shouldn't lie. But it was all right to lie to certain people, namely, Germans under the occupation. It was the "right" thing to misdirect occupying soldiers who requested directions. To protect Jews in hiding, it was right to lie about who lived in your home.

Even when differing societies share many behavioral options, the frequency with which its members choose a given behavior may differ substantially from society to society. Studying these differences helps us gain a perspective on how culture affects our thinking and behavior.

These cross-cultural comparisons help us to see the role of culture in the formation of moral and aesthetic preferences, as well as the way "objective" reality is filtered by cultural screens.

We can even compare cultures without leaving the bosom of our own family. Anyone who delves into their family history discovers that each generation has lived with its own precepts of right and wrong behavior, and even the languages used by our ancestors have changed from time to time. The centuries alone separate us from understanding the speech of our forebears. For most of us, olde English (or old any-other-language) is as incomprehensible as porpoise toots. Behavior considered appropriate by our families only a century ago now seems quaint, totally impractical, painfully bigoted, or just plain painful. Making your own furniture, spending all day Monday washing homespun clothes (and ironing on Tuesdays), thrashing or grinding grain to use in cooking, preserving the tribal scent through infrequent bathing, or binding girls' feet. In the Middle Ages one social pastime consisted of sitting by the hearth, delousing one's spouse and family. The daily life of our near ancestors may bear little resemblance to our own.

In short, comparing the values and behavior of diverse societies in both time and space is one way to get a sense of how culture affects the way we think and behave. It is a way for fish to discover water and for birds to discover air.

Multiple Socialization

The second way to put some distance between yourself and your cultural indoctrination is to personally experience your own socialization in two or more disparate societies.

One week a couple was dining in a posh restaurant in Washington, D.C., selecting the utensils that were appropriate to each specific course from a wide selection of shiny silverware surrounding the porcelain plates of varied size. The next week they were dining with a semi-nomadic tribe in the upper-Amazon jungle, using their hands to tear off succulent pieces from a smoked monkey perched on a plank. In each of these settings, there was a "mannerly," "civilized," "well-brought-up" way to perform the motor task of getting food into one's mouth.

In this case, however, the couple would have had to have lived extensively in Cofán culture to be able to claim dual socialization. To be socialized in a culture is to depend on others around you, and on their social system, for satisfying your basic needs.

The road from one culture to another is sometimes filled with unexpected opportunity and sometimes filled with potholes. It often contains both. Randy Borman, son of missionary parents from Illinois, was socialized by both the upper-Amazon Cofán and by a community of U.S. missionaries who lived in other villages. But primarily, Randy was socialized by the Cofán. He experienced difficulty with his U.S. peers the year he spent in college in Aurora, Illinois. Bicycling to school, he would put "good" road kill in his backpack for later cooking over a hot plate. Sometimes in winter he used the overheated radiators to cook his road finds.

One evening, as a young adult, Randy mused that to have the kinds of discussions he enjoys on intellectual topics he needed to talk to college-educated people, and he had to do that in either Spanish or English. But when he wanted to talk about the kinds of social issues that keep the spirit alive, he had to talk with Cofán people. The pull between two cultures can be strong.

A few years later, Randy built a house in the jungle, married a Cofán woman, and began to provide for his family through hunting; he augmented resources by working seasonally as a guide. Resolving the pull of two cultures is hard, and each of us goes our own way. Randy and Gonzalo opted for indigenous ways.

Lucky people—those who grow up multiculturally—can compare different societies and personally experience them. Their ability to entertain diverse, sometimes even contradictory, views of the world can be a resource to others of more limited perspective. Writing to a business readership, Stephen Rhinesmith (1993) states that the global effectiveness that is needed in the 21st century for economic interests to flourish requires the ability to balance contradictions.

Culture: Invisible Tyrant or Liberating Savior?

Just how sacrosanct is culture?

Is culture, to borrow analogies from ancient Egypt, like the cat goddess Bastet, wielding the destructive force of the Sun God's eye to those who do not show the requisite respect? Or is it more like the divine mother Isis, who civilizes the world through social institutions such as marriage? Whatever it is, it asks one thing of a multicultural person: a commitment to think about how culture affects our thoughts and actions. The resulting insight expands our consciousness and elevates us from being merely culture's automaton.

Humans, like all primates, are gregarious animals. The social conventions that have been developed to make it easier for humans to interact have grown quite complex, much more so than the social conventions of the other surviving 200 species of primates. These social conventions are the principal adaptive mechanism humans use to cope with life's circumstances. It is our cultures—abundantly more than our genes—that evolve to meet the exigencies of changing life conditions. Cultures can adapt immeasurably quicker to changing conditions than can our DNA—days versus millennia. Because of the swift adaptive ability of culture, Homo sapiens—for perhaps the last 35,000 years—has been sheltered from total dependence on biological evolution. (The high quality wall paintings in the Chauvet cave in present-day France date back 30,000 years.)

Even more important to humans than the species's biological structure is the way need satisfaction is structured by our societies, especially food consumption, sexual gratification, the acquisition of status, and protection from predators. These four drives—hunger, love, vanity, fear—are the major "socializing forces," according to Sumner and Keller (1927). It is in this sense that culture has become more critical than biology to the survival of our species. By extension, to the extent other life forms (chimpanzees, for instance) have developed cultures they too are shielded from total reliance on biological evolution. Shielded, not in the sense of preventing the deployment of genetic forces in the evolution of culture-bearers, but in the sense of introducing liberal amounts of a large and complex human artifact—culture—into the brew of evolutionary forces. While our understanding of the interactive effects between culture and evolutionary biological processes is still embryonic (Durham, 1991), the cultural resilience of multicultural individuals, we speculate, may well increase their overall "fitness."

Social customs for facilitating basic survival go with the flow of adaptive pressures. The more humans live in close proximity to each other, the more necessary are conventions of mutual respect, for example. When the pace of the hunt is leisurely, to take another example, one can dawdle over long meals. When these circumstances change, the adaptive mechanism must also change—fast-food restaurants, conveniently located. These cultural changes help individuals stay afloat in a changing world.

Culture provides the keys to our survival, and sometimes the keys fit easily, but other times they are rusted and make it hard to open the right doors. To the extent survival of a society is threatened by behavior that has become dysfunctional (for example, toxic waste dumps), traditional ways of doing things ("throw it in the garbage") become a liability to the group. Cultural change is indispensable to our species's survival.

Author Kurt Vonnegut, Jr. (1974) shares this thought while musing about developing a "Welcome to Earth" handbook for the world's children:

And one thing I would really like to tell them about is cultural relativity. I didn't learn until I was in college about all the other cultures, and I should have learned that in the first grade. A first grader should understand that his or her culture isn't a rational invention; that there are thousands of other cultures and they all work pretty well; that all cultures function on faith rather than truth; that there are lots of alternatives to our own society. Cultural relativity is defensible and attractive. It's also a source of hope. It means we don't have to continue this way if we don't like it.

The arbitrary, relativistic, invented nature of cultural values exerts a profound effect on the way we act. The enormous power of culture is that, unlike nationality, ethnicity, "race," and language, it conveys the "game plan," the rules of engagement that will determine much of our thoughts, feelings, and behavior. As the vehicle of our socialization, it would seem logical to base our sense of identity on culture. There are, however, three shortcomings to doing this.

The first limitation has to do with the way people are socialized within any single culture. Cultural values are not monolithic, even within a well-defined culture area, because of the cleavages of gender, age, social class, religion, sexual preferences, and many other groups whose values set them off from the rest of their neighbors. To the extent each of us has internalized the values of *subcultural* groups—and each of us has—the larger community entity (Arab, Chinese, Hispanic, Nordic, Slavic, Zulu) ceases to be, in many circumstances, an adequate explanation of where we inherited our system of beliefs. We get them from our families and other smaller groups within the larger collective. It is a bit fuzzy which influences stem from the larger cultural community—the shared "core" of values—rather than to a specific segment within the community. Most socialization occurs at the subcultural level.

The second limitation of using a recognizable culture as your identifying label has to do with the nature of "core" cultural values. They seem to be those standards that are acceptable to the dominant sector of society, the one with disproportionate power and prestige. What's usually described as "core" is either the Platonic ideal of the society's notables or their actual values. "Core" is what the map-maker projects; it's a function of the power and prestige of the cartographer, and it changes as social-political events hand other future map-makers the quill.

Culture is like an onion, with many overlapping layers. And when you peel an onion to get to the "core," nothing is there. The conventional metaphor of culture as a series of concentric circles within circles, with the centermost circle called "core," misconstrues both the locus of socialization and the adaptive nature of culture.

The third shortcoming of anchoring our sense of self in a given culture is that, as individuals socialized in more than one cultural system, even the otherwise reasonable and meaningful label of a given culture becomes falsely limiting, exclusionary. Just as one political or "racial" label implies too narrow a description, so too does one culture do injustice to the description of a multicultural person.

None of which is to deny that culture is a much more powerful boundary than either nationality or "race." For boundary crossers, however, a less "fixed" identity that goes beyond culture may provide a more satisfying descriptor, at least in some circumstances, such as when you are by yourself, between cultures. Research reported by the social psychologist Marilynn B. Brewer (1991) suggests that the more successful attempts to "label" oneself involve finding a comfortable balance between a sense of belonging and a sense of distinctiveness.

So . . . to say we are Mexican or Welsh or Dutch or Nigerian; or Hispanic or Celtic or Euro-Germanic or Ibo; or Asian or black is too fuzzy, too ambiguous, a label. It requires much additional demographic and psychographic data to be very descriptive. For starters, the age, gender, social class, ideology . . . etc., of the person.

There are, it should be clear by now, no fixed boundaries that can be pressed into service on all occasions to unequivocally delineate us. Our multiple boundaries depend too much on shifting contexts. The ingredients of self-identity include many odds and ends, but one quality it has to contain is flexibility.

Few people, and this includes social scientists and psychiatrists, have a good grasp on how culture affects our internal workings as well as our outward deportment. We shall, in the next chapter, look into a downside of being multicultural—the way some professionals misunderstand the multicultural experience.

Notes to Myself

1. My own approach to understanding how culture influences my thoughts and actions comes mostly from (check the most appropriate):

   ☐ Studying about different cultures and comparing them

   ☐ Having been raised in a multicultural family

   ☐ Having been raised in more than one culture

   ☐ Other: _____

   _____

2. I feel most socially affirmed with the following people and groups:

   _____

   _____

   _____

3. If I could invent any category at all to describe myself, it would be:

   _____

   _____

4. From my own experience, here is an example of a behavior that has meaning in one of my cultures but no meaning in another:

   _____

   _____

   _____

   _____

   _____

Boundary Strain

Are You Sick?

The pressures on self-identity and on one's "purity of perspective" that extensive contact with another culture imply can lead to a nether land, close to madness, according to some experienced sojourners.

Close to Madness

T. E. Lawrence (a.k.a. Lawrence of Arabia) donned Arab clothes at a time when the religious differences between Christianity and Islam were drawn much more sharply than their monotheistic similarities. It was a time when England intervened in a bitter Mideast armed conflict (Arabs versus German-aligned Turks in World War I). Some years later, Lawrence (1966) shared these reflections:

> In my case, the efforts for these years to live in the dress of Arabs, and imitate their mental foundation, quitted me of my English self, and let me look at the West and its conventions with new eyes: they destroyed

it all for me. At the same time, I could not sincerely take on the Arab skin; it was affectation only . . . . Sometimes these selves would converge in the void, and then madness was very near, as I could believe it would be near the man who could see things through the veils at once of two customs, two educations, two environments.

Lawrence of Arabia is not the only one who has feared the consequences of biculturalism. Do your friends and acquaintances sometimes make you feel like you're from another planet? One 18th-century Irish immigrant to the ethnically prejudiced New World said, "I was looked upon as a barbarian" (Fischer, 1989). Maybe a Nymphoid Barbarian from Dinosaur Hell, to borrow the title of a U.S. movie that only got a one-star rating. As a multicultural boundary crosser, you have to be prepared for mixed reviews.

The more homogeneous a society perceives itself to be, the stronger the tendency to respond warily to people who look or behave differently from "normal" folk. Many things contribute to this wariness: "Factors such as race, ethnicity, nationality, class, gender, sexual and religious orientation, tradition and modernism, all shade that identity. Sometimes these elements fuse harmoniously, but more often they clash" (Lavrijsen, 1993). Sometimes multiculturalism is hot, sometimes not. Culture contact always provokes mixed emotions. The national, ethnic, "racial," and language boundaries discussed earlier infuse discussions about multicultural people with negative overtones.

People who have been abroad and acquired other ways of thinking and acting can be quarantined by the Contaminated-by-Barbarians Syndrome when they reenter their home culture. A multicultural Japanese college student, Mayumi Fujii, says that "As a multicultural person, I am a mixed, somewhat confused, salad. I wander between two ideas, thinking both are great." Today in Japan, young Japanese who have been raised abroad as children of the men who are managing Japan's offshore economic empire are viewed as "polluted" when they apply to work in the same big Japanese companies that employ their fathers. These youths often go through adjustment difficulties on their return to an environment that does not affirm their broader-than-Japanese identity. Because mental and physical health professionals alike often are schooled by the tiny laboratory lens of a disease model, some monolingual, monocultural Japanese psychiatrists prescribe tranquilizers for returnees. This essentially puts the troublemakers "to sleep" so they don't disturb the social harmony.

Is a Rose a Rose?

There are, of course, many hues of border crossers. This diversity is illustrated by Oscar Martínez's (1994) descriptions of people who live on the Mexican-U.S. border. He considers three main forces: temporal, ideological, and economic. He suggests the following typology of borderlanders, or *fronterizos:* Mexican American assimilationists, Mexican American newcomers, disadvantaged Mexican immigrants, disadvantaged but upwardly mobile Mexican immigrants, advantaged Mexican immigrants, Mexican American binational consumers, Mexican American commuters, Mexican American biculturalists, Mexican American binationalists, Anglo newcomers, Anglo winter residents, Anglo nationalists, Anglo uniculturalists, Anglo binational consumers, Anglo commuters, Anglo biculturalists, Anglo binationalists, and Anglo residents in Mexico. Each category tends to share common dynamics, but the labels, of course, are not mutually exclusive. What about dual citizens, individuals who are simultaneously Mexican American and American Mexican? The key to placing an individual into a given category, Martínez explains, is to identify "the predominant force that currently drives his or her link with the neighboring country."

Martínez makes an interesting point about life in the borderlands. "Regardless of their political, economic, or social standing in society, individuals who have only a national orientation lack a full understanding of how the local [borderland] system functions and are therefore situated on the fringes of that system." To be monocultural on the borderland is to be peripheral to its culture. Whatever hue of multiculturalism you embody, there are novel relationships to be negotiated.

Is Multiple Socialization Inherently Stressful?

Being socialized into two or more cultures, even in regions with relatively little modern-day strife, is not without its stresses. In peaceful New Zealand where there are generally "good" relations between the indigenous Maori and the European settlers, tension erupts from time to time (Boucher, Landis, and Clark, 1987). Although intermarriage between whites and Maori is commonplace, and while there have been consistent government efforts at accommodation rather than extermination, indigenous land rights have been eroded by perfidy and a prejudiced judicial system, and the income levels of Maori relegate disproportionate numbers to lower socioeconomic status.

Intercultural contact inevitably provokes some degree of conflict, especially for people who are expected to internalize conflicting values. When the late Ruben Snake, a leader of the Winnebago Indian Tribe of Nebraska (USA), was asked why so many Native Americans experience so much stress in their daily lives, he replied, "If you had a cowboy boot on one foot and a moccasin on the other, you'd go around in circles, too."

"I am like a child lost in a maze. I believe there is a goal, but I do not know how to define it. I cannot ask for help from anybody; I just stand there and watch the people around me," says Machiko Yamada, a Japanese college student. A student from Finland living in Japan, Salla Toivonen, reacts this way: "I am an orphaned, wandering warrior, and the contradictory characters inside me get confused in situations that are unstable. This moves me, when I am frightened, to rely on authority, my teachers, elders, my father."

There are periods in history that exacerbate internal conflict. World War II was one such time.

The Stress of "Progress," the Strain of Migration

A common form of multiculturalism often is not even recognized as such. It occurs as a consequence of rural people all over the globe moving to the megalopolis.

All of us who live in urban areas have had ancestors who, at one time or another, crossed the boundary from rural to urban living. Perhaps the move has occurred during our own lifetime; perhaps we have been the one in our family who has crossed from rural to urban society. This crossing has not been easy, and the adjustments required are worthy of attention. In fact, Western sociologists have made careers studying rural people in their hamlets and following them on their urban migrations. This migration from rural to urban areas, however, often leads to multicultural space, where one is "caught on the horizon, part of neither Earth nor Sky," as a Navajo put it.

There are interesting variations on the theme of adjusting to rural versus urban life. For example, those immigrant groups that have settled in urban areas, such as the Danes in the United States, experienced stronger pressures to assimilate than did their Swedish cousins who settled into rural areas (Skårdal, 1974).

The exodus from rural areas is a result of economic pressures on subsistence farmers who see better opportunities for escaping poverty in the city. This is especially true in centralized governments where the lion's share of the nation's resources are kept in the capital, near the politicians and ruling elites. This daily drama enfolds in countries throughout Africa, Latin America, and Asia, where hundreds of thousands flock to cities in hope of a better life. The exodus exacts a sharp toll of behavioral adjustment on rural people as they pursue this most popular avenue for achieving upward mobility. In the process of making the necessary adjustments to urban life, they become multicultural—at home in both rural and urban environments, speaking different languages or dialects in each.

The agrarian, preindustrial culture of the migrants was a seasoned response to the conditions in which they formerly lived, but old behavioral recipes do not always prepare one for life in the big city. In addition to drastic changes in their daily routine, and frequently even in the language they must use, they are forced to interact with city slickers who have markedly different ways of viewing things. To make matters worse, city slickers sometimes lack the empathy that would mitigate the strains of adjustment suffered by the rural newcomers. Many students of the lifestyles of the rich and poor contend that rural cultures across the world share more cultural values than any one shares with the urban cultures in their own countries. This is perhaps especially true in countries whose economies are largely agrarian. Agrarian nations are the most highly stratified societies that humans have yet devised. Ancient Egyptian society, by way of example, contained a status spread that ranged from God-Pharaoh to unskilled slave laborer.

The Distressed Cultural Refugee

During World War II, people belonging to more than one culture were, most dramatically, the uprooted refugees. In the post-WWII era, many of these refugees were caught in the twin crises of urbanization and economic development. (European Jews were an exception as they had lived in urban areas for quite some time.)

When people of the day thought of cultural change, they saw stress. Strategies for coping with change became synonymous with the defense mechanisms described by Anna Freud (1946) and in her studies of children orphaned or made refugees by WWII (Freud and Dann, 1951). Most of the well-funded research throughout the 1950s and 1960s—and even to the present time—seems to focus on the pathology of culture change: alcoholism and substance abuse, neuroses, psychosomatic disorders, schizophrenia, depression, and diseases brought about through forced changes in diet and lifestyle, such as the incidence of diabetes among Native Americans.

Moreover, in addition to the stresses inherent in an adjustment to novel and often conflicting norms, the situation for many multicultural individuals was worsened by the unsympathetic metaphors that social scientists and members of the helping professions applied to them for most of the last 100 years. One pernicious set of metaphors we refer to as the "you Tonto, me Lone Ranger" metaphor. Another set can be called the disease metaphors. These metaphors were not, as we shall see, applied to rich and poor alike.

The "You Tonto, Me Lone Ranger" Metaphor

The space that multicultural people often find themselves occupying began to interest anthropologists from the onset of their discipline about 100 years ago. Franz Boas (1896) inferred that a process of change occurs in cultures in contact because such cultures tend to become more like each other. This was the beginning of research on acculturation, on the stress associated with the changes required to make the leap to "modernization," and on the behaviors that people manifest in dealing with these dynamics. We call this approach, as performed by the social scientists of the day, the "you Tonto, me Lone Ranger" metaphor because the individualistic scientists so often studied, with patronizing condescension, American Indians. Anthropologists studied "primitive" people in contact with the "developed" West, and sociologists studied immigrant laborers' participation in capitalism's urban industrial machine.

This interaction of rural, "primitive" man with his urban, "sophisticated" cousins led to the creation of the multicultural spaces first studied by social scientists and, thus, to the first social science theories regarding multiculturalism. Five phases in the culture contact cycle were identified by anthropologist Robert Redfield (1935), based on earlier work by sociologist Robert Park (1925, 1926):

- The initial contact (sometimes desired, sometimes dreaded)

- Semi-assimilation

- Rejection by the dominant group

- The subordinate group's being thrown back on itself

- The subordinate group's subsequent reemergence as a creative agent contributing to the resolution of the stresses associated with contact with a second culture

The whole cycle, it was thought at the time, occupies about 100 years. These phases in the cycle may now occur at "warp speed," and stresses, one notes, attend each phase.

Yet this model, presented in Redfield's famous 1935 *Outline of the Study of Acculturation,* contained at least seven biases that, in the myopia of the age, went unnoticed. These biases have had negative repercussions for multicultural individuals.

- The model dealt with group behavior and ignored the variations found in the behavior of the individuals who made up the group.

- The societies studied were in a relationship in which one society was clearly dominant over the other.

- Western norms were always seen as the dominant norms.

- Most studies focused on situations where only a pair of cultures were in contact. That is, they were really studying—according to their lights—*bicultural* space, rather than the *multicultural* space they thought they were studying.

- This "bicultural space," in fact, was a result of how dominant groups defined subordinate cultures. The error committed by those with the power to define others (the elite metaphor-makers) was to fail to distinguish one cultural group from another. Tribes were combined for administrative ease. The hundreds of indigenous tribes that met the Europeans as they came ashore were thus reduced, through definitional sleight of hand, to one "homogeneous" group—American Indian. For example, the U.S. government put Kiowas, Comanches, and Apaches, all speaking different languages and the latter two traditional rivals, all together on a single reservation and expected these "Indians" to behave as a unified community. Government employees could never understand why this "community" had so many factions. Reality was just too complex for the emerging modern bureaucratic mentality!

- The "studied" populations, whose "civilizability" was carefully moni-tored, were faced with edicts and regulations whose nightmarish con-tradictions and stupidities went unnoticed by the rulers and their scholars. Ask someone from Laguna Pueblo, New Mexico, about their problems in making the transitions from one status to another. Origi-nally they were, of course, a sovereign people. Then they became a subordinate people under the Spanish, followed by Mexican, then Texan, and finally U.S. federal administration. Today, the Bureau of Indian Affairs runs their primary school, the Pueblo runs their middle school, and the State of New Mexico runs their high school. Or ask the people of Vanuatu in the South Pacific (near Fiji) about their being under simultaneous British and French administrations with two sets of schools, courts, bureaucracies—two of everything!

- The contact situation was seen as transitional, to be resolved in "a new consensus" (read "domination") through the subordinate group's as-similation to the dominant culture.

You don't have to look far to find the origin of these biases. The model used for understanding culture contact was formulated by scholars and politicians dealing with non-Western peoples in contact with the West for the first time, and by social scientists living in the United States during the time of the great immigrations. Much of the negativism that "multiculturalism" conjures up in the minds of professionals laboring in today's schools and clinics, and lurking in the visions of politicians in charge of public policy, is the outgrowth of these earlier approaches.

An additional source of negative attitudes toward multicultural people came from another locus of modern science, the psychiatric couch.

Cobblers See Shoddy Shoes, Psychiatrists See Psychos: The Disease Metaphors

Psychiatrists, because they typically worked from a medical model of mental illness (rather than from a health maintenance model), were trained to see some coping strategies as merely responses to a diseased or damaged condi-tion. They reasoned that the defensive reactions (that is, the coping strategies themselves), as well as the underlying disease, needed to be treated. When the underlying pathology is obscure, the recourse is to treat the symptoms.

Conditions associated with World War II in the 1940s brought disease metaphors to the front, so to speak, as the helping professions tried to meet the needs of refugees and orphaned children.

A review of the mid-20th-century social science literature, prepared for a grant proposal in 1950 by a social psychologist, Donald T. Campbell, reveals a list of coping strategies utilized by marginal and uprooted persons. These strategies can be divided into three main categories of response: sick, rigid, and novel.

- **Sick.** Those coping strategies labeled "sick" allowed a sort of maimed survival in various states of neurotic indecisiveness, aimlessness, schizoid withdrawal, self-depreciation, cynicism, and destructiveness. An example would be the angry militant who rejects all cultural values.

- **Rigid.** Strategies allowing rather inflexible responses: the reestablishment of an orthodoxy (often more rigid than the "natural born" variety) characterized, perhaps, by a reactionary return to the parental culture, even if this meant a return to the ghetto; over-conformity to the "new" culture; the phenomenon of "passing" into the dominant culture; and the creation of a novel orthodoxy, one usually hostile to all existing orthodoxies. Example: Amish farmers following the customs of rural farmers of two centuries ago, even though the descendants of their ancestors who remained in Germany no longer share that culture. The expatriate writer Salman Rushdie (1991) wrote that "It is the natural condition of the exile, putting down roots in memory."

- **Novel.** Strategies that respond to the changed social milieu with novel behaviors: converting a relativism of values into a stable standard of reference; adapting to situations by recognizing the interplay between role and reference group and allowing behavior to be guided by several discrete "generalized others"; retaining goals, for instance, "wealth," while abandoning the culturally prescribed means of achieving them, and vice versa; and finally by being an innovator, an initiator of social change. Example: Nativistic Celts and South Sea Islanders—along with most everyone else who has gone about the business of creating a nation-state—who create a glorious, ancient culture the way they imagine it to have been.

. . . And Educators See Dunces

Worldwide, a common response to the culturally different is to view that person as socially underdeveloped, mentally ill, retarded, or otherwise alien. In the United States, as in other countries, the children of non-English-speaking immigrants disproportionately are assigned to classes for the retarded. Silvia, a graduate of Harvard University's law school, relates that as a Puerto Rican-born child, she scored 14 on an IQ test administered in English after her family moved to the United States. She was assigned to a Chicago classroom for the mentally handicapped. The sordid story of attempts by many mental health professionals and their colleagues in the public school system to pathologize multicultural experience continues even today.

A Chinese family moved into a western suburb of Chicago, dressed their little girl in a fine new dress and shoes, fastened her lovely black hair with a mother-of-pearl barrette, and sent her off to her first day of school. Her first-grade teacher could not get the child to understand even simple directions, so she referred the little girl to the school psychologist. The psychologist, himself bilingual in Greek and English, gave the monolingual Cantonese-speaking child a test—in English—to determine her developmental level. Based on her subsequent test score, the psychologist referred the girl to the school administration for reassignment to a class for the mentally retarded.

This event, along with many similar accounts, came to the attention of the Illinois state director of bilingual education. In response, he organized a three-day workshop for bilingual school psychologists and counselors. "Why," he asked, "did you make these assignments, knowing the testing instruments were invalid for non-English-speaking children?" After an uncomfortable discussion on whether the tests really were invalid—ingrained ideas are put aside with great difficulty—the psychologists replied that the law was clear: students suspected of special learning deficiencies had to be tested, and since there were no available tests in other languages, the students had to be tested in English. For the children to get redress, the law had to be changed. This account demonstrates that our professional credentials sometimes come at the expense of our own common sense.

Eventually, rather than just condemn the hapless victims of multiculturalism to classes for the retarded and to the sick wards, investigators began to take an interest in how people coped with multicultural stress. The well-known linguist and Wycliffe Bible translator, Kenneth Pike (1967), calls this stress a paradox: "Excessive tension can destroy us—this must be avoided. But without tension we, like a flaccid violin string, can serve no one." When Siddhartha was meditating under the bodhi tree 2,500 years earlier, this same perception accompanied his moment of enlightenment. In the midst of his meditation he heard the voice of a traveling musician instructing his student as their boat passed on the river: "A too tight string breaks; a too loose string will not make music."

The Marginal Man

One can be marginal in at least two ways: as "alone-in-the-corner-sucking-my-thumb" marginality, or as "let's-see . . . -my-daily-rate-as-an-international-consultant-is . . ." marginality. One can be marginal yet be a creatively productive individual. Are you part of the "mainstream," or are you marching to a different drum beat, creating new social space?

Multicultural people are regarded by some as marginal to all of the cultures in which they participate. They attain this status by breaking too many of the "rules" of mainstream life, and their reward for being untrustworthy is to forfeit membership in the larger group (Becker, 1963).

When Everett Stonequist used the term *marginal man* in 1937, it was a positive descriptor. Stonequist (1937) studied the biographies of the marginal men that Toynbee, the great English historian, had prepared—St. Paul, Gautama the Buddha, David, Caesar, Muhammed, Peter the Great, Lenin, Confucius—and he was intrigued. He saw great possibilities for "marginals." Marginal man was, in Stonquist's words, "the crucible of cultural fusion." It is these individuals, Stonequist maintained, who are on the cutting edge of cultural change. Approaching such persons with a psychology of adjustment does not work, Stonquist reasoned, because they have no *one* culture to adjust to.

Subsequent usage of the term *marginal man* by others gradually gave the term a negative connotation, and it remained clouded for 50 years until two specialists in intercultural communication, Milton and Janet Bennett, revisited the issue.

Janet Bennett (1993) differentiates between two types of cultural marginality, *encapsulated* and *constructive.* Individuals are "encapsulated," or trapped, by their marginality when they have "a compromised ability to establish boundaries and make judgments." Buffeted by conflicting cultural loyalties, the encapsulated marginal is unable to construct a unified identity. As a consequence, he or she is vulnerable to such mental pathogens of cultural alienation as powerlessness, meaninglessness, normlessness, cultural estrangement, self-estrangement, social isolation, anomie, and anxiety. Encapsulated marginals see themselves, according to Bennett, as so unique that they may be "incapable of envisioning a peer group with whom they can relate." It is this encapsulated wretch that many health professionals think they see when confronted with a troubled individual who, among other traits, is multicultural.

Bennett is more interested in what she calls *constructive marginality.* "Unlike the encapsulated marginal, the constructive marginal feels authentic and recognizes that one is never *not* at home in the world."

Different Latitudes, Different Attitudes

The school of cultural relativism tells us that each culture is a world of meaning complete in itself, and that trying to extend one culture's concepts and values to another culture is meaningless, like trying to judge tennis by the rules of baseball. Each cultural space is like nothing so much as itself. This is a lonely idea.

C. Douglas Lummis (1982) has thought about the pros and cons of cultural diversity and notes that the boundary, the exact line between two cultures, becomes a kind of cultural no-man's land, a bottomless void. "One who seeks seriously to build a common base between two cultures without compromising either finds only nihilism, despair, and madness." This statement may be a bit hyperbolic, perhaps, but there is, necessarily, some risk as you negotiate border spaces, building bridges and finding common ground. Marginal people, such as Lawrence of Arabia, rarely receive guidance and support while they sustain the challenge of dealing with disparate systems of thought and behavior.

It is certainly appropriate to don different attitudes when sojourning in different latitudes. This does not necessarily mean that madness awaits you if you attempt to build "a common base between two cultures," for there is more than one way to build a base. And "common" does not mean "identical," and what is common may differ from the cultural base of either party. It would be difficult in the extreme, of course, to try to reconcile out of context the diverse values that cultures promote. Each culture makes sense to itself. In Chapters 8–14 we will explore alternative ways of building a base by reconceptualizing the metaphor with which you can reconcile your contradictory conduct. More on this later.

Unusual Behavior

Multicultural "barbarians," in recent years, have been getting a little more respect, a little less criticism. While changes in the thinking of mental health professionals toward the "troubled" multicultural patient have been gradual, many psychologists and social scientists have begun studying multicultural persons with greater interest. Greater familiarity with multicultural people from a range of strata has led to an improvement in professional attitudes toward the multicultural process.

Functions of "Dysfunctional" Behavior

What, in multicultural life-space, defines appropriate behavior? To begin with, the animal behaviorist Konrad Lorenz (1973) cautions us to discover the survival function of seemingly counterproductive behavior. What problem does the behavior "solve," however inadequately? The dynamics of neurotic behavior are no different from healthy behavior, but such behavior may be deployed inappropriately, perhaps compulsively, in a given situation. Nevertheless, the ability to respond compulsively—and thus quickly—can diminish feelings of anxiety and enable the person to keep on functioning, however minimally.

Viewing the stressed behavior of multicultural individuals as a coping strategy that may even be appropriate to the situation removes it from the realm of pathology. And with the ideas associated with reestablishing balance after your cultural system has been jiggled out of whack, the grunts and groans associated with socialization into multicultural settings begin to take on the appearance of normalcy.

Hysteria

The functionality of some kinds of hysterical phenomena, from absentmindedness to multiple personalities, was acknowledged in one collection of essays (Soddy, 1961). These states were seen as providing temporary breaks in identity and a relaxation of control mechanisms, which allowed the person to reorganize him- or herself. The characteristic unstable behavior preceding periods of growth was called "productive instability" by a Danish psychologist (Rümke, quoted in Soddy, 1961). In fact, the inability to regress was found to be associated with rigidity. Flexibility is what is needed to adapt to changing conditions.

Many hysterical phenomena are not so different from many social conventions that under ordinary circumstances permit changes of identity. Examples of these identity change mechanisms include going incognito (to protect, to relieve from strain, to escape temporarily), *noms de plumes,* legal changes of name, the convention of speaking "off the record," initiations, ordinations, "taking the veil," or as is the penchant in Southeast Asia, periodically running amok (to borrow the Malay word).

Would YOU Follow a Half-Blind Guide?

One can conclude from the mental health and psychological literature that it is *monocultural* people who might be the victims of limited perspectives and cultural deprivation.

They may suffer cultural deficiencies such as limited behavioral repertories and severely restricted resiliency resources. People whose socialization has been limited to but one culture can typify a deficit model regarding cultural flexibility—a Model of Monocultural Impairment! These one-eyed people may be less effective in adjusting to change.

Any world view based on only one norm is deficient. Karl Oguss, in a 1993 lecture in Japan, invited the participants to imagine what might have happened if the first physical anthropologists had been Masai warriors. He describes it as if it had actually happened. First (in this imagined scenario), the Masai invented a stick to measure people. No matter who did the measuring, no matter how many times they measured subject A, their measurement stick indicated precisely the same measurement. Their stick met all requirements for reliability and replicability. The Masai anthropologists then began to measure all Masai people and discovered that on the average they were seven feet tall. The Masai physical anthropologists then were curious to measure other people in the world, so they set out with their validated measurement instruments and began to measure the world's many populations. As they did so, though, a very disturbing "fact" began to emerge. All the rest of the world's people were deficient in height!

This little story encourages us to remember that much of modern social and mental-health sciences still remain mired in ethnocentric concepts, "normed" no farther than the researchers' own backyards.

Schizoids "R" Us

We are still stuck with a dearth of terms for describing and labeling favorably a single person who has multiple ways of behaving in the world.

The psychiatrist R. D. Laing (1969) theorized that there is a comprehensible transition from the "sane schizoid" way of being-in-the-world to a psychotic way of being-in-the-world:

A good deal of schizophrenia is simply nonsense, red herring speech, prolonged filibustering to throw dangerous people off the scent, to create boredom and futility in others. The schizophrenic is often making a fool of himself and the doctor. He is playing at being mad to avoid at all costs the possibility of being held *responsible* for a single coherent idea, or intention.

Schizophrenics may not be as crazy as many would like to believe. They may be using weak coping mechanisms to adjust to a muddled society! All of this brings to mind Benjamin Whorf's (1964) statement that "we do not know that civilization is synonymous with rationality."

Mental aberration must be seen within its social context. Laing says, "our 'normal' 'adjusted' state is too often the abdication of ecstasy, the betrayal of our true potentialities, that many of us are only too successful in acquiring a false self to adapt to false realities." In some Eskimo villages, schizophrenia is seen as a gift and its recipients respected.

The current Western approach to schizophrenia is not to see it as a spiritual gift, but as a chemical imbalance tractable to drug intervention, and Laing's approach to schizophrenia has been criticized for ignoring the chemical components of this disease. Nonetheless, the role of adaptive mechanisms that deal with fear or guilt or confusion, emotional stakes that often accompany rapid transformations of identity, remains unresolved.

The line between the schizophrenic and actor may be thin. To identify precisely when a societal role enables one to hide or express oneself may be more complex than it appears at first sight. The next two chapters explore this in some detail.

The next chapter focuses on the multicultural person as actor, a metaphor that provides a way for many multicultural individuals to organize a concept of identity that must change from time to time.

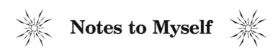# Notes to Myself

1. There are many cultural boundaries that one can cross. You can go from one form of society to another (e.g., from an agrarian to an industrial society). You can move from the country to the city. You can move across social class boundaries (e.g., from blue-collar worker to multimillionaire tycoon and philanthropist). The following ancestors of mine distinguished themselves by crossing boundaries:

_____

_____

_____

_____

_____

2. Some of the stresses that I, or border crossers that I know, have experienced include:

_____

_____

_____

_____

_____

3. I consider my peer group (my equals) to be mostly:

_____

_____

_____

_____

_____

4. I feel peripheral in some areas and very central in others. I feel peripheral in these areas:

_____

_____

_____

_____

I feel as though I fit right into the center of things in these areas:

_____

_____

_____

_____

5. Some ways that I have learned to cope with multicultural stress include:

_____

_____

_____

_____

6. When I talk to some of my friends who are multicultural, they suggest using the following techniques to lessen the stress that sometimes results from border crossings:

_____

_____

_____

_____

7. It'd be nice if I got some help in dealing with situations such as:

_____

_____

_____

_____

_____

8. Am I aware of ever having been personally victimized by one of the disease metaphors?

_____

9. On a scale of 1–10, with 1 being a raving maniac and 10 being the sanest person I know, I'd rank myself about a _____ .

10. I sense that some of the advantages I have because I have had multicultural experiences are: (Example: I have mediated a misunderstanding between people of two different cultures.)

_____

_____

_____

_____

_____

11. Some of the words I have heard or read that disparage any of my own ethnic backgrounds are:

_____

_____

_____

_____

_____

Some of the words that people have used to miscategorize me are:

_____

_____

_____

_____

_____

12. Some examples of how I have dealt with situations where people disparage my background or miscategorize it are:

_____

_____

_____

_____

_____

The Authentic Actor

Authenticity and the Theater of the Self

A Jewish Arab—and this is not an oxymoron—fell in love with a black Muslim woman. After their marriage, he went into the diplomatic service of his native Morocco, where he served in many posts throughout the world. Their children were raised in a dazzling mix of cultures: Indonesia, the United States, Japan, Spain, and Egypt. At a dinner reception in Cairo, one of the daughters was asked how she handled the issue of her identity: Who was she? "Well," she replied, "I have always considered myself a Moroccan actor. I go on the stage in one country or another and play the role of someone from that country."

Surrounded by a Stage

For the multicultural person, the stage is wherever you find yourself. The particular setting could be anywhere. A room, a restaurant, walking down the street, climbing a mountain, answering the telephone. You are called to speak different languages, carry your body in different ways, react to others in styles whose appropriateness differs from place to place.

Shakespeare's 16th-century metaphor for life (in *As You Like It*) holds that

All the world's a stage, And all the men and women merely players; They have their exits and their entrances, And one man in his time plays many parts . . .

Heroes and heroines, deformers and transformers of social space, villains, ingenues, scapegoats and victims—an actor plays many characters and roles. Yet through all these permutations, an actor can be perceived as a coherent entity.

The actor must wield a vast behavioral repertoire in order to be able to function effectively playing many parts in many plays. In the Japanese kabuki theater, one actor—particularly the most famous—plays many roles in the same play, with quick costume changes requiring many assistants. Many male kabuki actors specialize in female roles, not by portraying particular females, but by capturing the essence of femininity in their performance.

The dynamics involved in being able to play many roles is not unlike the dynamics involved in crossing cultural boundaries. Your acting may be stellar as you cross role and cultural boundaries, but without supporting players, you cannot perform your role. Even bit players form an essential part of the production. Perhaps you are part of a multinational family and you feel sometimes that you are just tagging along with the Breadwinner as he or she travels from country to country. *I am a bit player, rarely moving to center stage on any of the stages in which my troupe performs.*

The Idea of Consistent Personality and Role

Multicultural people often suffer from "authenticity anxiety." If they use languages and behavior so that they "play" well in different cultural contexts, are they being their true selves? Are they being sincere? Will others perceive them as trustworthy? The history of Western theater offers some clues for the resolution of this angst.

In the Western theater, so-called "method acting"—trying to actually become your character or role at a psychological level—has not always been required of the actor. As Yi-Fu Tuan (1982), a scholar of Western theater, notes, in medieval mystery plays a dozen actors might be used to play Christ in the same cycle.

No effort was made to present Christ as a single personality in the sense of being a single distinct individual. As for the role of God, Tuan quotes Kolve (1966):

> Those who played God would not have sought . . . to be God, to get inside His personality; such a notion would have seemed to them blasphemous and absurd. They presented not the character of God but certain of his actions.

Although God was the central personage of the medieval Western world, "He" was a triune personage. That is, God himself was perceived to be a three-in-one being, the Father, the Son, and the Holy Ghost—coherent, yet multifaceted. Multicultural people can also manifest themselves through appropriate, multifaceted actions.

What Do Actors Do?

It was not until the Renaissance and the ensuing revolution in science that the Western theater's focus shifted from divine power to the foibles of humans and, still later, to the tribulations of specific, individual humans with particular personalities. Instead of being "faceless" occupants of well-defined social roles, in the Western theater each character came to manifest assemblages of qualities and characteristics that make each person a distinctive individual.

So what do we assume the actors are doing on stage? Performing? Expressing themselves? Improvising? Or, like some rock stars, presenting their "real" self and interacting with the audience as a "whole human"? Can any "whole human," though, ever be fully encompassed in any one social role? Or maybe our actors are involved in the ancient and solemn play of allegorical figures who, if they are properly impersonated, will bring harmony to the human community. The purpose, in this latter case, is not personal emotional expression, but rather precise, unerring simulation, a fitting of one's self to the role or character, a perfect mastery, according to an ancient standard. This simulation, through behavioral artifice, remains an actor's stock in trade.

Many Roles, Many Plays

In our everyday existence we perform many parts in many plays (we even star in some), and although we may have favorite roles and plays, we are required by social exigencies to act according to a variety of scripts.

What's in a Role?

Each society bundles together different role-related behaviors into implicit or explicit clusters of conventional social identities. The roles and behaviors associated with these conventional clusters usually are claimed to "go together naturally."

Suk Yee Ma (1993), concerned with issues of "reentry shock," interviewed Hong Kong Chinese returning from study abroad. These were young adults returning after two to five years of study in Europe, the United States, Australia, Japan, Taiwan, and the People's Republic of China. They often spoke two forms of Chinese, English, and one or two other languages. They had successfully earned academic degrees abroad. Ma asked them if they now considered themselves to be cosmopolitan and multicultural. Most of these Hong Kong returnees did *not* consider themselves either particularly cosmopolitan or multicultural. They were just plain "Hong Kong Chinese," and being multilingual and being functional outside Hong Kong, as well as in the diverse Hong Kong cultural and linguistic mix, is simply an ordinary part of being a Hong Kong Chinese.

The tasks we assume to be associated with gender roles provide a nearly infinite list of examples of this bundling phenomenon. Thus, weaving is women's work among the Navajo but men's work among the Hopi. Hopi women, however, build houses, but in mainstream U.S. society that is men's work. Upper-Amazon Cofán men hunt, but it is women's work to prepare the darts for the blowguns. It is small wonder that in multicultural lives some of the greatest conflicts emerge as we orchestrate behaviors associated with gender.

Role Switching, A Talent We All Possess

In life, no one escapes the final curtain without having performed many roles. There are, sadly, no encores on this stage unless you believe in reincarnation, which, of course, provides another possible metaphor. We play the role of child, peer, parent, and relative; male or female; weaver, hunter, hewer of wood, drawer of water. The list goes on: coy coquette, student of antiquity, ambitious upstart, elder statesman. And on: budding young man at his bar mitzvah, admiring buddy at a friend's birthday party, patriot at Independence Day festivities, defender of local pride at an athletic contest. Playing all these parts requires flexibility, and this is constantly exercised by the ordinary switching among our roles. This fact of human existence rehearses the kinds of adjustments to our sense of self that also are required when we live intimately in a multicultural world.

Alas, the particular behaviors associated with moving between cultures may not be rewarded by *any* of the societies involved. The Japanese father of a daughter growing up in Hong Kong learned this the hard way. This young woman went to a British school in Hong Kong and had a boyfriend from the United States during the height of the popularity of punk pop culture throughout the former British Empire. Her father wanted her to speak several languages, but he preferred silk kimonos to the leather and purple hair she affected. He had not counted on his daughter's absorbing the popular culture of the foreign language she was learning.

The Jekyll-Hyde Phenomenon

Role switching within a culture prepares you for moving between cultures, but the way even commonplace roles are defined in a given culture may differ crucially from the same role in another culture. Do fathers wash the dishes, change diapers, hang pictures, take out the garbage, play games with their children, write poetry? It depends on how fatherhood is defined within their circles. Behavior considered normal and valued in one cultural context (for example, expressiveness or directness) might not be valued in another context.

Perhaps you've read Robert Louis Stevenson's book *The Strange Case of Dr. Jekyll and Mr. Hyde* or seen the horror film based on the book. It's about a man with two personalities, one murderous. For multicultural people, lack of social affirmation for the same behavior in different cultural settings can produce the lament, "I feel like Jekyll and Hyde."

Learning Role Subtleties

Throughout human history, from cradle to grave, people have been called on to perform in many different situations. The audience, as well as our fellow players, expects this performance to be reasonably appropriate to our role and the situation. Both comedy and tragedy are born of inappropriate behavior. The big problem as a multicultural person is managing to learn and perform properly all the behaviors that our participation in multiple theaters of life requires. *I am an actor on stage, with two different prompters giving me lines from two different plays; I am paralyzed by stage fright.* It is hard to learn these roles at a distance, outside of the milieu in which they are enacted.

Traditional Hopi believed that any Hopi leaving the Hopi's Arizona high desert mesa homeland were *ka hopi,* or no longer Hopi. Simply by the act of leaving, they "lost their Hopi hearts." Some of this observed alienation may have been because on their return they no longer behaved totally according to Hopi conventions.

Australian aboriginal groups define themselves as "people who follow the law." This implies observing many norms, including complex linguistic forms that take years to master. Elders are addressed one way, shamans another, women another, and so on. Youngsters who go away to an English-speaking boarding school, unfortunately, have to interrupt their first-language development, and for lack of practice they do not learn very well how to address various members of their home community. When they do return to their communities, they are no longer considered to be members of the group; they don't follow the norms. The norms include which roles are available to a person of a given age and gender and which range of behaviors are acceptable for those roles.

As with early 20th-century Hopi, it is still a quite common disposition in contemporary Japan to believe that Japanese who leave Japan become somehow polluted by the outside world. This is one reason Japanese children raised abroad, the so-called *kikokushijo,* or returnees, often have such a difficult time coming home. The cause of much of this difficulty is that they do not switch their behavior back to the conventions of the Japanese context quickly enough. Similar to the aboriginal children of Australia, some of this is due to forgetting or not knowing *keigo,* those subtle Japanese linguistic conventions for conveying respect. This lack of skill in using *keigo* can be further exacerbated by the returnees' additional lack of mastery of Japanese ideographic characters (*kanji*), 2,000 of which are needed to read a newspaper. Some of the negative reaction returnees experience also might be due to the envy elicited by speaking another language well, particularly English, because fluency in English is such a marketable skill.

Unfortunately, many monocultural contexts have little understanding of the time it takes to learn multiple roles and their associated behavior and have little tolerance for the changes in behavior in which multicultural people engage. Actors who play multicultural roles are then confronted with the task of eliciting tolerance for some lag time in first learning and then making the behavioral switches in each of their social contexts. The trick seems to be in giving those people with whom we interact practice in seeing such behavioral switches as of the same order of experience as the switches that are already part of conventional everyday behavior (student, friend, team captain). As a multicultural actor, you will need to study, naturally, the role requirements of the cultural setting in which you are performing.

But learning the behaviors associated with these roles is not the only challenge. Sometimes we are assigned roles we do not want to play.

Victim! Assigned versus Assumed Roles

Every so often, in life's dramas, we are pressed to play roles we do not choose, roles foisted on us by more powerful others.

In the Turkish folk theater, the shadow puppets Karagöz and Hacivat play out an interaction common to all societies—the class differences of the wealthy, educated (but perhaps morally a bit hidebound and intellectually a bit stymied) Hacivat, and the poor, uneducated (but clever and open to new ideas) Karagöz. The Russian popular jokes about aristocrats and peasants poke the same fun at the "dull-witted" upper class. Folk theater examines other relationships too: the British puppets Punch and Judy reenact "the battle of the sexes." Do we find ourselves cast in such stereotypic roles? *I am a shadow puppet, moved by the energies of others.*

We have outgrown many stereotypical roles: the "venal Jew," the "frightened black," a "deceiving Greek bearing gifts." They were not, of course, ever characteristic of their groups. But there are always unfavorable roles that casting directors want us to play. Sometimes we don't want to play these roles but because of our social identity—gender, race, religion, ethnicity, nationality, social class, sexual preference—we are coerced into the role. It seems that the script is written and someone must take the part. You are that someone because of who you are perceived to be, not because of who you *really* are or can imagine yourself to be. To add insult to injury, unlike the actor in a play, you are expected actually to be the personage assigned in the script, not just behave like him or her.

One highly individualistic woman, raised in New York City by Japanese parents, reports that thinking in the language of her parents—Japanese—produces profound conflict, anger, and rage in her, especially about role issues. Avoiding the role of a proper Japanese woman, for instance, or at least not identifying with the role while paying lip service to it, has become important to her. "Generally," she says, "I've spent the last 25 years defining my core self in ways flexible enough to stand up to my father's definitions."

Some of us, for varying lengths of time, may view ourselves as victims. Many people consider themselves to be members of *several* oppressed minorities. An oft-quoted calculation by Aaron Wildavsky based itself on the numbers of U.S. citizens who considered themselves to be a member of an oppressed minority: 374 percent of the population! Some respondents clearly indicated membership in more than one group. In a "victim" state, we inhabit a hazardous landscape, are exposed to discomfiture of all kinds, whether bacterial, accidental, or as the objects of social and psychological duress. The ugly exploitive face of human experience comes to the fore, with its accompanying issues of class structure and control and the radical acts thought to combat domination.

Sometimes, in the confusion of negative feedback, we may lose sight of who we are. But we know who we are not, and that is a starting point. Beryl Hammonds (1993) writes:

from nigger to colored,
from negro to black,
from black to afro-american,
from afro-american to a person of color,
from a person of color to african-american,
to refining who you are by first
defining who you are not . . .
I am not a dark-skinned white-girl.

There are victims, of course, and through no fault of their own. Reynolds Price (1994), paralyzed from the neck down with agonizing cancer, shares this advice: You are no longer who you were; you will never be that person again. "Have one hard cry, if the tears will come. Then stanch the grief . . . . Find your way to be somebody else, the next viable you." Beryl Hammonds puts it this way: "I need to let go of suffering—it is not my destiny." Wilfrid Sheed (1995), in a book that describes overcoming the effects of long-term debilitating illness, concludes that "God, or the Great Whoever, has been so lavish in His gifts that you can lose some absolutely priceless ones, the equivalent of whole kingdoms, and still be indecently rich."

Many otherwise resourceful people, however, seek the mantle of woe. They revel in the companionship of despair. By the 1980s the "damage model" had permeated U.S. popular culture (Wolin and Wolin, 1993). A palliative for feeling too sorry for yourself may be to read Charles Sykes's book, *A Nation of Victims* (1992). Sykes says that assuming the burden of a damage model bogs people down in three ways:

- It focuses attention on past injuries rather than on living well in the present.

- The image of victim diverts people from the hard work of changing.

- It leaves people who have survived bad experiences feeling like they are walking away from a time bomb.

Sykes's message: *lighten up.*

Am I Simply My Role?

Whatever else actors may be doing on stage as they flit from role to role, they are certainly doing one thing that is invaluable to multicultural people—rehearsing flexibility of identity. But this very flexibility poses a problem: Who is the real me?

The American writer John Barth (1994) says, near the end of *Once Upon a Time,* "I've always thought, the first and final narrative question is not 'What happened,' but 'Who am I?' " The great existential question, so much a part of understanding Western angst, is now complicated by an awareness of the complexity of multicultural experiences. If I play a different persona in different cultural settings, am I being false?

Split Asunder

How is the schizophrenic's "split" personality different from an actor's skill at switching roles? Is it a strength or a weakness to possess multiple personas? Does each of us have but one personality, a set "assemblage of qualities or characteristics which makes us a distinctive individual" (*New Shorter Oxford English Dictionary,* 1993)? Does a successful management of multiple personalities depend on one's ability to integrate them in a holistic sense, or simply on one's ability to respond appropriately, to be the right person at the right time? Being able to display "appropriate" responses may also depend on society's tolerance for "inconsistency" in a person's behavior. This capability for multiple response, according to Soddy (1961), may well be a strength in a society that is diverse and/or undergoing rapid change and showing some cultural dislocation.

When individuals come into frequent contact with another cultural system, they begin to question some of the basic assumptions of their own culture. When this happens to someone who lives on a cultural boundary, questions of authenticity inevitably arise. In the 1950s, there arose in Francophone Africa a literary movement around the theme of *authenticité.* A crucial question for these Francophone African poets was, "In which language do I dream?" They reasoned that it is when we are unconscious that our "pure self"—not our self in a social role—reveals itself. This question, In which language do I dream?, can have only one answer: "It depends." It depends where the dream is taking place and with whom the dreamer is talking. His or her tribal language may be used if the dreamer is talking with mother at home, a more widely spoken language, Hausa or perhaps Mandingo, if bartering in the marketplace, French if reciting multiplication tables in school. We are left with the questions that dreams do not unravel: Are we somebody outside our social roles? Do we have a "self" independent of social affirmation? A Japanese student, Shizu Kawata, searching for a metaphor to encompass her sense of self, says "I am like an important building. I shelter, enclose, and protect the happiness and sorrow of others. I am purposeless without those I shelter."

Is There a Me?

The search for self began to absorb playwrights such as Ibsen and Chekhov, and their attentive audiences, in the late 1800s. Ibsen's Peer Gynt, near the end of his journey, peels an onion and is horrified to discover that it does not have a heart—a vision of the self unoccupied at its core. At the end of Chekhov's *The Seagull,* one of the characters asks woefully: "Who am I? What am I?"

Do we have a sense of self that is independent of our interaction with others and with nature? Most social psychologists would say no. (Those who would say yes are probably evolutionary psychologists who remind us that there are genetic predispositions to take into account.) For many multicultural people it is this "person in society" that is the aspect of self that proves the most problematic. A young man, born and raised in France of Japanese parents, always felt Japanese until at the age of 18 he went to Japan where people viewed him as a *gaijin,* or outside person. He then realized the complex interactive nature of labels of identity.

It is the need for social affirmation that generates the entire issue of authenticity. The authenticity issue rests, therefore, not only within the multicultural person, but within the often monocultural contexts in which we commonly find ourselves. Society often displays ambivalence toward "half-breeds." They evoke issues of humanity's divided nature, "civilization" versus "the wilderness," light versus darkness. Will the "savage" elements in a half-blood burst forth in violence? Contention in the United States for real estate remained hostile (Euro-American settlers were stealing Indian land) until 1890 when the settlers had obtained all of the worthwhile land. (Land grabs by whites continued well into the next century as "worthless" Indian land was found to house mineral deposits.)

Although the "savage" but "ennobled" Indians could be and were written off as a part of history (or even as prehistory), the ample existence of people with mixed Indian-white parentage clearly represented the present or even the future of the developing nation. Throughout the 19th century, U.S. dime novels often portrayed people of mixed Indian and white ancestry. These popular novels document the dilemma posed in the minds of many whites of the day by the presence of "half-breeds" (Scheick, 1979).

Most of these marriages were between white men and Indian women. While there were many reasons for the intercultural alliances, whites of the day simplified them to two: expediency (the absence of "women of the cleaner colored race" as one writer put it in 1857), or, especially in the last half of the century, calculated acquisitiveness so whites could gain Indian property and prosperity. Neither of these reasons increased the status of the offspring of mixed marriages in the eyes of whites. Unlike the Spanish and French, English-speaking Americans were reluctant to accept the existence of these "twice-blessed" inheritors of Indian and European cultures. In fact, in the dime novels of the day, American authors frequently used the "half-breed" to make covert attacks on the despised French and Spanish. One mid-19th-century half-blood echoed a plaintive identity dilemma common to many boundary crossers (quoted in Scheick, 1979): "Here I am, neither an Indian nor a white man—just nothing." Sometimes others in the period regarded the half-blood as more than the sum of two cultures. In 1849, Francis Parkman (quoted in Scheick) said that mixed-bloods were "a race of rather extraordinary composition, being, according to the common saying, half Indian, half white man, and half devil."

Let us not forget, however, that many of these half-bloods spoke English and at least one Indian language (some also spoke French and Spanish), and their services as broker between the cultures was critically needed by both sides.

Even when mixed-heritage people are allowed a measure of multicultural duality, people socialized in a monocultural social context may insist on seeing this duality as duplicitous. When the social context requires that a person should only feel at home in one place, some multicultural people, who may feel at home in many places, actually resolve the dilemma of an either/or choice by having *partial* identities that they use as appropriate, depending on the social context. For instance, a German-Brazilian may identify himself as Brazilian while in Brazil, using the appropriate expressions and gestures, and as a German in Germany. The writer Marina Warner says that home lies ahead, in the unfolding of the story in the future, not behind, waiting to be regained (Warner, 1995).

Is There a Self?

What is the self, anyway? Buddhists don't believe there is a real conceptual self, only the illusion of it. This belief contrasts with Western traditions that hold sacred the notion of an absolute soul and, by implication, a self. Such an identity, in the Western way of reasoning (Descartes, for example), has defined borders, characteristics, solidity, cohesion, and continuity.

Although most contemporary neurophysiologists do not claim to have found a distinct anatomical part of our body that may be the locus of consciousness, or a likely repository for the self, some scientists are keeping an open mind on the issue (Crick, 1994; Hobson, 1994; Penrose, 1994, thinks consciousness resides in the brain's microtubules). Behavioral geneticists believe that there are clusters of genes that enable what they call "conscientiousness." Being conscious, of course, is not the same as having a sense of self-identity, but it is hard to have a self-identity without some consciousness of it.

How much of our sense of self is built into our bodies as a biochemical system determined by our genes? How much of our core self is learned? The current thinking among behavioral geneticists is that human behavior is about one-third genes and two-thirds socialization (Wright, 1994). Modern research suggests certain inborn temperamental properties. T. Berry Brazelton (1984) has shown us how the personalities of newborn infants differ in terms of how active or passive they are, how easily excited by external stimuli, and how easily calmed they are, and several dozen other traits. Clearly, there is a biochemical engine driving, or at least providing the outline for, "the real me." Yet "the real me" is perceived by most of us to encompass more than drives and inherited characteristics and predispositions. A large part of our self contains values that appear to be acquired from the social environment. Honesty, ambition, thoughtfulness, religiosity, honor . . . the list goes on.

The word *self* is a culturally loaded term, particularly regarding what anthropologist G. G. Harris (1989) refers to as "the self's unity or non-unity in the face of multiple social identities." The list of terms used to deal with the self in the social science literature, especially in the Euro-American literature, is extensive. There has been study after study dealing with the self, identity, personality, self-esteem, individuality, individuation, differentiation, self-actualization, as well as with something called "ego-strength."

Is "self" a collective noun, like fish and deer and herd, like The Theater or The Dance or Art? If so, is this intrinsic multiplicity handled on a periodic schedule or in a particular order? Simultaneously or synchronically? Consistently or intermittently? Does one part come to dominate or replace the rest? How are these various identities conventionally bundled together? Explicitly or implicitly? Or is this "bundling" something we multicultural pioneers must do for ourselves (with a little help from our friends)?

The Three Faces of Me

G. G. Harris (1989) helpfully describes three aspects of this me-myself-and-I around which we build our identity, no matter how many cultures have modified our upbringing.

The Biological Me

First, we have a sense that we are a single, separate biological entity distinct from other human beings, a physical individual. This sense was developed long before the appearance of humans (Sagan and Druyan, 1992). "Cells of 3.5 billion years ago must have possessed some knowledge of the difference between 'me' and 'you.'" Otherwise, cells would have digested other cells within the same organism for their food value. In humans, this consciousness of being separate from others develops early in childhood in many Western countries. It is buttressed by other aspects of upbringing that emphasize individual expression. In the United States, adults are constantly querying children: "What do you want?" "Why do you think that?" "Stand up for what you believe!" This societal push toward lone self-actualization is further reinforced by other Western imperatives such as competition. *Among all other actors of whatever national origin, I am one of a kind—and I am one of the best!*

The Conscious Me

Most of us sense that there lies within us a conscious "self," a core, a center of being or locus of experience that is more than the sum of our biological and chemical parts. Perhaps this sense is an anthropomorphic projection, but it is this sense of core-self that allows us to experience a feeling of coherence, of continuing identity, even as the details of our "someoneness" refashions itself with age and experience and social context. Without some kind of persisting self, how would it be possible to have consistent relationships with others? Or, in Western societies, how would we be responsible for our actions? *I am an old actor, remembering my triumphs and failures on the world's stage.*

The Me in Society

It is the necessity of maintaining reciprocal relationships that highlights the third aspect of our me-myself-and-I, the aspect of being "a person in society." *I can't be a Romeo without a Juliet.* This is the aspect of ourselves, the one needing social affirmation, that is so fraught with challenge for multicultural players.

This "social someone" may be perceived as being anything from totally independent of other people to being inextricably enmeshed with other people. Most definitions of the social self in the world's societies can be sorted along this continuum, independent through dependent. It is the collective wisdom of our culture that influences which perspective we will adopt: whether we see ourselves as subject and the rest of the world as object, to maintain "dominion over . . . every living thing" (often stereotyped as "Western" thought in the social science literature), or whether we see "our self in all and all in our self," as the Hindu *Bhagavad Gita* counsels (often labelled "Eastern" thought).

The Japanese word for self (*jibun*), to illustrate one end of the independent-dependent continuum, maintains a connotation of "the part that is part of a whole." In Lone Ranger Country, on the other hand, the self is supposed to be "actualized," to "stand out" from the whole. *I am a star! My name is in marquee lights, and I am at center stage as I tour the best of European theaters.*

Those of the Lone Ranger persuasion feature egocentric definitions of selves with negotiated and often rather contractual relationships with others. They behave relatively independently of the social context. Lawyers and gun merchants thrive in this setting.

People who incline toward the view that we are all inextricably enmeshed, on the other hand, entertain sociocentric definitions of selves and maintain organic relationships with others. The behavior of people falling into this group is relatively dependent on social context. For this latter group, being a person is not a "bootstrap" operation—they readily acknowledge that they get "a lot of help from their friends," as the Beatles put it. *I could never have played my many parts so well without the help of my supporting actors from many supporting cultures.*

The metaphors that multicultural people choose for themselves come from the full range of the dependent-independent continuum. Many ideas of what the self is fall in the "interdependent" middle range, like those of the Lakota, who see us all as related, autonomous, and socially connected simultaneously. North American Indians are constantly reminding their Euro-American sisters and brothers: "Remember, every person has a mother. We cannot survive without others."

How we deal with these three aspects of self—biological distinctness, consciousness of a coherent experience, and the way other people affect our sense of self—is what gives each of us the unique details of our selves.

In the next chapter we explore further the issues of the persisting self and the social validation of the self. We do this by posing the question, "Who are we between roles?"

✳ Notes to Myself ✳

1. If I were to see myself as an actor on some sort of a multicultural stage, I'd try on the following metaphor for fit:

   _____

   _____

   _____

   _____

   _____

2. Some qualities and characteristics of my core self, as I see it, are:

   _____

   _____

   _____

   _____

   _____

3. After asking my friends' impression of "the real me," some of the traits they see as part of my core self include:

   _____

   _____

   _____

   _____

   _____

4. The major roles I play as a multicultural actor are:

_____

_____

_____

_____

_____

5. One's behavior does not always have to be connected to belief. One example where this separation has occurred in my life is:

_____

_____

_____

_____

_____

9

Who Are We between Roles?

Authentic In-Betweenness

In the rush to change costumes between acts and to learn new roles before the next play, we sometimes forget who we are between roles. And who we really are can be confusing. "I resist anything better than my own diversity . . ." the popular 19th-century American poet Walt Whitman said in "Song of Myself" (1892).

Consciousness of being simultaneously both actor and an "authentic" person leads some to see themselves as occupying a special realm of existence. This may be particularly true of those of us who do not feel prepared to play the assigned role. *I am a stand-in and I know neither the plot nor the lines. I don't even know the setting or the language.*

After we strip away all the role-specific performances in all the many plays, what is left? What core of self remains when we are by ourselves? This question is especially intriguing when the individual performs in more than one culture. In Japan, many feel that it is only when you are by yourself alone in nature that the true self shows itself; any time you are with others you are constrained by some kind of social role. Does this mean, then, that the entire concept of "acting authentically" is an oxymoron?

Who are we when we are not acting? Are we "off" when we are offstage? If we remain actively involved in maintaining social relationships, then are we "on," whatever the setting? *Show time is all the time.* That part of our self that is molded by our relationships continues to be influenced as long as we maintain the relationships. People who influence us don't have to be present to exert their influence; even people in our lives who have died often continue to be an important part of our reference group.

How do we manage the adjustments needed to perform across multiple roles in various cultural settings?

Orchestrating a Functional Self across Roles

In a world where a multiplicity of roles are being enacted, a dynamic, changing, fluid sense of functional self requires some orchestration. But this orchestration is dependent on adjustment to the specifics of shifting cultural scenarios.

To what standard do we conform when we are between roles? Between acts? Between plays? Between theatrical traditions? People's lives, of course, do not fit a single mold. We all live with many contradictory thoughts, from many disparate traditions. *I am an actor, delivering paradoxical lines. The audience laughs and I am a hit.* Many so-called traditional societies have become remarkably adept at the construction of fluid identities.

In some traditions, one's "self" is expected to change with time. Betty Friedan, in her book *The Fountain of Age* (1993), expresses it this way: "I am myself at this age." Sometimes new identities arise out of a particular feat or event. These events may give rise to new names, just as the main character was gifted with a new name—Dances with Wolves—in the U.S. film of the same name. The "self" becomes both age- and event-appropriate. Traditional Western marriages usually involve the bride's giving up her surname for that of her husband—a defining event. *My present character arose out of the ashes of a cultural event so challenging that it redefined my very essence.*

Muneo Yoshikawa (1987), a linguist and director of the Holonic Paradigm Research Institute in Tokyo, developed a model of face-to-face interaction, which he calls a "double-swing" model, that is suited to East-West dialog. The model is based on Martin Buber's ideas of how to deal with forces of unity and diversity while dialoguing with another person, without eliminating the uniqueness of either, and on the Buddhist logic of "paradoxical relationships" (*soku*). Yoshikawa's model allows two people of different cultures to "experience relationship" by suspending their cultural roles. They face each other standing on the common ground of "between" cultures, where each partner allows the other to reach out. The self can become expert at "dynamic in-betweenness."

This "in-between" aspect of identity is present to various degrees in all societies. Sometimes you may feel that you are between everything. *I exist in interstitial space.* Contemporary Japanese psychology, deeply rooted in Japanese cultural notions of the existential mutability of all life, provides a metaphor for those who cross cultural boundaries: the self as a switching station, with different identities manifesting themselves depending on the social context (Hamaguchi, 1981). To mix the Yoshikawa and Hamaguchi metaphors, *I am "dynamic in-betweenness," an intercultural switching station in a gigantic multicultural railway yard.*

Eliciting Changes in Behavior

What is it that elicits changes in our performance? Who and what gives us our cues? Let us examine the effects of other actors, the setting, the role, conceptualizing role as coat versus core self, and some of the functional metaphors of authentic in-betweenness.

Other Actors

Just as an actor is not the same character and does not perform the same role in all plays, so we are different personages and play different roles when we interact with different people. We perform one way in front of our parents, another way with our peers, yet another way with our confidants and significant others. Strangers get yet a different performance. *I am a different character with each person with whom I interact, a Sancho Panza to El Quixote, but El Quixote to Dulcinea.*

The Setting

Sometimes it is the play's setting that elicits behavior change. When cast as Macbeth, you behave one way in the castle, another in Dunsinane Forest.

The Role

Other times it is the role that exerts the most effect on performance. If you're cast as one of Cinderella's stepsisters, you are programmed to perform rather differently from the title character.

As a competent actor on the stage of life, you get inside your roles to perform "in character." If you are playing a truck driver, you assume the dress, the speech and mannerisms, and the world view of a truck driver. You do not declaim the lines of a hairdresser or those of a college professor.

Role as Coat or as Core?

How can you balance the demands of social role with the drive to be "yourself"? This drive, although currently perhaps a particularly North American preoccupation, is of increasing concern to young people in urban areas all over the world.

How do we avoid a confusion of social role with self? As multicultural people, we learn to deal with very different relationship rules, particularly those regarding the interaction of social roles and age and gender. We have to find social roles in each of our contexts with which we are—or can learn to feel—comfortable, roles that are relatively compatible with our preferred way of expressing our personality. It's either this or creating new roles for ourselves.

In mastering all the physical and linguistic skills involved in accomplishing the demands of new social roles, which are the "easy" skills, the ones we can put on like a coat? Which are the ones that confront our core values, the ones that feel as though they would require plastic surgery?

Where this line is varies from person to person. Skills that are easy for some may pose wrenching pain for others. What we can frame as a surface accommodation can include a wide range of behaviors that will enable us to move smoothly in diverse contexts without disturbing our core values.

James Fletcher, now a communication specialist at the University of Georgia, is a rough-hewn, big-boned man, well over six feet tall. While he was a U.S. Army officer in Thailand, he lived in a modest residential neighborhood of Thais. Once a year, during the Songkhran Festival to celebrate the end of the dry season, the eldest woman of the neighborhood is paid homage by its residents. The procedure requires asking permission to enter her home, then crawling into the small living room, carefully keeping all of your body lower than the head of the tiny elder woman who is seated on the floor. Would you have joined these celebrations? Major Fletcher's acceptance by the local Thais was greatly enhanced by his willingness to follow these and other surface cultural procedures.

There may be social costs when, for whatever reason, we do not enter fully into a proffered role. One American living in Italy, whose religious views proscribed alcoholic beverages, lost a potential friend by refusing (as nicely as he could) to drink wine at the home of an Italian policeman and his wife. They were offended. After a relationship has progressed to a certain point in Japan, a similar refusal to join someone in a trip to an *onsen* to share a bath together will probably insert some distance into the relationship. Willingness to interact with someone, whole human to whole human, hiding nothing, is essential to building the kind of mutual trust that exists among Japanese. This trust is based on a feeling beyond verbalization. It is based on your total sense of another human being, beyond, behind, without any artifice or cover.

Public selves hide and protect the inner being. Roles that only require pretend depth can be easier to play than roles that require you to alter your core self. Within Japan there is an interesting convention for handling changes of social context. As you change social contexts you are supposed to adjust your behavior to the new context, not to negotiate an accommodation of the context to your own preferences. As the person entering a group's social space, you are the one to do the adapting, not the group.

Kejime

In Japan, a mark of a mature person is the ability to do *kejime,* the often radical shift or change in behavior and loyalties done in order to fit into a new context. This is the meaning of the pure white under-kimono that a bride wears. Because her name will be removed from her own family's register and entered into her husband's family's register, the white kimono symbolizes her making herself blank. She is symbolically removing all of her own family's patterns so she can absorb those of her husband's family.

Accommodation to the new reality is aided not only by the ability to do *kejime,* but also by two associated Japanese psychological mechanisms: *tatemae* and *honne.*

Tatemae and Honne

Here we enter the realm, so well explored by Erving Goffman in *The Presentation of Self in Everyday Life* (1959), of the difference between public and private space, the difference between formal and informal space, or, to continue the theatrical metaphor, the difference between onstage and backstage.

The first of these psychological mechanisms—"polite fiction" or "obligatory self" (*tatemae*)—enables a person to conform to social expectations. The second—"true feeling" (*honne*)—enables a person simultaneously to acknowledge his or her own deep, unchanged, and often quite different, unexpressed feelings. These two mechanisms allow one to acknowledge one's feelings while acting according to group norms. The mechanisms enable one to meet the Japanese moral imperative of conforming to the group consensus.

Yoshiko Kawai was among the first Japanese women to return to school as an adult. She began undergraduate studies the year before her son entered university. She says, "I am like an energy that seeks to break through the container of *tatemae* in search of truth."

It does not take much imagination to see a giant conflict emerging for anyone seeking to function effectively in Japan who has been socialized in a country like the United States. In the United States, the moral imperative is to "stand up for what you believe" (and to express it publicly). In Japan, the moral imperative is to "kill" your self for group harmony. Tuan (1982) reminds us that in many cases public selves hide and protect the inner being, a view shared by Takeo Doi (1986), who also believes in the protective efficacy of social forms that preserve public harmony by confirming socially constructed "harmonious" public selves.

Role Redefinition and Negotiation

To be harmonious there has to be some collective consensus about what constitutes accord. As we continue to enter a globalized environment whose major feature seems to be constant change, old social roles and their accompanying scripts will be increasingly inadequate to meet our needs. Role stress, conflict, and failure will be endemic and will result in the need to redefine our roles and to negotiate these changes with others.

Besides well-developed interaction skills, the redesign and reconstruction of our relationships requires substantial cooperation from role partners. One cannot play a social role unless others play reciprocal roles, so a change in one role entails changes in other roles. You can't do this without the cooperation of others. Jerald Hage and Charles Powers (1992), in their book on roles for the 21st century, call this process of role redefinition the "pivotal micro process" and the "true locus of social creativity."

Three Other Kinds of Selves

According to Hage and Powers (1992), "the complex self" is the kind of self that is capable of successfully negotiating this redefinition of roles. The complex self can be contrasted with "dominant" and "situational" selves.

The "dominant" self is the same across all contexts. The "situational" self conforms to the demands of each social context (like Hamaguchi's "contextual" self, above). The "complex" self, however, is like Nakashima's (1991) description of Eurasians who identify themselves as Asian, Caucasian, and Eurasian. They are made up not only of old identities (Asian, Caucasian), but also of a new synthesis (Eurasian). Complex selves find it natural and appropriate to maintain several identities at once. This is neither inconsistent nor schizophrenic. Ability to move in more than one direction provides adaptive power in the dynamic contexts in which multicultural people find themselves. For one thing, multiple identities reduce the sense of failure if we do poorly in a given area of performance; they give us the capacity and emotional strength to move into whole new adventures (Thoits, 1983).

The core self itself is, then, a complex configuration of evolving self-concepts and flexible identities.

Can't Be a Cowboy in a Noh Show? But You Can Create Your Own Role in Your Own Show

Yes! You can write your own script and be the star of your own play or film. You can write your own roles, define your own characters. This is adaptive. Of course, this has to be done in dramaturgically effective ways in whatever traditions you are moving between, combining, and creating. But you do this by making choices, taking positions, like the Japanese-American woman in Chapter 8 who has spent the last 25 years defining her core self in ways flexible enough to stand up to her Japanese father's role definitions while still being an American woman.

Or another woman who was raised in an exceptionally supportive family that helped her create and sustain vital expressions of her core personality. She did not see herself as the poor, black, victimized woman that many other people, especially men, tended to see. One result of refusing to act in accordance with the negative view that others often had of her is that she got into lots of trouble with her peers, especially men. In spite of this occasional negative feedback, she feels good about herself.

Altering Old Roles, Creating New Roles

The key to being effective in situations where existing roles have to be altered or new roles have to be created is to know what your options are and where strategic change can occur. Awareness of your connections to forces that shape your identity is an important component of this knowledge. You may make the connection through language, religion, sexual orientation, nationality, ethnicity, gender, or family. Orchestrating these forces is a performing art. Altering them through expansion or contraction, elimination or invention, is a creative art.

When existing roles do not fit or suit us, when the role pinches our "core self," when we have to put the make-up on too thickly, what can we do? We can change or alter a role though shrinking or expanding the role, adding to or subtracting from the expectations associated with the role. We can refuse a role, or we can work to eliminate certain roles in a given society (for example, slaves) and work to create new roles in society (for example, economically independent women).

For the multicultural person, there are, inevitably, times when existing roles simply do not fit, and the only authentic option is to play yourself in a manner that is intelligible and convincing to the people in your various contexts. As one of Wasilewski's (1982) Japanese-American informants stated: "I was never going to be 'traditional' enough to please my grandmother, and I was never going to be 'American' enough to please my peers, so, damn it, I was just going to have to be myself!"

If you never take this position or make this choice, you may never get to be yourself. The key to effectively altering or creating a role is to change it in a way that somehow connects with or complements—somehow fits into—the existing cultural milieu. Native Americans call this "getting the sense of the group," getting a feel for how everything and everyone fits together so you can figure out how you can make your contribution in a way that can be absorbed by the setting you are trying to enter.

Personae

The idea of *persona* is a very handy one for entering new settings. The dictionary defines *persona* as that aspect of our personality that we display to others. Another strategy in the role alteration or creation endeavor is simply to manifest the most complementary aspect of ourselves in each of our cultural environments. To insinuate our "selves" into each environment a bit at a time, gradually allowing the environment to "digest" us. Think of yourself as a rich piece of chocolate cake or as a strong drink that cannot be gobbled or guzzled, but must be tasted and sipped slowly in order to be enjoyed! We don't get to display our "whole" selves publicly, at least all at once, let alone all of our internal selves, but in the high tradition of aspiring young performers, we at least get "a foot in the door."

As a *gaijin* (outside person, or foreigner—usually European) in Japan, it is important not to get stuck on trying to be "Japanese." The role of *gaijin* and guest are very well-defined roles in Japan. You will probably never be an "insider" except instrumentally, and only if you have skills of value to a particular *uchi* or inside group, of which there are hundreds. No one in Japan (not even a native Japanese) is an insider at all times, in all places, and on all occasions. Japan, culturally, may be somewhat homogeneous—although far less than its preferred myth would have us believe—but structurally it has hundreds of competing hierarchies, each its own *uchi* (Miyanaga, 1991; Bachnik and Quinn, 1994). However, in your role as an insider's outsider (because you always have to be introduced by an existing insider) or outside insider (sort of a token *gaijin* who lends status to an enterprise), you have all kinds of opportunities to move across local Japanese social boundaries. This mobility gives *gaijin* the potential to have a more comprehensive experience of Japan than an ordinary Japanese, because the group a Japanese "belongs to" locally limits his or her access to other local groups. These local groups are often involved in very competitive relationships. Thus, invented—but complementary—roles often deliver unanticipated freedom of movement.

Entrances and exits involve dramatic dynamics.

You have to constantly be aware that your novelty, no matter how smoothly presented, deforms, and in a small way transforms, the existing cultural space (Kishima, 1992). You are creating change. Not necessarily through direct confrontation or overt revolution, but simply by behaving differently in a given social space. Change, unfortunately, always makes people somewhat nervous, so you may want to be patient, letting them slowly absorb this new persona in their midst.

Set Design

It is the same with "sets" when you are figuratively designing your own "production." The real world provides us with certain "sets" or environments within which we "perform" or behave. We can play a given role within a given set. We can invent a new role in that set. We can also tinker with the set. Move props. Tear down buildings. Hang a different backdrop. Redefine the meaning of the space by carrying out novel activities in it. One advantage of the current era is that because once-isolated cultures are now interacting with "alien beings," their interacting contexts, or "sets," are less definitive. There are more cracks, more border spaces in which creative activity can occur.

Many Theatrical Traditions

At the dawn of the 21st century, the human predicament of orchestrating all the parts that life calls on us to play has expanded geometrically. Now we are not only called on to play many parts in the same play, and to perform in many plays, but also we often are called on to perform in plays belonging to radically different theatrical traditions. Off-Broadway one day, Noh theater the next, and a Hopi ceremonial the day after that. *I am an actor in many different theatrical traditions. I am equally adept at declaiming parts scripted by Racine or improvising in a stand-up comedy house in L.A.*

From Bunraku to Improv

What different assumptions do these various "theaters of life" make? What is kept backstage and what—through convention—simply is not seen, like the black clothed and masked Japanese puppeteers who manipulate one-half to two-thirds life-size *bunraku* puppets? Are you obsessed with total expressiveness, or do you seek to express the focused nuances of masked performances? Do you strive for perfection in your performance? Or do you value spontaneity and, consequently, improvisation? *I am a member of a multicultural improv troupe; we play off each other's multilingual cues.*

And speaking of improvisation, the director Linda Yellen is one of the foremost practitioners of this mode. In a made-for-TV video called *Chantilly Lace* (because such lace is both beautiful and strong, and it gets stronger as it ages), she explores friendship among women. There was no script for this production. Through collective improvisation, Yellen and seven actresses created seven characters to explore women's friendship. Six days of shooting resulted in 28 hours of film that was later edited into a two-hour production.

Emerging Theatrical Traditions

The Western theater, by way of example, has undergone tremendous mutations from communal ceremonies to placate and manage the gods, through the Greek open-air dramas and medieval Christian mystery plays of cosmic proportions, to our contemporary little theater of the self. And the theater continues to mutate. Its dynamic nature serves to increase the theater's relevance for those in search of metaphors that can stretch around a changing human scene, as participation in multiple theatrical traditions bend the participant.

Some of these modes of participation, moreover, are onstage, some are backstage, and others are offstage altogether. Members of the human community have variously defined themselves as participant, performer, audience or spectator, impresario, director, playwright, set designer, costumer. And other roles as well. We flit about the set.

Even as you read these words, new theatrical traditions (like Yellen's) are emerging that give clues to multicultural people for the combining of disparate elements into new kinds of productions. Peter Brooke is famous for his productions that combine international casts and the theatrical traditions of many cultures. Brook's 1991 Tokyo production of Shakespeare's *Tempest* was performed in French (with simultaneous translation into Japanese) by an international cast. Most of the players, however, were neither native French nor English speakers. The part of Miranda, for instance, was played by an actress from India. This production combined the conventions of at least five theatrical traditions, including the "rain sticks" of West African ceremonials and the black-clothed manipulators of *bunraku* puppets.

Another example is German director Wim Wenders's film *Notebook on Cities and Clothes.* This film is a documentary (for lack of a better descriptor) on the life and work of Japanese fashion designer Yuji Yamamoto as he and his atelier prepare for Paris and Tokyo fashion shows. Most of the time this "film" features three simultaneous visual images: regular film, a video image, and the image of the video monitor as the video is being made. The film is trilingual (English, French, and Japanese—and all this by a German director). In one scene the setting is Tokyo. The camera pans to the sky, and when it returns to earth, the viewer is in Paris. This "documentary" becomes an extended discourse on the nature of identity, work, and art in our highly mobile, electronically connected world. The film explores the paradoxes of identity, of what is real, true, consistent. With painting everything was simple, Wenders says, but with photography it got complicated. "The original was a negative. Without a print it did not exist. Just the opposite. Each copy was the original."

The prologue to his film begins as follows:

You live wherever you live.
You do whatever you do.
You talk however you talk.
You eat whatever you eat.
You wear whatever clothes you wear.
You look at whatever images you see . . .

You are living however you can.
You are whoever you are.

. . . We live in the cities.
The cities live in us . . .

time passes.
We move from one city to another.
We change languages.
We change opinions.
We change clothes.
We change everything . . .

Another metaphor comes to mind. *I am a player in a motion picture, filmed simultaneously in three languages, set in two nations, with an international cast of characters.*

Now that we have peeled back some of the layers of the theatrical metaphor, are there roles or insights that you may have previously overlooked that might provide the dynamic construct you need to enhance your participation as a multicultural player in life's various theaters?

In attempting to capture the tension between self-definitions and social definitions of self, we want to honor the complexity of persons living in a world where individual modes of participation have to be affirmed by groups outside themselves in order to achieve full identity. A person choosing to behave differently, unexpectedly, can gradually elicit social respect for that difference. This can be done by creating—convincingly—a new character or role or mode to aid that person's participation in the human drama even when this involves rescripting the whole drama or redefining the entire performance space itself.

We have explored the territory "in-between" and have seen that it is necessarily a fluid place. Although we get plenty of practice switching roles within each of our cultural contexts, we need more metaphors of authentic in-betweenness to assist us in expressing our complex and dynamic realities to others as we alternate cultures. We need help from others in orchestrating our multiple multicultural roles. Without this help in expressing a complex self, how will we elicit cooperation in affirming our identities?

Metaphors for people who cross cultural boundaries are generated by all traditions of thought and experience. Part 2 of this book explores nontheatrical terrains and will expand the reader's skill in finding apt metaphors of identity.

Recognizing Complex Selves

Hage and Powers (1992) describe some of the characteristics of "complex" selves. Complex people:

- Entertain equally valued different identities simultaneously, taking apparent contradictions in stride
- Accept periodic shifting of their social position without reacting defensively
- Can look at situations from more than one point of view and can, therefore, be more creative in envisioning solutions to problems and be more effective when enacting those solutions cooperatively with others
- Expend more effort in the construction of self than in the presentation of self; construction of self flows from participation in problem solving and the role redefinition associated with problem solving
- Personalize and customize a role or the meaning of an attribute, rather than project some script-like definition
- Judge themselves on overall performance, rather than on performance in any particular sphere
- Deem less important to their self-esteem the evaluations of others, replacing them with a sense of efficacy in dealing with change, in overcoming problems, and in being flexible
- Exercise choices that require negotiation and co-determined agreements
- Act effectively within a collective (rather than individual) setting

---

Notes to Myself

1. The metaphor that best describes who I am when I am between roles, at least for now, is:

_____

_____

_____

_____

_____

2. When I think of those times when I am between roles, it is most often in circumstances such as:

_____

_____

_____

_____

3. Sometimes my own personal complexity includes notions that appear to be contradictory. Some examples that come to mind are:

_____

_____

_____

_____

Part 2

Beyond "Fixed" Boundaries

"Complex selves are too individualized to match an archetype," Hage and Powers (1992) say. Traditional archetypes based on nationality, ethnicity, "race," or language no longer suffice . . . if they ever did.

One way to elicit the social affirmation needed to develop a strong sense of self is by explaining ourselves with an apt metaphor. An apt metaphor not only stimulates a vivid picture in our mind, a picture of our resplendent inner plumage, but it also provides a verbal handle for the image. Metaphors allow us to form mental images that we can communicate to others to give them a sense of who we are. They come in handy, if only while talking to ourselves in front of the morning mirror.

Most multicultural people can readily see themselves through theatrical metaphors, the subject of the prior two chapters. There are, moreover, many other sources of metaphors that hold promise for the multicultural person, and Chapters 10–13 explore a sample of these.

Some of these metaphors get kind of wild: "I am Trickster Coyote; I am both sides of the coin." "My only name is the Scroobious Pip." How we see ourselves does make a difference. Why? Because the suppositions that underpin the mental constructs we employ in thinking about ourselves set boundaries to our self-image. A guide to help you construct your own metaphor is provided in Chapter 14.

We offer you a sampling of metaphors for you to use as you see fit, in the hope that this will stimulate you to develop new—or to tune up old—descriptions of your own faceted self. Many of the illustrations we supply may not click for you. Perhaps they come from a cultural or intellectual tradition with which you do not identify. Not to worry. We sprinkle metaphors throughout these chapters like spice on a vegetarian pizza. The aim is to tease your brain's taste buds into feeling alive. In the spirit of brainstorming, we want to spark your creativity, help you loosen the bounds of fixed identities, and explore the world of dynamic metaphoric thinking.

Metaphors that speak to the multicultural person abound. Just today, a National Public Radio program told of a little "Neorican" girl (born in Puerto Rico, living in New York City) who came home saddened that she had been called a "spick" in school. Her father consoled her by saying, "You are not a spick. You are a mango tree grafted onto a magnolia tree. You not only taste good but you smell good, too." The healing power of metaphors!

From Rat Deva to Pure Energy

Cosmologies of the Spirit and of the Mind

Multicultural people have an even broader context within which to conduct themselves than do people who have never had their view of the world challenged by other traditions of thought. One problem they often face is looking for appropriate metaphors of self in but a limited number of places.

Metaphors from any tradition of thought or expression can be powerful tools for visualizing nuances of the multicultural self. Three sets of metaphors are sampled in this chapter: those from various mythological and spiritual traditions; those from classical scientific cosmologies, including mechanical and organic systems; and those based on images of pure process.

The Power of Mythology

The gods and goddesses of ancient mythology provide an unexpected source for building identity. As Gloria Steinem says in her foreword to a book on this approach by Jungian psychiatrist Jean Shinoda Bolen (1984), "You may find a myth that will evoke the reality in you. . . . At a minimum, these archetypal goddesses are a useful shorthand for describing and thus analyzing many behavior patterns and personality traits. At a maximum, they are ways of envisioning and thus calling up needed strengths and qualities within ourselves." Bolen (1990) has also written a book along the same lines for men.

You can look to whatever tradition of mythology that catches your eye. You can be a combination of the independent, achievement-oriented goddess Artemis and the goddess of love and beauty, Aphrodite. You may find a sustaining myth in your own past, as Maxine Hong Kingston (1976) did in her mother's stories of her ancestors, which Kingston relates in *The Woman Warrior: Memoirs of a Girlhood among Ghosts*.

Spiritual and Religious Cosmologies

Some of the most compelling metaphors throughout the ages have been inspired by various traditions of spiritual belief. For some philosophers of religion, the search for one's self is a search for God; God resides in our self. The search for self knowledge—Socrates' 2,500-year-old injunction—is to move toward the light that is divine.

In most areas of the world prior to the 18th century—and in much of the world today—a grand-scale view of the universe is supplied by spiritual or religious traditions, and they equip people with a satisfying orientation of self. Each person—and consequently one's self—can be seen as participating in a cosmic plan, as in the communal ceremonies of ancient Greece.

Sometimes a cosmic plan is considered to be preordained; other times it is seen to be subject to free will (to use vocabulary from the Christian discussion of these issues). Sometimes, as John Farella (1990) points out, the "preordained" plan entails an intricate balance between change and changelessness. Navajo philosophy, for instance, postulates that human beings always get into trouble when they ignore the three givens:

1. There is male and female, or two.

2. This gives birth to many, or diversity.

3. This, in turn, engenders constant change.

For some traditions, the cosmic drama has been cyclical. Each person is reborn after death as another life form, the complexity of the new life form depending on the spiritual growth or deterioration attained or fallen to in the previous life. *I am made of life energy itself and in my many reincarnations I will take many forms in many places.*

In societies heavily influenced by the Judeo-Christian tradition, the person's task might be stated (monotheistically) as: *I am a child of God and my destiny is to become more Godlike though His grace and by following His teachings as best I can in the cultures in which I find myself.* In some Protestant Christian translations, this task could be restated as: *My core self is a "striving-to-be-better" self, and this I can do within whatever cultural boundaries I find myself.*

What is "better" is, of course, defined in precept and parable. Each religion has flesh-and-blood models of "better" behavior, and some individuals derive guiding metaphors from them. Deities provide models: I am a daughter of Obatalá (a West African Yoruba god); I follow the teachings of Buddha.

Finding Flexibility in Set Systems of Spirituality

For many people, spiritual metaphors imply absolute values rather than situational values. Because of this, spiritual metaphors may not appear to be especially accommodating of the multicultural experience. But for many traditions, especially polytheistic traditions, this absoluteness is not a feature of the belief systems.

One U.S. teenager, imbued with religious fervor, would frequently ask acquaintances what religion they espoused. As a *judoka,* he met many Japanese, some of whom were fellow judo enthusiasts. The responses of the first half-dozen Japanese to the religious-membership question were identical. First, the person would respond with a blank look. Then, recognizing that the question had its source in U.S. culture, they would explain that in Japan religions were more like philosophies. Each had different functions. You might be married in a Shinto ceremony, buried in a Buddhist ritual. The teenager began to realize that his question did not make a lot of sense to people outside a Western sectarian milieu.

Japanese are not alone in blending elements from different spiritual traditions. Consider the different feel of Roman Catholicism in the United States and in Mexico. Besides the preeminent importance of the Virgin Mary in the Mexican Church (among the populace she typically gets top billing in her apparition as the Virgin of Guadalupe, over God and Christ), accommodations have been made to incorporate selected practices from pre-conquest Aztec times. The Day of the Dead is one example. Two other communities familiar to many tourists also mix Catholic and Indian religious traditions: Taos Pueblo, New Mexico (United States) and Chichicastenango, Guatemala.

Religious dictates notwithstanding, conscientious believers of any spiritual tradition tend to interpret a creed with some flexibility. The broader social as well as religious context is often taken into account. This leads to honest differences of opinion. A recent poll of U.S. Catholics suggests that 87 percent did not agree with the Pope's position on birth control. The point is that there usually is considerable flexibility in practice, if not in theory, among conscientious adherents to religious traditions with absolute, deity-given dogma.

This honest difference of opinion was demonstrated at a recent international conference held in Cairo, Egypt, for English-language teachers from various parts of the Islamic world. Participants got into heated arguments over whether specific behaviors portrayed in English-as-a-second-language texts were immoral. One male Saudi participant, for example, referred to U.S. dating customs incorporated in the dialog of one text as "behavior absolutely prohibited by the Quran." A young woman teacher from Turkey rose to her feet and said that devout Moslems in her country do not believe that the Quran prohibits the social contact between boys and girls described in the text. Clearly, there was a difference of interpretation of just what members of the Islamic world believe and practice with regard to behavior associated with gender.

We can be functional in a culture without embracing all of that culture's values. In fact, within most cultures a diversity of values is accepted. This is one reason why people in similar circumstances act differently within the same culture; their beliefs and reasonings, combined with their emotional disposition, lead them to reach dissimilar conclusions on the same issues. The pro-choice and the pro-life advocates on the abortion issue in the United States are one example of similar people reaching dissimilar views.

The Case of the Kitchen Rats

Even sheltered spiritual societies of like-minded people do not remove all controversy from their midst. One such example is the New Age community in northern Scotland at Findhorn, famous for its large vegetables and harmonious interaction with all life forms. On one occasion, an infestation of rats, especially in the kitchen area, threatened both food supply and public health. Some members of the community argued that for the public good the rats should be exterminated. Others argued that all life is sacred, and the rats should be allowed to live. As the rat colony prospered, the controversy took on increased urgency. The community tried to communicate meditatively with the rats, letting them know what the situation was and urging them to depart. Carmen Hendershott (1989), an ethnographer from the New

School for Social Research (New York City), was there at the time. She relates that:

> though some of the founding members had had striking success in reaching the mole deva and persuading the moles to confine themselves to particular parts of the Findhorn property away from the midst of the garden, history did not seem to be repeating itself. Efforts to reach the rat deva in meditation seemed unavailing, yet many members were vehemently opposed to calling in an exterminator. They delayed doing it until the Board of Health threatened to close down the kitchen.

Desperate, the New Age community gave the rats an ultimatum: "If you stay, it's your choice." That last effort, according to Hendershott, enabled the members to rationalize their killing the rats: It was the rats' responsibility, "who, having been warned, had used their free will and stayed." In this case, controversy over the underlying assumptions of a mental construct ("Do not kill") was mitigated by another construct ("A being has the freedom to make its own decisions").

However they are interpreted, spiritual metaphors cannot eliminate all dilemma from human decision making. Nor can any other philosophical insight or ideological imperative. Life is just too complex to accommodate a one-situation, one-response solution to human existence.

These spiritually inspired cosmologies can be so pervasive that their adherents experience difficulty in separating spiritual belief from secular belief. *Wherever I am, I manifest in my own life the essential plan of the universe.* In the Islamic world, for instance, there is much consternation evoked by the matter of teaching about other cultures. Culture is regarded as intertwined with religion, and to study other cultures is seen by many believers to be akin to teaching the creeds of heathen religions. English teachers who want to prepare students to function in European or American cultures, or even to read English-language textbooks in college, run into this controversy.

The line of demarcation separating religious values from secular practices is much harder to perceive in theocratic societies. In many parts of the Islamic world, and in some Native American tribes, for instance, the word "culture" is regarded as virtually synonymous with "religion." In these societies, one must look a little harder to see where the line is drawn. Oft times, the line can best be discerned by a member of the group who has lived with his or her coreligionists in another geographic setting.

In *Beyond Culture,* Hall (1976) argues that we must learn to differentiate our selves from the cultural protocols we use to satisfy our perceived needs.

Conceptually, in other words, there is a significant difference between saying, "I am hungry, therefore I must eat," and "I am hungry, therefore I must eat a cheeseburger." The former axiom allows for substituting a gyros for a cheeseburger without courting a conflict of core values.

Many public behaviors, such as avoiding food proscribed by the dominant religion or the etiquette of eating with forks, do not usually raise the issue of individual preference to the level of existential conflict. (Forks, incidently, were used by Spaniards and Italians since the 17th century, a practice resisted by the English, who at the time ate with bare hands or knives [Kass, 1994].) The multicultural person can make easy accommodations to most surface manifestations of his or her internal values. The value "Don't revolt or insult your hosts by the way you eat" is a more comprehensive rule than the specific admonition (in Ethiopia) to "use *indira* bread to grasp your food."

Classical Science Cosmologies

In the 18th-century Western world, a less sacred, less divine view began to make inroads among the elite. The classical scientific views of the universe as a giant clockwork provide terrain we can mine for metaphorical nuggets, views that may be useful for crafting multicultural selves.

Mechanical/Structural Metaphors

Some rather well-educated people, influenced by the physics of Isaac Newton, thought they saw a mechanical order built into the world, an order humans could control. *The cosmos is a machine, and although each culture provides different levers, I know how to move them.* Or, if the last image seems to lack proper humility, a somewhat less reassuring image of a mechanistic world is offered by another metaphor: *I am like a cog in culture's contraption, caught in the grindings of the World Machine in the place where circumstance has dumped me.*

Unfortunately, this supposedly observable mechanical order has proved elusive. Upon closer observation the world increasingly seemed to be all flux and change. Astronomer Sir James Jeans (1931) once wrote, summarizing findings in physics, "The world begins to look more like a great thought than a great machine." Fellow astronomer Eddington (1933) preferred to think of the world as "mind-stuff." Yet even the mind, sociologists keep telling us, is not so much a thinking instrument as it is a pliable medium programmed by social forces—an art object, in a sense. "The mind is a blue guitar upon which we improvise the song of the world" (Dillard, 1982; see also Stevens, 1968, 175). Perhaps there is no immutable or unchanging order. "Our knowledge is contextual and only contextual," observes Annie Dillard. This is a rather familiar concept in some of the old cosmologies, and one never given up in the East.

One downside to mechanistic metaphors is that they often generate structural images that are rather bureaucratic and hierarchical. Most of the time they provide a much too rigid metaphoric coat for multicultural people to wear comfortably.

There is an alternative to rigidly mechanistic interpretations of the universe in more flexible, organic models based on biological observations of living creatures. Both Western and non-Western traditions readily embrace biological, procreative, organic life forces. These forces affirm diversity, adaptation, and rebirth. Symbols of rebirth, for instance, can be seen in Christian Easter rituals and in animistic spring rites alike.

Although the "machine" metaphors have obvious weaknesses, science metaphors in general are appealing because they are so readily amenable to change in response to new information. This is because all science metaphors, in essence, are metaphors of hypothesis. When proven to be less than satisfactory explanations of reality, they are edited or discarded. (This is discussed further in the "pure process" section later in this Chapter.)

Thinking of ourselves in a more organic mode, it is possible to see ourselves as part of an immense developmental system.

Organic Systems

Western thinkers, traced by George Lockland (1973) in *Grow or Die,* began seeing this other kind of order, one that resembled Darwin's organic evolution rather than mechanical functioning. They began to describe an orderly process of growth and development. More recently, simple genetic copying was observed to evolve into more dynamic forms of recombination. Cycles of replication became the double helix of genetic transmission and transformation. Biological metaphors lead to another view of self, one that incorporates more and more diversity as it grows. *Just as a single cell becomes an organism, so do I evolve as I develop more internal structure; I become more complex as I become more multicultural.*

In one of her short stories, Sandra Cisneros (1991) describes a young girl's 11th birthday. She likens this dynamic, organic, personal growth to earth-based and expanding metaphorical tree rings in which all of our experiences are brought to bear on the present moment. "I am a tree where each internal ring encompasses a part of my experiences, and all the rings are brought to bear on the present moment—my three-year-old self, my seven-year-old self . . ., all these old selves were in attendance at my eleventh birthday. . . ."

Trees add one ring during each cycle of growth. This ordered expansion contrasts with another form of growth—evolutionary development. Canadian writer Robertson Davies says, "One is a bead on a string. You partake of innumerable people in the past, and you contribute to goodness knows how many in the future" (Gussow, 1995). Some evolutionary forces alter the structure of the organism. Partly because multicultural individuals experience unusual combinations of cultures, they may feel like "new" organisms. *I am a newly discovered species; I need special care.*

What do these "new" species look like? They have different shapes. Organic metaphors involve ideas of growth and development and evolution (and of "progress"), and they may involve ecological points of view that emphasize the relationship between you and your environment.

Many of the "new" metaphorical species are found beyond the animal kingdom. These metaphors go well beyond conventional organic categories to encompass entire biotic regions with their myriad of complex, interrelated, adaptive, organic communities. *I am like a plant. In the mountains I am laurel; in the desert, a yellow buttercup; in marshlands, lacy fern; by the shore I am heather, purple and sturdy.*

At first glance, if one assumes that one cannot go back and forth between different species of life forms during a single lifetime, the above metaphor appears not to work. It does, however, evoke the interrelatedness of all life forms with their immediate environment. Something on the order of a coyote eating a mouse eating a plant growing from compost.

Mentally, of course, we are making the connection between organic biosystems and human social systems. Both systems are dynamic rather than static and participate together in this process we call life. If we consider organic metaphors from the perspective of diverse manifestations of the "energy" of life's "underlying essence," the images suggest the potential ability of an individual human being, nurtured by several cultures, to display, as a result, more aspects of the "possible human" (Houston, 1982).

Cultural traditions of expression often associate physical movement with metaphoric concepts that can be either mechanistic, organic, or both. Ballet and modern dance provide contrasting examples. The highly stylized movements of ballet, with leaps toward heaven and emphasis on precision and perfection of movement, illustrate a mechanistic metaphor. Modern dance, on the other hand, with its earth-based floor work, is organic and biological in its metaphoric allusion. The slow-motion stylization of a Chinese martial art, *T'ai chi ch'uan,* often seen practiced by older people in Chinese parks, has both mechanistic and organic elements. The movements themselves are rigidly prescribed, but the accompanying metaphors are organic. Different movements evoke specific thoughts. Thrusting one's hands above the head, then lowering them, may signify energy entering oneself from the solar system; an outward horizontal sweeping movement of the arm may symbolize the growing of branches out into the world. *T'ai chi* offers a combination of exercise protocol and a succession of organic metaphors concerning one's place in the universe. *Through T'ai chi ch'uan, I see my vital force (chi) as a tree, spreading roots in different directions, getting energy from the earth, lifting leaves and branches skyward, drawing energy from the heavens and from the earth's many cultures that have enriched me.*

Alternatively, as LaDonna Harris notes from her Comanche nomadic tradition: "People do not have roots, like plants. A person is mobile, free as the wind, and meant to manifest who they are wherever they happen to be." The "people of the wind" metaphor contrasts with the "roots" metaphor. People of the wind make relationships wherever they go. Root people are deeply involved in a particular place and a particular set of relationships. One example of root people are the Acoma Pueblo families that have lived in the same North American town (now in the State of New Mexico), at the top of a 400-foot mesa since before the time of Christ. But what if a person were half Comanche and half Acoma? Half wind and half root?

Metaphors of Pure Process

Going further beyond the organic, we find metaphors with an even more pointed focus on process. *I am an intergalactic cultural force field, a system of cultural energy undergoing a continuous process of transformation.*

Or, *I am a constantly changing pattern of cultural energy interacting with all things in all cultures.*

In actuality, identity itself is not static. Identity formation implies a lifelong process. Aging in itself assures us of change. As we follow our friends and ourselves throughout a lifetime, the simple fact of aging reveals the self's adaption and change to the clearly different stages of life.

Awareness of life's metamorphosing events may go deeper than a simple recognition of a fact—aging—that is, after all, amply modeled in extended households. One's sense of self may not be a particular content of consciousness, rather, *I am consciousness itself, and I am aware of different manifestations of it in each of the cultures in which I exist.*

Self, in this metaphor, owes much to Descartes: *Cogito ergo sum* (I think, therefore I am). It is the continuously renewed encounter of the ever-structuring mind with the reality it perceives (Dillard, 1982). In this world view, based on consciousness itself, the integration of new "reality" into our core self does not imply complete harmony, but simply the organization of diversity into some coherent pattern.

How do we imagine a life perceived as total process? What is the basis of coherence in a life of total process? There are many approaches to visualizing coherent process: as a novel following classical Greek proscriptions for drama—a linear narrative with a beginning, a middle, and an end. Or as a TV set; a flip of the switch and the program is changed. The collage-like electronic imagery of the current MTV era may free us from the burden of maintaining a single identity or "story" for the duration of our time on earth.

Even if we imagine ourselves as all flux and change, unfolding according to some internal logic of the change process itself, we still need some sense of continuity. Otherwise, *I feel moved about by cosmic cultural forces, achieving coherence wherever I can.*

For some people, in rapidly changing circumstances the self can be seen as the only enduring element in shifting social contexts. *I am the rock that endures.* Pueblo Indians, deeply rooted to communal life and its cosmic relationships, have wrapped themselves in blankets of secrecy. Waiting out the 500-year Euro-American "storm," they endure.

Through the cosmological, scientific, and pure process metaphors just discussed, we can see how the particular way we describe our self-image carries much philosophical baggage. Another metaphoric category highlights the idea of faceted uniqueness. The next chapter investigates ways to describe this prismed self.

So, How Do You Imagine Yourself?

Perhaps you do not see yourself, even in analogy, as a member of the plant kingdom or as a rock, however enduring. How *do* you imagine yourself?

Do you imagine yourself to be a single organ, such as a brain? Do you focus on yourself as an information processor? decision maker? designer? Do cybernetic images come to the fore as you imagine yourself as a learning entity with an intrinsic ability to learn how to learn? Or maybe it is the brain as a holographic system that captures your attention. In this image the brain is like a mirror reflecting the universe. If a mirror is broken, *all* its fragments continue to reflect the total image. Our brains, too, are analogically organized to reflect redundantly. When we are transported to another culture, we retain the ability to see things whole; we are not a fragment of our former selves.

An obvious strength of these dynamic metaphors for the multicultural person is that they are firmly rooted in the inescapable fact of change. This is one reason why the Platonic and Christian fascination with immutability or changelessness strikes many American Indians as so odd. According to new world cosmologies, all of which are based on the natural world, that which ceases to change is dead. This process of constant change tends to be more highly conscious in those persons who undergo continuous contact with two or more cultures. This is in contrast to those monocultural persons for whom changes in values and in orientation may not be so necessary or dramatic.

Notes to Myself

1. As I look over metaphors of spirituality and those based on science, my own preference of a metaphor for my multicultural self is:

_____

_____

_____

_____

_____

2. Comparing organic metaphors with metaphors of pure process, I think that for my multicultural self I prefer:

_____

_____

_____

_____

_____

3. Reviewing the metaphors of this chapter, my own composite image of my multicultural self goes something like this:

_____

_____

_____

_____

_____

11

I Am Like a Diamond

Metaphors That Sparkle in the Light

There are many ways to sparkle. Some cultures provide a limelight for certain aspects of your personality; other cultures feature some of your other qualities. Some cultures may bring out the worst in you. Various facets of you shine under the different lighting that each culture radiates. As Takeshi Izutsu, a Japanese college student, put it, "I am like a diamond that is too hard to hurt the surface, but inside, every light is refracted and the color of the light is always changing."

Personal Uniqueness

At first blush, the idea of personal uniqueness strikes one as a quintessential Western conceit. Its relevance to multicultural individuals, however, extends—necessarily—well beyond the West.

What two people (except maybe identical twins) have precisely the same genetic combination? (Even identical twins are not perfectly identical, because their genes are sensitive to ambient influences during embryonic development, and each twin interacts with a partly different prenatal environment.) And who—including identical twins—has had the same experiences in life as another person? The possibilities for human uniqueness are infinite both in spite of and because of our dependence on, as the standard institutional disclaimer states, "circumstances beyond our control."

The Spanish philosopher José Ortega y Gasset said, "I am myself and my circumstances" (*"Yo soy yo y mis circunstancias"*). No matter where you are on the nature-nurture debate, no one can deny that both our heredity and environment interact in complex ways.

Multifaceted Individuals

Multicultural people are not only individually unique. The different cultures in which their natures have been nurtured may place very different values on the behavioral dispositions they were born with as well as on their learned behaviors. A person who is naturally extroverted, who has mastered "speaking out" in a culture that values such behavior, may be roundly criticized in another of his or her cultural settings where expressive, direct behavior is discouraged, perhaps in favor of "active" listening and observing. This may be especially the case if the person is young or female—or even worse, young *and* female. Even in "expressive" societies, expressiveness may be limited to certain times and places.

Teeter-Tottering between Expressiveness and Being Seen But Not Heard

A professor at the University of Colorado was socialized in both Pueblo Indian and Mexican cultures and schooled in Anglo-U.S. institutions. His Mexican relatives were verbally expressive about emotions such as love and anger. His Pueblo relatives, on the other hand, believed emotion should not be overtly displayed, and although they valued the opinions of young people, there were times, places, and protocols for expressing opinions. These parameters involved important elements of timing and avoidance of direct confrontation. His Anglo school teachers and peers talked a lot about beliefs and opinions. His Pueblo relatives constantly criticized him for talking too much. One had to be quiet initially to discover how to insert one's opinion into the discussion in a way that contributed to mutual respect. Because of these differing constraints governing verbal expressions, as a young child this individual had to learn to display his natural extroversion appropriately in each cultural context.

In the Mexican setting, he could give reign to emotional expression, especially as a teenage boy in his relationships with girls; he could be a poet. At school he became active in school politics and became a student-body officer. His natural exuberance enabled him to participate easily in "mainstream" U.S. political settings—a skill that later benefited both his Mexican and Pueblo communities. At home with his mother's relatives in the Pueblo, his "people sense" enabled him to be *appropriately* expressive. This, paradoxically, involved *not* expressing himself. That is, it involved closing his mouth and discovering the skill of active listening. Once having demonstrated his skill as an active listener and *appropriate* speaker, he was often called on to articulate the community's needs to "the outside." *I am like a diamond. Depending on how the light strikes, I radiate different shapes and colors.*

This person even used his natural expressiveness to manipulate the dominant culture when he was a young child in Indian boarding school. There was a rule that you could not "talk Indian" at school, an "offense" for which you could be expelled. So any time he wanted to get away from school for a few days to visit his Pueblo grandmother, he just spoke to one of his classmates in "Indian" within earshot of a teacher. This was the only area where he was a "behavior problem" to school authorities, authorities who never did realize that this nine-year-old was manipulating "the system" to his own advantage.

Multifaceted Cultures

Today it is a rare environment that is *only* bicultural. North American cities such as Miami, New York, Chicago, Los Angeles, Seattle, Vancouver, Montreal, Toronto, Mexico City, and the entire region on both sides of the U.S.-Mexican border are all current locations of massive immigration. Virtually all large cities of the world are multicultural, and it is not uncommon for the children in one school system to come from families that together speak 100 languages. There is a long history of urban multiculturalism. When New York City was still called New Amsterdam and had a population of 400–500 inhabitants, the ethnically mixed "metropolis" spoke "as many as 18 languages" (Quinn, 1994). By the 19th century, half the inhabitants of New York City were foreign born. From engineers to dishwashers, the current immigrants to the world's metropolitan centers constitute "a new sort of tribal frontier where new combinations of cultures attempt, often uneasily, to coexist in a manner and on a scale never before seen" (Kotkin, 1992).

Between Facets

Because cultures themselves are multifaceted, and because more and more supposedly homogeneous cultures maintain intensive contact with each other, the space between cultures is itself becoming progressively important. The "between" space houses increasing numbers of people who experience the phenomenon of multiple belongingness, a concept explored in Chapter 9 from the perspective of an individual person between roles.

Intercultural Space

Communication between cultures entails the rather formidable task of building bridges. Not just any bridge. But a bridge between orders that are not simply different structurings of the same reality, but structurally different realities. Communication between cultures involves someone first learning the conventional forms and orders of the other culture. Knowledge of the language of both cultures typically is critical. People from both sides of the cultural boundaries, by dint of their experience and skills, become "brokers," mediating between cultures. They often create a unique culture.

These new "in-between" cultures have their own style and language mix, as Wagner (1977) argues. The forms and habits of these "cultures of communication" obey the same rules as other cultures, with members, customs, beliefs, and lifestyles. Members of these mediational cultures include the "cultures" of translators, anthropologists, missionaries, traders and trade communities, administrative, and diplomatic missions (Karttunen, 1994). In the 1950s and 1960s, the anthropologist Ruth Useem (1967) first called the children of these people "third culture kids." In the 1990s, the intelligent and wealthy international students who hang out in Harvard Square call themselves "Euro-kids." Many others currently call themselves "global nomads." Artifacts of these third cultures can include anthropological monographs, lifestyles, and languages, including pidgins, creoles, and jargons.

Similarly, communication in certain multicultural situations may give rise to new patterns that are understood by all participants. A lingua franca such as Tok Pisin (pidgin talk) in Papua New Guinea is an example of this pattern. It incorporates English, Spanish, German, and local languages and pronunciations into a new mode of discourse. Our favorite Tok Pisin expression is *tok gavman* (government talk); it means *talk of a suspicious nature.*

Margaret Olebe and Jolene Koster (1989) also have gone on record as believing that multicultural situations constitute a unique culture of their own. Thus, people living in a multicultural setting, engaged on a daily basis in intercultural interactions, may employ a set of communication skills reflective of neither culture of origin. Nancy Adler (1980) has written extensively on this kind of cultural "synergy" as it manifests itself in corporate cultures.

Specific situations do invite their own communication patterns. Interactions on a soccer field, for example, are not identical to those in an executive boardroom, even if the participants employ the same underlying competitive strategies. Although the specific ways people interact may vary situationally, the underlying interaction strategies are actually quite similar. These strategies include recognizing the extent to which knowledge is personal, developing skill in functioning in both task-related and relational roles, a posture that facilitates interaction (respect, empathy), and reacting to new and ambiguous situations with little visible discomfort (Ruben and Kealey, 1979).

Are You Liminal?

There are mountains to climb, borders to cross, and visions to invent. Many social scientists are working to understand these dynamics of change and invention.

Takako Kishima (1992), a Japanese political scientist who is working on an explanation of change in human societies, theorizes that change occurs through the intrusion of borderline or in-between people. She calls such a person a "liminal" being, one who lives in society's cracks, and such a person is not unlike Stonequist's (1937) marginal man, that "crucible of cultural fusion" who is on the cutting edge of cultural change. Kishima emphasizes that her liminal beings live outside, below, above, or in-between the structures of conventional or mainstream society.

The term *liminal* describes dynamics that often occur in Japanese society that link the heights and depths, the inside and outside of society. In the past, Samurai could not go into battle without the armor made of the leather produced by *burakamin,* Japan's untouchables. This interdependence of people of very different social status is reflected today in Japan, Inc. Most innovations in Japanese industry are invented by high-risk small and medium-sized companies of but modest status whose prototypes are bought by large, prestigious companies. The risks associated with change and innovation are typically taken by low-status people. Perhaps the most famous examples of influential liminals are the geisha of Tokugawa Japan, the girls of poor families sold to geisha houses who became the discreet hostesses of the rich and mighty.

Circumstances can be liminal, too. War or famine, or attending a birth or a death, are examples. Such events often cause ordinary people to begin to live in the crack between established realities, cultural and otherwise, and to behave differently from what is expected by those living on either side of the crack. In Japan, World War II was this kind of liminal event. It catapulted many low-status people to the center and heights of society. Honda, the lawnmower repairman who went on to making motorcycles and then automobiles, is one such example. He had the nerve to handle the risks inherent in creating new social space, just as the children of Japanese colonial administrators in China, Manchuria, and Taiwan often became the frontmen of Japan's global economic expansion in the post WWII era. The participation of these liminal people in everyday life and their different behavior in their social roles deforms the existing social context. If many people are simultaneously behaving differently, the surrounding society becomes so deformed that it becomes ripe for transformation or change.

Takamatsu (1994) studied the lives of Japanese women in their 50s who had consistently engaged in activities that promoted social change. Most had fulfilled traditional roles as wives and mothers but had negotiated with their families for the time to do their social actions. None had a grand strategy for social change. They thought of "the problem" as a big wall. Quite independently, but aware of others' actions, individuals and their associated groups poked holes in "the wall," until the wall fell down "all by itself." *I live in the space between one set of cultural conventions and alternative possibilities, and by my very existence I create new social space.*

Multiple Belongingness: The Sunflower Self

In lectures, Marshall Singer of the University of Pittsburgh describes the self living in a multi-group society as being like a sunflower with many petals. The "face" of the sunflower is the core self, the place where all the petals attach, the locus of coherence. Each of the different petals is the self as perceived by the members of one of the groups to which one belongs. Or, to use our previous metaphor, as the facets of oneself that one can reveal in that setting. Singer (1987), in his book on the relationships between culture and perception, questions whether the self in multicultural societies ever really perceives itself as belonging to only one group.

Yoneji Masuda (1980), the Japanese futurologist, postulates that the information revolution in which we are all presently engulfed will engender "multi-centered participatory democracies" as the societal form of choice for the next great era in human history, where multiple belongingness will be the norm. *Like a peer-to-peer LAN (Local Area Network for linking computers), I have many centers.*

The conviction that multi-belongingness is a common human experience is gaining credence. We question if it has ever been much of an exception. As noted in Chapter 2, for millennia many people have had exogamous marriage customs (that is, they systematically married outside their own group), and they have managed to cross cultural boundaries and skillfully maintain multiple relationships.

Intermarriages continue to generate interesting examples of multiple belongingness. When it came time to register the birth of the child of a mixed-race couple in a midwestern U.S. city, the hospital registrar asked what the child's race was. The father, who had just spent several years in the then-segregated U.S. South, wanted to know what the options were: the father was white, the mother was Hispanic of African ancestry. At the registrar's suggestion, the father talked on the phone to someone who worked in the Cook County birth registration department. He explained the situation to a lady whose voice identified her as African American.

"Well," she said, "there are a lot of choices." She read him a list of about 20 races and ethnicities. "Filipino has been quite popular lately," she told the father. It made him feel good to know that the world's major cultural identities were his son's for the asking!

Some years later, when this now young man of mixed race and culture began looking for a summer job in Chicago to help him continue his college studies, the father sympathized. He guessed summer jobs were hard to find when so many high school and college students were out there looking, too.

"Not for minority students," the son said.

"And which minority are you?" the father asked.

"Being Hispanic never got me anywhere," the son replied. "I'm putting down 'black.' "

Ah, back and forth between identities. *I am a gregarious animal who joins alliances of convenience to acquire the requisite "union cards" to join the groups I want.* Years later, when asked about his identity, the son said that he used the label that got him the farthest in the situation in which he found himself. An instrumentalist to the end!

A paradox faced by many multicultural individuals who want to feel a part of the community in which they find themselves is that to the extent they are viewed as "outsiders" they are accorded more latitude in their behavior. "Outsiders" fall outside many of the local behavioral expectations, especially those that are role-related, so they often benefit from this exclusionary mechanism in terms of greater freedom of action. The cost of this freedom, of course, is paid in sacrificed intimacy. Some cultures will not allow you to assume the role of outsider if your ancestral heritage is of that culture and if you look like one of them. Japanese-Americans visiting Japan are expected to have an intimate understanding of Japanese culture; Mexican-Americans visiting Mexico are expected to speak Spanish fluently.

In some places and times, identity switching among specified entities such as ethnic, religious, or racial may not be allowed. But remember, if you are multicultural and mobile, choice is momentary and situational; you get to leave cultures as well as join them.

In this backing and forthing, we often, by chance or on purpose, find ourselves on some sort of a quest, where others may regard us as some kind of otherworldly creature. "What planet are you from, Bucky?" Sometimes the search for organizing metaphors leads to strange places. To stories and games and circuses, for instance. The entrance to the Big Tent is in the next chapter.

Notes to Myself

1. As a diamond, some of my facets are:

_____

_____

_____

_____

2. Some of the ways I feel unique are:

_____

_____

_____

_____

_____

3. Given my druthers of "fitting in" or "standing out from the crowd," I am more comfortable with:

_____

_____

_____

_____

_____

4. I belong to the following bridge or mediational cultures:

_____

_____

_____

_____

5. What borders do I walk?

_____

_____

_____

_____

_____

6. I feel that I am on the border when:

_____

_____

_____

_____

_____

7. One example of when I jumped back and forth across a
   cultural/psychological border was when:

_____

_____

_____

_____

8. What in-between-space experiences do I bring to the
   social settings in which I participate?

_____

_____

_____

_____

9. Looking at the behaviors that are associated with the effective building of cultural bridges or connections, which ones are a part of my personal repertory? (The behaviors are recognition that knowledge is subjectively personal, skill in functioning in both product-related and process-related roles, a posture that facilitates interaction, and the ability to display little discomfort in new and ambiguous situations.)

_____

_____

_____

_____

_____

10. Placing myself in Marshall Singer's sunflower metaphor, this is my drawing of my particular sunflower, labeled with the group identities that constitute the petals of my flower:

12

Imaginary Creatures, Questers, Games and Circuses

Exotic Visions

Sometimes our metaphors are not even remotely based on the real, on things as we believe we know them. Some metaphors are more about beginning the beguine, as a once-popular song put it, imagining the imaginary. Look at the world maps drawn by European cartographers during the initial years of the Age of Discovery. Maps of imaginary places filled with imaginary beings. Dragons guarding the Seven Golden Cities of Cibola. Our imaginations seem to go into overdrive when we are confronted with the dangerous, the mysterious, or just the curious.

The Dangerous

New worlds of the past, new worlds of the future, new worlds peopled by strange and wondrous shapes. Remember the Intergalactic Bar in the first Star Wars movie? Lingering about the new and strange is an aura of danger, but also a spirit of excitement and adventure.

People need a sense of drama in their lives, and facing the exotic is one way to obtain it. After mountaineer Edmund Hillary and the Nepalese Sherpa mountaineer and guide Tenzing Norgay conquered the highest peak on earth, Sir Hillary was asked by reporters why he did it. "Because it was there," is his famous response.

Humans will do the darndest things for drama. Skydivers, riding gravity through a curtain of wind, jump for more than the view. A child looks at a roaring lion in a zoo in Cincinnati and feels he has conquered fear, for a moment.

The Mysterious

Sometimes even the real is beyond imagining. Old men and women examine a small woodland flower of the subtlest unnamed color and feel they have found something wondrous and mysterious. The paleontologist Loren Eisley and the writer-critic Annie Dillard both comment on the patterns found in the world and the magnitude of Divine Imagination in the conception and creation of a creature like a giraffe and on the iridescent colors of a wood duck's feathers. Or even the fact that dinosaurs once existed. In Key West, Florida, late each afternoon a crowd gathers on the dock to watch the sunset; they applaud at its successful conclusion.

The Merely Curious

The smell of the greasepaint, the beat of the drum, draw us to curiosities . . . bearded ladies and two-headed snakes. It may simply be the opinion of an outsider that stimulates our curiosity. The notions found in popular adages and in the musings of clever men and women of each culture contain intriguing points of view, views that can enrich our lives. A young American in Mexico offered his opinion on some issue of the day to a friend, ending with a saying popular in the United States: "Take it for what it's worth." The friend smiled and said, "In Mexico we say 'Take it for what it cost me.' " A nicely nuanced thought.

Novel pronouncements provide greater comprehension and resolution to our own version of reality. These culturally generated notions provide copious images, some of which we can synthesize to create future images of our own. These alternative constructs enhance our ability to imagine novel configurations of reality and of the self. An expert police hostage negotiator was asked what had prepared him to do that kind of work. He thought for a minute.

"My parents' divorce. It was where I first began to deal with a world that was not like it was 'supposed' to be."

Metaphors of Pure Imagination

Charles Proteus Steinmetz was a rare electrical genius who died in 1923. His employer, General Electric, instructed his bank to honor his checks in any amount—without limits! That is how irreplaceable he was regarded. Steinmetz was physically misshapen (he was a hunchback) and suffered because of it. In spite of his physical disabilities, he once said, "Man is only limited by his imagination."

We have generated metaphors from theater, from spiritual traditions, and from science and the natural world. Now we will let our imaginations soar and see if we can salt the tail of an intriguing image or two.

The Trickster Coyote

Multicultural people appear, in many contexts, to emerge from beyond everyday reality. Multicultural people move from one realm of convention or assumption into other realms each time they cross cultural boundaries. They may be, consequently, the epic deformers and transformers of our time. Inspired by Native American stories, you may create a metaphor that acknowledges the perversity of convention. *I am coyote, the trickster; I live on the edge, just beyond the firelight; I am both sides of the coin.*

Cognitive Complexity

Some thinkers, like George Kelly (1955), suggest mobile-like metaphors for shifting constructs of self. *My core creates a kind of cognitive geometry— dynamic mental mobiles incorporating the shapes and colors of many cultural traditions.*

Using these "cognitive geometries," we formulate constructs about "reality" based on the way we anticipate events (Mancuso, 1970). These anticipations are similar to Cartesian axes. They are not reality itself, but rather are points at which measurement can be made. The more points, the more complete our description of reality. The possible coordinates are infinite in number, so we do not need to chart all of them to get a good sense of the terrain. In addition, these axes, or intellectual constructs, need not emerge from past reality, but rather they can actually design or mold "reality." This point is emphasized by Alexander Christakis (1984; 1986) in his work on designing the future. If we design the future using the patterns of the past, we will keep ending up where we have been. Step one in designing an *alternative* future is to *imagine* it.

The Dream Machine

Many traditions of thought, including some Japanese Buddhist traditions, tell us that the past is just a dream, and the future is nothing more than imagination. This thought was expressed, in 1635, by the last prominent dramatist of Spain's Golden Age of Literature, Pedro Calderón de la Barca, when he said *Toda la vida es sueño, y los sueños sueños son* ("All of life is a dream, and dreams are [just] dreams") (Calderón, 1992).

We may even successfully employ a variety of designs that are inferentially incompatible with each other. Theorists speculate that it is often, in Kelly's words, the "uninferred fragments" of a person's metaphoric system that make him or her great! As Ralph Waldo Emerson (1981) said (in "Self-Reliance"), "A foolish consistency is the hobgoblin of little minds." *I am a mixed metaphor—a centipede that swims to a different drum beat—one whose parts appear incompatible but that respond to a deeper law of complexity.*

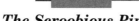

The Scroobious Pip

Perhaps none of the metaphors yet described in this book resonates for you. Perhaps your own unique self is its own metaphor. Consider Edward Lear, a 19th-century English artist and writer of "nonsense" ("The Owl and the Pussycat"). He took a two-month vacation on the isle of Corsica 130 years ago and over the course of three days penned a wonderful verse for the children of friends. It did not see formal publication until 100 years later (Lear, 1968).

The title character was an oddly configured being. His head was kind of birdlike: a blunt beak, delicate feathers that reached down, beardlike, to his upper chest, but moth-like antennae, donkey ears, and a fine pair of curved horns splendidly poised at the crown of his head. His two legs were hoofed, his tail decidedly aquiline, and his wings iridescently insect. The other animals of the sea and the land and the air gather around him and say:

> Tell us all about yourself we pray
> for as yet we can't make out in the least
> if you're fish or insect, or bird or beast.

Each time he is asked, he replies: "My only name is the Scroobious Pip." Finally, all of the resplendently different animals accept his own statement of identity: "Chippetty tip! Chippetty tip! Its only name is the Scroobious Pip!"

For some, this may be the quintessential metaphor. *My only name is the Scroobious Pip.* Like Wasilewski's Japanese-American informant in Chapter 8, you just state for all and sundry that you are yourself—with whatever multicultural idiosyncrasies that may imply. "Call me Ishmael."

Metaphors can open up the possibility of including contradictory traits, traits that fall on supposedly opposite ends of some continuum. We are, metaphorically speaking, anything we can imagine.

I Am a Traveler and a Tinker, Therefore I Guess

Another dynamic construct of the self, according to Bennett Berger (1968), who is critical of efforts spent trying to "find oneself," is the model of "a person who does not know who she or he is. [This person] might just be anything and, hence, is fit for the unanticipated opportunities and eventualities which rapidly changing societies provide." A Scroobious Pip, perhaps.

The Good Guessing Way

Paul Ryan (1973) describes what may be the life strategy of such a person as "the good guessing way." This way is characterized by openness to the unknown, a feel for what is relevant as things develop, a sense of significant difference, and access to relevancy or freedom to self-correct. *I am a nomad, traveling the little-known byways of the world, figuring things out as I go along.*

Perhaps you view your identity as that of an assayer, conducting a series of experiments and explorations, each of which may be readily abandoned in favor of still newer quests.

The Taita of Kenya are not very willing to speculate, so they only make cautious guesses about the identity of others, based on observations of their behavior. In the U.S. middle class, attempts to "read" other people are readily practiced, and this is even supported by a psychologistic social science. Much of these efforts at "guessing," where popular books are written about how to manage "the first four minutes" of social contact with a stranger, may have a bit too much of the recipe book flavor to it for some cultures.

I, Pathfinder

"I am like a lone quester who strives to perceive great thoughts so she can internalize God's world," says Meiko Noji, a Japanese college student.

For other individuals who sense a need for more control than that of the uncertain seeker, perhaps the illusion of control insinuated by the following metaphor will be supportive. *I am a pathfinder, and I shall map the unknown.*

The pathfinder does not map unknown territory, though, without being changed by the process of exploration. The ultimate reciprocity inherent in culture contact is an important point to remember for the multicultural person who is developing a conscious and affirming sense of self.

The people of the West may have been carrying the "white man's burden" when they went out to "discover" the rest of the world, but they also found the "noble savage." (And the "discovered" found metal pots and kitchen knives—the first Western innovations usually adapted—as well as unwelcome diseases, booze, and weapons.) Perhaps the most significant English literature of the 19th and 20th centuries, according to Goonetilleke (1977), is set in the developing world. Kipling, Lawrence, Forster, and Durrell leap to mind. While this literature tells the West more about itself than it does about the cultures in which it is set, the important point to note is the energy that people from one culture draw from contact with "exotic" others.

In the last half of the 20th century, the interactive effect of culture contact has become even more pronounced. When Kaiser Zaman, a graduate student from Bangladesh, was at American University in the 1970s, he commented, "I came from halfway across the world, from the land of Hare Krishna and Maharishis, seeking the West, and I met zealous young men and women going the other way" (Zaman, 1974). *I travel East and West, seeking the twain.*

Don't Be a Wimp—Be Dynamic!

Dynamic, rather than static, constructs provide frames of reference for our personal quests. The metaphors modeled in this chapter furnish a notion about how we can launch out from our admitted ignorance and transcend our own dogmatisms.

We are no longer doomed to either provinciality or alienation by the accident of having been born in a certain place at a certain time. Explorers of multicultural space—even at the dawn of the 21st century—are still pathfinders.

Games and Circuses

We appropriate personal knowledge based on our own experience. "Traditional" cultures provide prototypes of how to search for knowledge.

The Clown

One approach they model is that of providing lighthearted feedback. The sacred clowns at a Pueblo ceremonial mimic and mock the participants, reminding them of social infractions committed during the preceding year and providing the mockees with the necessary awareness to mend their ways. This brings to mind the ancient Greek chorus. Here we have come full circle back to a theatrical, or performance, metaphor. The smell of the greasepaint! *I play the clown, a particle of social anti-matter.* Like the sacred clowns and tricksters in tribal myth and ceremony, multicultural people, just by their very existence, call everything into question. Perhaps you are a stickler for detail. "I am a perfectionist clown!" wrote Mieko Ogawa, a Japanese college student.

Clowns remind us that life can be viewed as a circus parade. *The world is a pageant and I wear a purple coat.* The non-royalists among us may be attracted to the self-designed "world"—electronic "virtual reality"—that lies just around the corner.

Virtual Reality

Virtually all of the foundational discoveries and inventions of our species— fire, bronze, marriage, and clans, for example—were spread by neolithic people traveling across cultural boundaries in their pre-Gucci moccasins. The average speed of this cultural diffusion was a little over a mile a year (Edmondson, 1961). The airplanes, automobiles, e-mail, computer networks, faxes, and cellular phones at the end of the 20th century have not only made the pattern of interchange and contact with people from disparate cultures more rapid, but also more interactive. Technology has created, in the jargon of our times, "virtual" societies. A complete stranger, noticing the boarding pass sticking out of the shirt pocket of an airline passenger awaiting his flight, approached him at the departure lounge of an international airport in Jamaica and introduced himself. They were old friends, although they had never met face to face. They had for years exchanged messages on a computer bulletin board. They were "virtual" friends in cyberspace!

Serious thinkers have meditated long centuries over whether life is a game. The Buddhist Bodhisattva, for example, have given this some profound thought. They see life as a game in which one avoids confusion of social role with self-identity. Their appreciation of the illusionary, game-like character of all reality leads us right to a metaphoric view of the multicultural person from the perspective of the computer game. *I am a player in a virtual reality computer game programmed with the dynamic coordinates of a dozen cultures.*

The metaphor quest can lead us beyond outmoded social adaptations, beyond what is charted on the maps, out of the present dream, to the next levels of perceptual resolution or awareness. The three *P*s—perceptions, perspectives, and polyphony—are the topics of the next chapter.

Notes to Myself

1. Some of the things I do to provide drama in my life are:

_____

_____

_____

_____

_____

2. One thing that happened to me that gave me a heightened sense of the beauty and mystery of the universe was:

_____

_____

_____

_____

_____

3. The aspect of crossing cultural boundaries that fires my imagination most is:

_____

_____

_____

_____

4. An imaginary creature that manifests many of my multicultural traits might look something like this drawing:

13

Perception, Perspective, and Polyphony

Kaleidoscopic Visions

Prominently displayed on the desk of a CEO of a large multinational corporation is a kaleidoscope, encased in a hand-oiled walnut tube fastened with brass fittings. It was patterned after an early one crafted by the Scottish inventor of the kaleidoscope, Sir David Brewster, in 1816. Everyone enjoys looking through a kaleidoscope. Brilliant and yet subtle colors in novel geometric patterns delight the eye. New realities, with a flick of the wrist.

Perception and Multiplicity

Think of telescopes, microscopes . . . and kaleidoscopes! Think of colored lenses of different magnifications, of fun-house mirrors, of patterns and their backgrounds. Call up the images of the Dutch graphic artist, M. C. Escher. Remember his famous woodcut, *Day and Night*, with the light-colored birds flying in one direction and the dark-colored birds in the opposite direction, and the viewer's inability to discern the point at which the day birds turn into the night birds (Locher, 1988).

If we think of our core self as a set of perceptual lenses and our social context as multiple patterns waiting to be perceived, then we open up the possibility of seeing a nearly infinite number of patterns, all of which carry the force of real things.

Now forget about color, about which spectrum of light we are viewing, although this is a very interesting aspect to consider as well. Think only of the level of magnification or resolution. Think about what it was like to look through a microscope in your high school biology class. As you changed the level of magnification in the microscope, the background at one level of magnification became the foreground at another. Similarly, the self as a system of focused perceptions existing in a social system of multiple patterns has an interesting kind of depth (internally or vertically) as well as breadth (externally or horizontally). This may best be visualized as a set of serial planes. *I and my environment have many planes and many patterns, and each pattern provides the background for the design at the next plane of perceptual resolution.*

To understand ourselves as multicultural individuals in our various social environments requires us to review the very nature of perception itself (Singer, 1987). A multicultural environment cannot be perceived well if one is wearing cultural blinders. Perceptual metaphors highlight an important fact: the multicultural person has the potential for seeing more of a diverse environment—and seeing it more accurately—because he or she can look at the world through more than one lens and at more than one plane of resolution. *I look at the world through many different lenses of many different hues and magnifications.*

These perceptual metaphors raise some provocative questions. If our perceptions are distorted by cultural lenses, can we trust that our multiple lenses will mutually self-correct each other? Or do multiple lenses place an even heavier burden on us to be aware of the degree to which distorted views are embedded in the perceptions favored by each of our cultures? It falls to the multicultural person—the one using multiple lenses—to say, when circumstances warrant, that the Emperor has no clothes, or that an arbitrary cultural bias has crept into an otherwise persuasively reasoned thesis.

Albert Einstein once said that any problem posed at one level of thinking cannot be resolved at that same level. As we tinker with our perceptual microscopes and telescopes to adjust for the proper resolution for viewing this and that, we may be able to bring into focus the whole "deep logic" of multicultural identities.

A Matter of Perspective

Going back in time a few centuries, a great Renaissance discovery was made in the arts—three-point perspective. This ability to present the illusion of three-dimensional space on a two-dimensional canvas generated a growing awareness of individual points-of-view. The vanishing point, the illusion of three-dimensional space, usually could only be appreciated by a viewer in the right position, usually from front and center. Arguments arose about whose version of "objective" reality was correct. Don't the eyes "follow" the viewer in the painting by da Vinci that Americans call the Mona Lisa and Europeans call La Giaconda? The recognition of multiple perspectives of the same object is inextricably related to the concepts of "self as locus of experience" and to the normal human capacity to notice one's own noticing (Harris, 1989).

This viewer-in-the-right-position is looking through a "picture window" that commands an image. This image does not belong to the world, but rather, as Tuan (1982) reasons, the viewer "organizes and orders [the world] from a pivotal and circumferential point." While this ability to organize the world into a coherent, unified picture gives an illusion of power, the resulting unified picture depends on where the viewer is standing, as all artists know. "Reality," Tuan concludes, "loses its givenness and stability when the way it appears is recognized to depend on the position and sight lines of the spectator."

And so it was that artists experienced the principle of indeterminacy two to three centuries earlier than physicists. A person experiencing perspective, or experimenting with it, cannot help having an awareness of the self as a unique source of knowledge—a knowledge not shared exactly by another person standing only a few feet away. "Look Mabel, up in the sky. It's a bird . . . it's a plane. No, it's . . ."

The Truth or the Beauty Quest?

Cultures have inspired individuals in their communities to espouse an over-riding "mission." A mission may include helping others, maintaining family honor, getting rich, courting wisdom, making the world a better place . . . the list is quite long. Some missions focus on developing individual potential, others on promoting group harmony. Two overriding missions, or quests, are the search for Truth and the search for Beauty.

Truth, A Cyclops's View

One constraint (for Westerners) in the search for understanding the essence of life is the way Western thought has defined the search. It is, we are taught, a search for Truth. And although we recognize paradoxes and dilemmas, it is hard for us to reconcile contradictory truths.

Most of the societies it is our conceit to call "modern" (we really mean states that have a high gross national product derived from industrial enterprise) emerged from monotheistic traditions. These religious traditions have focused a great deal of philosophical effort on exploring questions of truth and meaning, but always with the underlying assumption that there ought to be but one truth.

Perhaps because of this focus on discovering "the Truth," industrial societies have created an atmosphere that paradoxically believes itself to be all encompassing. In reality, the perceptual world of "Truth societies" is severely edited and oversimplified, a mere sketch rather than a full rendering of reality.

Let us say this in a different way. It is widely believed in many industrial societies that their way is *the* way, while in fact and of course each of these societies manifests only one of many possible human patterns. Societies tend to project, monolithically, their severely skewed perspectives onto complex reality. Every colonial government in the world has projected its own view of how society (and the world!) is organized onto its colonies.

There appears to be an interactive relationship between the development in Western art of perspective and the emphasis on the question of whose truth is truest. This may sound abstract and too philosophical, but much of the angst felt by multicultural people about their own authenticity stems from the basic question of what is true. That is, what is the truth about what they were taught to believe? In addition to the issue of "truth" in your sense of personal authenticity, there is the other, related, tension discussed in Part 1: the need for social affirmation. In fact, "social truth" is created from the interaction of these two tensions. The very manner in which the issue of *the truth* is phrased illustrates the Western industrial penchant for single truths and consistent behavior: the assumption is that there is only one reality. This penchant is in marked contrast to many societies—the ancient Chinese, for instance—where there is no distinction between the rational and the irrational.

Objective Truth

Stuart Pickens (1992), a professor of ethics at International Christian University in Tokyo, says that if you look at the categories of classical Western philosophy you find metaphysics (what's the first principle of things?), epistemology (what's true?), ethics (what's good?), aesthetics (what's beautiful?), and rhetoric (how to persuade or influence others?). The West has spent a lot of thought and effort on metaphysics (the first cause, or God) and epistemology (the nature of truth). Since the Renaissance, epistemology has been the West's central concern.

The Western quest for the Truth—that which is absolutely true—from the time of Greek science till now, has been an epistemological quest for "objective" reality, and this mostly for its own sake.

The thinker, poet, prose stylist, and literary critic Annie Dillard (1982) explores this issue in her book *Living by Fiction*. Many historians of culture, she says, think that this interest in "the truth" sprang originally from the meeting of cultures. In the port towns at the peripheries of major civilizations, people of varying cultures and religions met. Faced with such a divergence of beliefs, they soon asked themselves, what could be true? The mindset inspired by this innocent inquiry led to great advances in understanding the physical world. In fact, the inquiry led straight to unexpected places. Dillard sums this up.

> Science, that product of skepticism born of cultural diversity, is meant to deal in certainties, in data which anyone anywhere can verify. And for the most part it has. Our self-referential mathematics and wiggly yardsticks got us to the moon.

Dillard points to the shaky nature of the underpinnings of science as it deals with multiple reality when she says: "I think science works the way a tight-rope walker works: by not looking at its feet. As soon as it looks at its feet, it realizes it is operating in midair." As Dillard puts it,

> What can we know for certain when our position in space is limited, our velocity may vary, our instruments contract as they accelerate, our observations of particles on the micro level botch our own chance of precise data, and not only are our own senses severely limited, but many of the impulses they transmit are edited out before they ever reach the brain? . . . We are having a slow century of it, digesting the information that our yardsticks are not absolute, our mathematics not absolute.

She goes on to wonder whether we can trust our brains even if we could depend on our senses. Even if science could depend on its own data, would it not still have to paw through its own language and cultural assumptions to approach things as they are? To what, Dillard asks, could the phrase "things as they are" meaningfully refer, apart from all our discredited perceptions to which everything is so inextricably stuck?

In some cultures, inquiry into the nature of reality is resolved in the realm of social or subjective reality, rather than in the realm of physical or "objective" reality. Dillard observes that many people in the West agree now that there is "more than one way to skin a cat, or raise a baby, or alleviate pain, or live."

Subjective Truth

The Danish physicist Piet Hein addressed the issue of the nature of "reality" in his little book of line drawings and poems, *Grooks I* (1969):

Getting Down to Fundamentals

It will steadily shrink,
our earthly abode,
until antipode stands
upon antipode.

Then soles together,
the planet gone,
we'll know the ground that we rest upon.

That is, the ground on which we rest is each other, along with our mutual human perceptions of each other and our respective "realities." Earlier (in Chapter 6), we referred to culture as a largely self-contained system. However, each of these "self-contained" systems has blind spots, areas of reality that go unnoticed. As Daniel Haeberlé (1993) argues, it is only as we develop models that "accord true legitimacy to a greater variety of constructs" that we can hope to fill in the blind spots in our analytical frameworks. Only by filling in these blind spots will our perceptions achieve the flexibility and reliability necessary to enable us to navigate adequately through multicultural space. Space cadets, take notice!

Because the answers we get depend on the questions we ask, let us dwell on this assumption for a moment by contrasting it with another approach.

The Beauty Way

Navajos and Japanese both illustrate variations of the Beauty Way.

In one of Tony Hillerman's (1993, 319) detective novels, the Navajo tribal policeman, Jim Chee, tries to explain the Navajo concept of *hozho,* beauty, to his city-raised girl friend.

I'll use an example. Terrible drought, crops dead, sheep dying. Spring dried out. No water. The Hopi, or the Christian, maybe the Moslem, they pray for rain. The Navajo has the proper ceremony done to restore himself to harmony with the drought. You see what I mean? The system is designed to recognize what's beyond human power to change, and then to change the human's attitude to be content with the inevitable.

Hillerman's character Jim Chee goes on to note a dynamic aspect of the Navajo Beauty Way, at least among younger shamans. "So I think the concept of *hozho* means you adjust the ceremonial system like you adjust everything else. You keep it in harmony with the inevitable." This may mean breaking up an eight-day ceremonial into two or three weekends so working people can participate.

Ethics professor Pickens (1992) insists that in order to understand Japan you have to understand that the center of Japanese philosophy is not epistemology. Rather, it is aesthetics, or answers to the question, what is beautiful? The underpinning of Japanese ethics is not Truth, but Beauty, particularly the social beauty conveyed by the Japanese concept of *wa,* or social harmony. *Wa* does not mean that people are in agreement at the level of meaning, but rather that a great deal of effort is put into maintaining a smooth and, thus, beautiful, social surface.

In many Western countries people are willing to deal with a great deal of conflict manifesting itself on the social surface in order to achieve eventual agreement at the meaning level. In fact, many of the people in Western history who have led their society into such confrontational and noisy conflicts are labeled heroes, Martin Luther King being one of the most recent from the United States. In Japan, most public displays of conflict on the social surface are seen as merely signs of social immaturity. Kishima (1992), by way of example, quotes a reporter's criticism of a strident Japanese politician: "[He is] inefficient in human relations." From a Japanese perspective, Westerners often allow truth to be a tyrant that totally disrupts the social order. As Akiko Dohi, a Japanese college student, says, "I am a resilient tree that loves organic contexts filled with harmonious energy with which I am joined in trustworthy relationships."

Perhaps, along with the Navajo and the Japanese, a quest for single truths does not command your energies. You may seek an aesthetic model of the self, one shared by artists. Perhaps not just any artist, though. Maybe your model is the creative artist rather than the performing artist, the pattern creator, rather than the pattern masterer. Creating art is a venerable enterprise.

Among the oldest words in Chinese, dating back 3,000 years or more, is the word for art, *wen*. It refers to "pattern wherein meaning and form become inseparately united, so that they become one, indistinguishable," as Sam Hamill, in the introduction to his 1991 translation of the 3rd-century AD classic, Lu Chi's *Wen Fu,* puts it. (The idea of "art for art's sake" was a 19th-century Victorian aestheticism, articulated by Walter Pater.) You aspire to the expression of your own unique pattern. As one Japanese college student, Mari Tanaka, puts it, "I am a painting drawn with many different colors. Some are original colors, some are newly created by mixing other colors together. I am not yet a completed painting. I do not want to be finished yet; I want to add more colors and create unique colors along the way toward a perfect canvas."

There are other images. A traditionally romantic notion of oneself as raw material for a creative process is the view of life as a novel. *My life is a picaresque novel whose next sentence is poised in midair, waiting to be beckoned by the experience of strange lands.*

Christakis's paper, "The Cosmology of Design," suggests another aesthetic metaphor. *We are designing the future, like potters shaping the clay.*

Do We Have to Choose Truth or Beauty?

Can these quests, these two concepts—truth and beauty—be combined?

Both quests are present in most cultures, but in those where either truth or beauty is assigned a priority rating distinctly higher than the other, where truth (or beauty) becomes the central concern, other quests tend to be relegated to "also ran" status. What do you do when your central concerns do not match those of the society in which you live?

One way, of course, is to stake out your interest in a quest that is peripheral to society's principal area of concern. Many intellectuals do this quite successfully, and even John Doe is left to indulge his idiosyncratic interest in bird watching. Another approach taken by some multicultural people who pursue both Truth and Beauty quests is to lean to one side or the other when articulating a sense of what they are about, depending on which culture they are functioning in at the time. In single-perspective societies, you can search for truth (maybe the truth about some aspect of beauty); in harmonic-beauty societies you can emphasize the other part of your organizing metaphor and search for beauty in simple truths.

If your quest is either epistemological or aesthetic—but not both—then you have to consider how to communicate who you are to people who are in the other philosophical camp. Perhaps you will find another comfortable metaphor, one that also will connect with the social group with which you wish to have a relationship. After all, the highly cognitive Dr. Spock (Vulcans tend to be like that) was able to "translate" himself well enough to be seen as a valued crew member among the emotion-bound humanoids on the Starship Enterprise.

Polyphony: A Blending of the Beauty and Truth Ways

The search for social knowledge takes us to many curious corners. Music, a nonverbal means of human communication, is a potential source of powerful insight. Isaac Stern, the master violinist, said that it is only through music and the arts that you can express your soul. (In his autobiography, Bertrand Russell [1967, 158–159] says that mathematics is "capable of an artistic excellence as great as that of any music.")

A Sunday Afternoon in Tokyo

We see the influences of many cultures reflected in popular music. This was vividly brought home to Jacqueline Wasilewski on her first Sunday in Tokyo in the fall of 1990.

> Standing here in Harujuku, I am having a hard time convincing myself that Japan is an aging society. Crowds and crowds of young people as far as the eye can see.
>
> As I stand on the left-hand side of Harujuku station waiting for my friend, I begin to absorb cosmopolitan Tokyo. The one thing I do not see is "the homogeneous Japanese race." It looks to me that, like the rest of the Pacific Basin, Japan has been the site of the comings and goings of many peoples.
>
> My friend arrives, and we set off for Yoyogi Park, the place where Japanese youth go slightly wild on a Sunday afternoon to the music of a hundred rock bands playing simultaneously. (Well, maybe not a hundred, but it seems like it.) Orange hair is fashionable.

The band playing at the entrance to the park (which is not far from the Meiji Shrine) this particular Sunday afternoon was made up of seven members in black pants with white polka dots. Two Japanese, one white boy and four blacks. The group did break dancing as well as play jazz and rock and roll. There were two saxophonists, a Japanese boy (maybe Japanese-American) and a black youth with reggae-Rastafarian hair. The black musician with the reggae hair also played electric guitar. Other members played drums and base, but they were break dancing while we were watching. The second Japanese was a young woman who seemed to be the business manager, judging from the exchange of business cards that was going on at the sidelines with people who could have been bookers or agents, or perhaps simply potential customers.

The white boy wearing Michael Jackson's trademark single white glove (!) worked the crowd in Japanese (!). He was the announcer. One of the black male dancers could do all kinds of polychronic muscle movements as part of his break dancing routine, and at one point he swallowed a cigarette, rippled his stomach muscles and then later made the cigarette (still lighted) reappear. He had a 1990s version of a '50s flat top, partly bleached.

Watching this performance was the rest of Tokyo. Young girls in green school uniforms. Parents with young children on their backs and in strollers. Grandparents gazing at the performance with smooth faces. And the first Japanese "bag lady" I had ever seen. (At least that is what we would call her in New York.) She was a woman about sixty years old, squatting in the inner circle of watchers, mirroring the movements of the break dancers, really "getting down" or "jiving," as they say in Black American English.

Music offers intriguing metaphors for sensing our place under the sun. While the generations of the 1960s and 1970s identified themselves politically and ideologically, some members of the generation of the 1990s identify themselves aesthetically through the music they listen to. "I like Pink Floyd," or "So, you listen to Metallica!" are the initial lines in the end-of-millennia friendship dramas of youth culture. Like the appearance of jazz in Wasilewski's initial impressions of Japan, this gives us an idea for another approach to ordering the multicultural self—through metaphoric links to musical traditions. *I am an Odetta kind of person, social consciousness in harsh and soft nuanced tones, down-home folk; I sing to black and white alike.*

The appeal of contemporary music is global. Not only are these music groups themselves often multicultural and multinational but so are the audiences. The Irish groups Hothouse Flowers and U2 are as easily accessible to Japanese as to European, American, other Asian or Australian audiences. The musicians use instruments from all over the world, playing musical idioms in which the musical traditions of non-elites are predominant.

These musical groups represent different . . . can we call them aesthetic ideologies? Except they are not strictly political ideologies, but rather ecological and social—connected to the way life is lived on this planet.

A research team studying Japanese social systems, led by Eshun Hamaguchi (1992), describes a class of "harmonized" behavior that people use while they are interacting with others. Hamaguchi's research team characterizes Western societies as organized like vertebrates with a central nervous system. Japanese society it characterizes as having an invertebrate organization.

For instance, when an invertebrate starfish is turned upside down,

it is not predetermined which of the five limbs becomes the leader in righting the starfish. It seems that leadership is assumed by the limb best positioned as a pivot for righting the animal. The process occurs not only in the righting action of the starfish, but in the walking action too, where the movement of the countless ambulacral feet on each of the limbs, at first random, is gradually integrated into the movement of the limb as a whole.

The movement is similar to "the information-exchanging interaction itself which . . . creates the overall harmonized movement and the structure of the system." This movement is similar to the synchronizing behavior of schools of fish, the branching and negative viscosity of slime molds, to bioconvection, and other rhythmic movements. *When my Japanese self decides I am like an invertebrate starfish, I am wonderfully harmonic, analogic and nonlinear, quite in contrast to my more vertebrate, centralized, binary, and linear U.S. self.*

We see here the beginnings of a descriptive formulation of Japanese "harmonic mutual adjustment social processes" that is accessible outside the Japanese sociocultural context. The descriptions of these processes may help us understand how to overcome egocentrism with systemic wisdom, as we constantly deal with issues of identity and closure, trying to create the feedback loops that sustain the logics of systems based on mutual causality. These processes sound rather like the jamming of a jazz band. Maybe that is why jazz is so popular in Japan! In improvisational jazz, one lays aside all thoughts of "a necessary future" (to use Alan Watts's turn of phrase) to fulfill the potential of the moment. *We move between the structure of choral singing, where a missed beat can throw the rest of the group off, to the openness of a jazz jam session.*

Consistent with this view, Tatsuro Kunugi, the former Japanese Assistant Secretary General of the United Nations, chose the following title for a 1993 U.N. conference in Tokyo: *Harmonizing Population and Development.* When was the last time you heard of a U.S., or U.K., or German development expert talking about "harmonizing development"? We asked an American devotee of New Age philosophy just that question, and she launched into a discourse on "harmonic convergence," a meeting of new epochs on the Aztec and Mayan calendars!

Yi-Fu Tuan (1993) conceptualizes all cultures as "a moral-aesthetic venture to be judged ultimately by its moral beauty." Even the state "is an aesthetic-moral construction," albeit on "a grand scale."

> Politics is at its core, but politics viewed as the serious effort to articulate excellence, for society is itself a moral-aesthetic aspiration, and its achievements are properly deemed artworks that make claims to being both beautiful and good.

Through the interaction of peoples from traditions that have pursued different "quests," interests tend to converge. W. H. McNeill (1965) hypothesized the possible development of a worldwide cosmopolitanism run by a "more than Chinese" bureaucracy, the West's technical genius absorbed by another group with a genius for institution building, a social imagination capable of inventing a self-governing, participatory world order. Fosco Maraini (1971), an Italian writing on Japan, characterizes the Japanese as being masters of the "ceremonial logic of human intercourse." He doubts that any real "Westernization" is going on in Japan. Rather, what is at work is a process of "mondialization," a neutral territory, now in the "nothingness of nowhere," a potential world culture only partly Western. The West, too, will have moved from its "enclosed gardens of the mind," and there will enter the "polyphonic richness of many voices in what is now a mere point in space-time."

Hindu psychology provides ideas about how such polyphonic diversity may be organized (Rawlinson, 1981). Imagine a sound-mixing system that has three levels. *Manas* decides whether the system will handle something, *ahamkara* decides where to put it, and *buddhi* assesses the value of the categories *ahamkara* is using to sort things.

> Not only can the treble be turned up or the bass down so as to change the overall impression of the music, but in sophisticated mixing systems individual instruments can be brought out from other instruments or sunk back into them—and even single notes by a particular instrument can be highlighted or merged into the background. It is in this sense of subtle interplay . . . that we should understand the statement that they [*manas, ahamkara,* and *buddhi*] are different levels of the mind.

Perhaps the understanding that reality is ultimately subjective and social, based on aesthetic and ceremonial logics, will enable Maraini's vision of "a polyphonic richness of many voices" to come into existence in "what is now a mere point in space-time."

This emerging metaphor of a singer in a polyphonic choir offers multicultural people a promising vision for integrating their multiple perspectival melodies into a synergistic whole. Multicultural lives are enriched by a complex instrumentation of knowledge, feelings, and skills—a potentially harmonic polyphony, a blending of different tones. If, of course, we humans have the aesthetic imagination to make it happen. Kenji Taniguchi, a Japanese college student, puts it this way: "I am like a piano that plays various music according to the whim of the listeners. I have ebony and ivory keys that together create harmony in contexts that always contain both tears and joy. I provide my listeners with the accompaniment to which they can sing."

While the West has pursued, with focused resolve, a Cyclopean search for Truth, the East, with equal resolve, has searched for Beauty. To lay claim to even a single perspective, to have the depth perception needed to apprehend the world's profundity, requires at least binocular vision. We have difficulty keeping our physical balance without two-eyed vision. Will two or more perspectives prove more ocularly perceptive than either view by itself? Will a multiple, 360° view enable us as cultural gymnasts to keep our balance while tumbling in midair? This is not to say that the complex beauty born of multicultural experiences is not achieved without cost, as Chapter 7 pointed out.

Before we go on to our "final thoughts" on the issue of multicultural identities, let us pause a minute. Let your sense of drama guide you in applying new combinations of greasepaint, in beating new rhythms. In the next chapter, you will have the opportunity to create your own metaphor.

Notes to Myself

1. I sense that my own personal "quest," the central flow of my life, revolves around the following:

_____

_____

_____

_____

_____

2. In my own personal "quest," "truth" and "beauty" fit in in the following ways:

_____

_____

_____

_____

_____

3. An example of an intriguing notion from one of my cultures that I find enriching:

_____

_____

_____

_____

4. To me, polyphony sounds like:

_____

_____

_____

_____

_____

5. Here are some ideas I have for how I would participate
   in the creation of harmonious multicultural blending:

_____

_____

_____

_____

_____

Another Metaphor, Anyone?

I Ching, Therefore I Am

As we go through life, picking up knowledge the hard way, we may want to tune up our own sense of who we have become. The rocky roads of life may have jarred the old metaphor out of alignment.

Sometimes our organizing metaphors don't work. If we experience a series of unhelpful outcomes from ventures based on a particular construction of reality, even the most dim-witted designer will realize that something may be wrong with his or her vision of reality. In this case, we can stop experimenting (at least temporarily), loosen up our reference axes, and increase the permeability of our metaphors.

An increased understanding of the influences that have affected your sense of self will, we hope, enable you to be aware of the assumptions from which your personal metaphors emerge. We may need to remind ourselves sometimes that no single metaphor can ever capture fully even our limited consciousness of our own "reality." Remember, you are not the metaphor and the metaphor is not you. It's simply a tool for conceptualizing salient aspects of your multicultural self (see Appendix, "Why Metaphors?"). Human beings are many things at once, and we are constantly conjuring ourselves anew.

An intelligible perception of your own personal identity, and how it interacts with the cultural contexts you are inhabiting, does not come without a basic commitment to insight. Know thyself, as the pudgy Greek said in the marketplace.

It is useful to make more explicit the perceptions and the experiences and the underlying assumptions on which our metaphors of multicultural identity are based. A clearer sense of this helps us cope in a multicultural milieu.

This Century's Major Categories of Metaphors

Milton Bennett (1992), a specialist in intercultural communication, puts into three categories what he calls the major paradigms with which humans in the "modern" era view the world: the classical science emphasis on structure; the Einsteinian emphasis on relativity and the relationship between objects in space; and the post-Einsteinian emphasis on dynamics or pure process. According to Kavolis (1977), personal narratives also have three aspects across time and cultures: structure, relationships, and movement. These three aspects parallel the three major constructs governing Western thinking as described by Bennett.

A paradigm can be thought of as a meta-metaphor. Of course, all of these aspects—structure, relationship, process—exist simultaneously. The *focus* in each group of paradigms is simply different. The template for generating your own metaphors that follows includes all three categories.

The first two parts of the template—subjects and objects—are parts of some *structure* of reality, the gears in a machine, the characters in a play, or a plant in the landscape. The third part of the template emphasizes *relationships* within a system, such as the way members of a family interact. The fourth part emphasizes *process*—dynamic relationships like those between an entity and its environment, or like transformations of mass and energy.

How do we learn and organize the highly distinctive repertories of behavior required of effectively functioning multicultural people into something that both feels coherent and gets some social respect? This book's metaphoric explorations have perhaps increased your ability to express and describe yourself convincingly to others in alternative ways, ways that capture some of the resplendent and evolving multiplicity of your multicultural self.

Generating Your Metaphor of Identity: Who Am I?

As we bow out of this book's discussion on metaphors of self-identity, the spotlight turns to the guest star of the show—you. Now generate a metaphor of your own.

If you are an anarchist at heart and like little structure, perhaps the following outline will suit you:

I am like a _____ that _____.

Or, if you want your new metaphor to be based on broader considerations, you may find the following outline, with its suggested menu selections, helpful:

I am _____ [a subject, an object, a set of relationships, and/

or a process] **that has** _____ [certain qualities] **that lead me**

to _____ [behave in certain ways] **in contexts that are seen**

to be _____ [kind of situation], **which have** _____

[givens] **and** _____ [artifacts], **with which I am related in**

the following ways: _____ [relationships].

We are all beings with internal characteristics that both affect and are affected by an external world of givens and interactions. Add your own descriptive items, if you choose, to the "menus" provided below. Brainstorm a new metaphor for yourself!

To tailor a metaphor to fit your particular circumstances, put a circle around those descriptors from the menus provided below that best describe your own character and situation. Choose one or more from each menu. If you wish, draw visual responses to each prompt.

I am . . . [a subject]

    actor
    clown
    creator [artist, painter, potter]
    deformer
    impresario
    improviser
    individual, one of a kind
    multiple personae
    pathfinder, explorer, pilgrim, quester, pioneer
    performer
    person
    phoenix
    playwright, raconteur, story teller
    reformer
    Scroobious Pip
    spirit
    transformer

[or an object or a structure]

    body
    brain
    creative work [painting, novel, watercolor, haiku]
    diamond
    facets
    fragment [half-breed, split personality]
    machine
    mask
    melting pot
    mixed metaphor, mixed salad
    plant
    puppet
    rock

role
stage prop
tree, rings in a tree

[or a set of relationships within a system]

center, core
circumstances
cog in machine
God's child
gregarious animal
kaleidoscope
motherless child
network [peer-to-peer LAN]
participant in myth
planes of optical illusion
player, programmer [of computers]

[or a process in continuous interaction with my environment]

chi
computer
consciousness
continuous interaction
continuous process of transformation
dynamic in-betweenness
emotion
energy
great thought
locus of experiences
organism
pattern of energy
pure process
switching station

that has [certain qualities]

border [liminal]
centered/peripheral
double/half
expedient
flexible/rigid
marginal, in-between
multiple, diverse
resilient
reversible/irreversible

that lead me to [behave in certain ways]

believe
deform
express
feel *honne*
follow [God's teaching]
guess
imagine
improvise
interact
internalize [structure, complexity]
perform according to *tatemae*
reflect
reform
replicate
arise [out of the ashes]
seek [truth]
strive [to be better]
survive
think, perceive
transform
transmit

in contexts [that are seen to be concrete or metaphysical, local and/or global]

consistency of changing scenarios
drama of cosmos
expressway
great thought
machine, machine-like
organism
social network [family, society, political system]
stage
virtual reality game
work of art
world of the spirit

which have [givens: constraints and resources]

gender [maleness and femaleness: creativity]
diversity [others]
change

and [artifacts generated within the system],

abstractions, paradigms
cognitive geometries
cosmologies
creations/imaginings
designs
myths, stories
relationships
supermarket of cultures, cultural lenses
technologies
words

with which I am related in the following ways:

boundaries/interfaces
homogeneous/heterogeneous relationships
multiple/exclusive relationships
permeable/impermeable body/self
synchronous/monochronic/polychronic
synergistic relationship
unified/oppositional/complementary relationship

Now edit the story you are telling about yourself so that it is reasonably coherent for a first draft. Then reedit your metaphor to be a shorter, streamlined version.

_____

_____

_____

_____

_____

_____

_____

_____

_____

_____

_____

_____

_____

Check that Assumption

The basic assumptions that shape our perception of "reality" often surprise us when they are examined. Kidding around, we asked a friend, Rosendo R. Rivera, a math teacher in his early years before he entered the field of U.S. migrant education, whether he still remembered what two plus two equaled. His immediate response: "Base what?"

It is so easy to lapse into the same-assumption rut. We were thinking base ten, but Rosendo was drawing on more perspectives: In base two, base three, or base four the sum would differ from the base-ten product of four. (The Mayans used base nine to calculate their 52-year cycles.)

In this case, the fact that Rosendo understood math better than we did gave him the added perspective. So, too, being multicultural heightens our general ability to see things from different perspectives. It underscores our uniqueness. The number of possible combinations of major cultural and subcultural mixes is staggering. Imagine the copious number of perspectives that multicultural people, in the aggregate, can roll around in their heads. Your whole world takes on new significance when your experiences have not been narrowed by social and geographic immobility. (A word of warning to mental couch potatoes.)

Rosendo's question, "Base what?" really means "Based on what assumptions?"

Some Metaphors from Japan

After working through this exercise, you will probably want to write your own metaphor, one that reflects your own style. Here are some examples of metaphors that multicultural students living in Japan composed after going through this excercise and wrestling with their sense of self.

"I am a thinking stone searching for a heart." (Reiko Shinki)

"I am like a philosopher who doesn't have his own opinion." (Hong-suk Choi, Korean)

"I am like a tumbler who can't decide which way to fall and wavers in many directions." (Hiroko Matsumoto)

"I am like a cloud that has no concrete figure and wonders where to go. I don't like to "get down to earth" when conflict occurs. I want to float free and happy, blown by the winds." (Midori Umeda)

"Like a cloud, from above I observe people who have complicated psychologies and uniquenesses. I am related to them in a way that is both boundless and distanced." (Takako Kamei)

"I am full of freedom, an eternal poem who dreams fantasia." (Chieli Suzuki, Japanese-Philippine)

"I'm like a pillow that needs to be cuddled and huddled;
I'm like a rabbit who runs away quickly when danger arises;
I'm like a blue balloon that bulges with imagination
and floats up into the sky
as long as happy thoughts are nigh." (Yuriko Nagasawa)

"I am a resilient clown with a permeable body, expressing myself on a stage filled with diverse and creative possibility." (Junko Kakita)

"I am like a ray of light that is bound for where truth abides." (Eri Tomizawa)

"I am like an improviser who perceives and thinks deeply." (Akiko Izumi)

"I am like a Black Panther which stands Black and Proud. When challenged, I will take ground. I appear more frightening than I really am. It is my color and confidence which makes me appear so fierce. Like the Panther, I must face the dangers of the wilderness—race and class injustice. I must be better, more intense, more intelligent than the next person. It is this struggle which defines me as a person.

"I will leap over boundaries without blinking twice. But inside I need to feel needed and accepted. I receive my inner strength from the energy of others. Their love, affection and praise. I have a great tolerance level. I am a good source of strength to those who know me." (Niambi Daniels, African-American)

"I am a rock with diamonds inside. I am like the sun that never burns out, but sometimes lowers the amount of energy released so that people can see me without filters." (Yoshiki Yamamoto)

"I am like the seed of a plant that travels around the world seeking somewhere where I can find comfort in the future, where I can reside and bear fruit." (Kazuyo Imai)

"I am contradictory fragments in between rationality and instinct, striving to be better." (Makiko Ota)

"I am like a balloon that is floating in the Japanese air while being held down by an invisible but tough thread on a heavy Korean weight. The boundless world is open in front of me. I keep attached to the weight while I look at the world and wonder what it would be like to be free of the ballast. I fear that if the thread were cut I would just fly up into the sky and find nothing at all. Because my world is limited now, I can face reality while dreaming about a boundless world." (Suni Park, Korean-Japanese)

"I am like a changing sky, affected by atmospheric conditions, and affecting others too as my own temperament changes." (Yasushi Komatsu)

"I am like a long-distance cycler who travels far and wide, resting at times in the shadow of a tree." (Kazue Tani)

"I am like a lost child who desires the places where I feel I belong." (Moyona Ishimaru)

"I am a covered pot of water, at times threatening to boil over. Before it does, I lower the heat. The lid of the pot is like a barrier shielding my inner contents from others." (Peggy Wang, Chinese-American)

"I am like a philosophy that doesn't settle." (Shinichi Nishiyama)

"I am like water that is ever changing its form." (Nana Aoba)

"I am like ocean seaweed, providing oxygen to other living animals and plants." (Yuko Iwakura)

"I am an improvising kaleidoscope in a virtual reality game full of diversity and myths with which I am related synchronically." (Kellie Smith, English)

"I am a friendly Mickey Mouse with a smile to balance ambiguous and stressful situations." (Kenichiro Nakata)

"I am like a performer who always looks good in front of people and who has the ability to please people, but who in his personal life is lazy and sometimes reckless." (Maki Tsukada)

"I am like an artistic work that has many colors, but at the very beginning, only a simple thing was there . . . white paper." (Yumi Uetani)

"I am an actor with a large repertoire, striving to observe and interact on a stage of life which features much diversity and many possible relationships with others." (Mitsuko Ootsuka)

"On the outside I look like a tree, calm and solid, tall. Inside, my many layered self distances me from my friends and family, yet I intensely care about them." (Erin Killackey, USA)

"I am like a quester who is always seeking his own truth." (Mina Mizote)

"I am like a lump of clay.
As I go along, kneaded and molded, I pick up a lot of things.
If I am put on a hay stack, I will pick up the straw, and it will be molded into me.
If I am put in a puddle of colorful waters, my colors might slightly change.
It may not necessarily be something good, and again, it may be something that will streghten me.
Whatever it may be, it becomes an integral part of me.
The molding makes me strong and whole.
I am now in the final stages of kneading and molding, on the verge of going on to the next step of taking shape.
This forming of a shape will take the rest of my life, at times with major design changes, but usually at a slow and sure pace.
What I may turn out to be is still a surprise." (Keiko Fukuda)

"The story I am telling about myself goes something like this: Like the rings of a tree, I am between. I perceive the consistency of changing scenarios which over time offer stable exchanges with which I have complementary relationships." (Junko Seta)

"I am a spontaneous fairy tale that shimmers in a consequential dream. All the stories flow together in the great scheme of things." (Thomas Kolar, an American who grew up in Okinawa)

"I am a flexible translator who mediates the confusion in dynamic discussions." (Satoko Yoshihara)

"I am like a brain moving on roller skates, trying to come to "logical" solutions but constantly constrained by time. I want to learn to trust more my sense of feeling." (Remco de Wit, Dutch)

"I am like a person in a house of many rooms, surrounded by front and back yards. When I interact with people, we may talk at the gate, or when I know them a little better, at the front door. I show more of the house as I become more comfortable with them, but there are always things in drawers that are never shown. It makes me uncomfortable when somebody pops inside unexpectedly and unceremoniously." (Mai Uchiyama)

"I am a flexible spirit that internalizes the drama of a diverse and imaginative cosmos through my permeable self." (Hikaru Okono)

"I am like a dog
that looks pedigreed from the outside, but who is a mongrel inside;
that flatters people around her because she always worries what others
    will think of her;
that is searching for a safe place with good companions;
that thinks about being a "good" girl so much that she is afraid to digress
    from the "right" way and risk making mistakes;
that acts prudently (she is a bit of a perfectionist), but once convinced—
    she dashes for it!;
that once she bites a bone, never lets it go (she hates to lose);
that barks and pretends strength to hide her weaknesses;
that always waits for someone to lead the way to where she can be
    satisfied and successful.
I want to be a happy-go-lucky dog!" (Junko Meguro)

"As an actor, I always have to be seen. I become my role, and at the same time I am not what I am playing. I have to see myself from others' points of view for that is how I can improve myself. Nevertheless, I always have my own place where I return to. I tend to be selfish in that place." (Miwa Todani)

"I am a masked actor, like a politician that only says *tatemae*" [who only tells people what they want to hear]. (Takeyoshi Okutomi)

"I am like dust that flows in a vast universe, or like a sheep that wanders to a safe nook. I am frustrated and angry at my powerlessness." (Takayuki Ashima)

"I am like a chameleon that has the ability to change its colors and hide its feelings. I look for safe havens." (Mika Aoki)

"I am like a moon that looks down on the town but never goes down there." (Akiko Kawata)

"I am like a sponge that soaks in the fear of others and changes it into caring when squeezed out." (Shino Kimura)

Chiharu Sugiyama explains her metaphor of self, "I am the water; I am the sea," as follows:

I have felt something special about the sea ever since I was little. I was very familiar with it since my mother's hometown (her *jikka*) is a small beachtown in Kanagawa. My father works for a merchant vessel company and was on the ship himself as the first navigator for thirteen years. I believe that the sea is in my blood. I still feel it is very relaxing to go to a beach, just to watch the crashing waves, so I usually try to go when I feel stressed about something.

I believe I have many sides to myself, just as an ocean changes herself depending on the days and seasons. I can be rough and mean; I can be calm and kind. I can be transparent and bright; I can be black and dark. Sometimes it's easy to see through me; sometimes it is very difficult to see what's on my mind. I figured that ocean fits me perfectly, and I love what I am.

I was also attracted to this notion of water, as it is so flexible. Once I pulled an *omikuji* [a slip of paper with one's fortune] at Meiji Jingu and it contained this advice: "Be like the water. Water can change forms depending on the shape of the container. But water can be so strong that it can make a hole through a rock." It left a strong impression on me.

She then writes her extended metaphor of self.

"I am like the water; I am the sea
I hold no shape; I hold no place
I am nowhere yet all over
And I am still yet I am flowing

I am clear; I have no color
But I love to reflect assorted tints
I can be azure like the cloudless sky
And I can be gold like the setting sun

I am capricious, so-to-speak
I change myself as I feel
When I'm happy, I'll be gentle
But when I'm not, I'll be rough

I am caring; I am concerned
I look after all those around
I try to guide all lost vessels
Back on the route safely home

I want to be the nest for those
Who seek for me and care for me
For those in trouble; for those in tears
I want to comfort as much as I can

I wander; I drift
I search; I look
I fight; I protect
I rest; I dream

I am strong; I am weak
I am trying; I am challenging
I search for myself; I see my shadow
I am who I am: I am myself

I want to be the water
I want to be the sea"

15

Final Thoughts

Set on a Multicultural Path

Nancy Yamada defended her master's thesis (1992) on Japanese women's lives in a society where there are still two quite distinct worlds for men and women. A member of the thesis committee, Japanese anthropologist Kuniko Miyanaga, asked the master's degree candidate, "and so, which world is real, the men's or the women's world?"

Yamada, after a moment's startled pause, responded, "Why, of course, they are *both* real!"

If this is true of gender-based worlds, then it is true for larger cultural worlds as well. Dealing with this multifaceted reality is, of course, the main task for our multicultural selves. Perhaps this is expressed in the following poem, called "Perspectives," by Jacqueline Wasilewski.

Standing in a well lit room
Staring out the window
At the black night

Look closely
Not only the void
But the reflection of oneself
Staring back
The prism, the lens, the veil
Through which we perceive
All "reality"
Sensation is
Events are
Their meaning
Be it problematic or beneficent
Is a phenomenon of the structuring human mind
A creative act
Even meaningless
Is a chosen metaphor
The human eye can respond to upwards of 7 million stimuli
Which ones do we choose "to see"?
The senses number not a mere five but more like twenty
To which do we choose to attend?
The sensations are there
The raw materials
The rhythmically beating patterns
Of a universe
Playing with itself
In infinite combination
Ready for the artists' eyes
The universe looking at itself
From a hundred million points of view

Is it worth the effort to become multicultural—assuming you have a choice in the matter?

Have you ever been unable to decide between two options? You have not known what you want to do? So you flip a coin to decide, then measure your immediate gut reaction to the lay of the coin. If you were pleased with the way the coin landed, you go in one direction; if you are disappointed by the lay of the coin, you ignore the coin and go the direction you now realize you prefer.

Ned Seelye had an informative gut reaction to the wisdom of his multicultural path through life, not from the flip of a coin, but from a kind of Zen moment he experienced for a few seconds several years ago. At the time of the moment of enlightenment, the peripatetic pilgrim was residing in the United States. In the middle of taking a shower, the water suddenly stopped. Instantly, a profound and wonderful flood of nostalgia for Mexico (where it was commonplace for the water to shut off unannounced) swept over the soap-stained author. The *feeling* for his teenage years in the country that had had such a formative effect on him returned as a felt but undefined sense in a fast-rewind blur of past events. A small epiphany, but it all seemed worthwhile.

A multicultural author, Salman Rushdie (1994, 211), ends a book of stories with a statement on the pull of cultures:

> I, too, have ropes around my neck. I have them to this day, pulling me this way and that, East and West, the nooses tightening, command- ing, *choose, choose.*
>
> I buck, I snort, I whinny, I rear, I kick. Ropes, I do not choose between you. Lassoes, lariats, I choose neither of you, and both. Do you hear? I refuse to choose.

Lord Byron, after several years traveling about Portugal, Spain, and Greece, lived the last eight years of his brief life in Italy in voluntary exile from England, where his intemperate ways led British society to ostracize him. Writing almost 200 years ago, the great poet said that

> Between two worlds life hovers like a star
> 'Twixt night and morn, upon the horizon's verge.
> How little do we know that which we are!
> How less what we may be.

Afterword

If we have written the book we envisioned, you now have a much clearer understanding of how the pull of two or more cultures affects your sense of self. You have an increased appreciation for the fact that, as a reflective, multicultural person, you may have perspectives that can enhance the quality of life—even the ability to survive—of your communities. As long as recorded history, and before, humans have counted on multicultural exchanges for much of their social and material progress. The wheel has not often been reinvented.

Wheeling and dealing in multicultural settings oft times produces some stress, and we have tried to give you insight into this aspect, too, of being multicultural. Mental health professionals are beginning to appreciate the creativity involved in the multicultural process and to see the adaptive responses of multicultural individuals as less pathological and more enterprisingly functional.

Generally, as is the case with the U.S.-Mexican border, borderlands establish an ecological relationship that transcends political lines on the map. Whenever one draws a line, it connects as well as separates. One woman in Rio Grande City in south Texas, while waiting for her car muffler to be replaced, was asked, in English, where she was from. "Rio Grande City," she replied. Twenty minutes later she was asked the same question in Spanish by another person. "Ciudad Miguel Alemán," she replied, identifying the sister town on the Mexican side of the river. She lived on both sides of the border. Was she Mexican or American? The "imagined communities" on the map are, for borderland people and multicultural people alike, unrealistically exclusionary. Buttressed by the ease and speed of modern transportation, and by the multicultural nature of the world's metropolitan areas, she could as well have lived in Mexico City and Chicago, simultaneously.

As a multicultural person, your sense of self is complicated by feedback from people who see life in different—even contradictory—ways. Because you yourself hold two or more sets of values and behaviors, the issue of who you *really* are can sometimes tease, even taunt, you. The identity of most people leans heavily on nation-state, ethnic, or "racial" notions. Yet we have all descended from the same paleolithic ancestors; there are no families "older" than others. (Some just have better oral or written records.) Fixed notions of identity basically transform an ethnocentric myth into a social "fact" whose main function is to separate "us" from "them." In ways we have discussed earlier in the book, "fixed" definitional boundaries deliver inadequate metaphors for most multicultural men and women. For one thing, both cultural and geographic identities change drastically over time. Single-tribe labels become frail as the shadows of forgotten ancestors touch identities that have been oversimplified by expedience and ignorance.

We have provided an alternative approach to help you deal in a creative way with your sense of self—through alterable metaphors that are less constrictive and more dynamic than the lexicon of exclusionary labels. Perhaps the single most important message of this book is: Stand up for your own complexity!

This is not to say that if someone asks you whether you are Swiss or Laotian you should respond, "No, I'm like the spring rain that blows across the land bringing new growth to hibernating roots." It's all right to say, "I'm Mexican and my father was German." However, besides opportunistic settings such as the muffler shop, there are at least two contexts for using non-ethnonational metaphors. First, in moments of reflection when you think about the complexity of your own multicultural antecedents, it is germane to employ a metaphor that cuts across fixed boundaries on the map. These transnational metaphors can better capture the essence of a person who functions regularly in several cultures. The second context is when someone asks you how you manage the ethno-national-racial-religious-caste-class-clan-role-age-gender paradoxes of your identity, you can respond by saying that you see yourself as a river fed by many streams . . .

Appendix

Why Metaphors?

A special tool—metaphors—can capture mental images of how your self-identity develops in concert with your own multicultural life experiences. A metaphor, in essence, says that X is *like* Y. For example, even though people who function in two cultures (X) may not be actors (Y), they may see themselves as similar in some respects, or *something like,* actors who declaim their lines on different national stages. We consider similes—usually introduced by *like* or *as* and considered to be a more direct analogy—to be just a variety of metaphor, and the distinction irrelevant to this book's purposes.

Metaphors are at the heart of the mental construct for achieving *Between Cultures'* purpose. Why metaphors? First, because they offer dynamic, rather than static, labels of identity. Static labels such as nationality or "race" are exclusionary, but dynamic labels can cut across all fixed boundaries. Second, because thinking creatively sometimes requires us to loosen our hold on what we perceive to be reality. It's like brainstorming new ideas. Creativity is aided by relaxing the limits imposed by thinking that is overly logical and by suspending criticism of thoughts that may appear, at first, to be a little bizarre. The figurative language of metaphors allows us to do this. We walk you through many types and examples of them, sort of like browsing in a supermarket of metaphors, looking for ones that fit and satisfy your taste.

Metaphors can transcend some of the limitations of language by providing a way to think about things that are hard to express within the constraints of the often linear logic of words and sentences. Even when a metaphor is easily paraphraseable, such as "I am a round peg in a square hole," the figurative expression is more easily grasped and communicated to others than the paraphrase. There are metaphors that are not so easily paraphrased. Can you paraphrase, for instance, "The mind is a blue guitar upon which we improvise the song of the world"?

Like any theoretical construct, metaphors are, strictly speaking, fictitious, just as visual images are imaginary. Metaphors represent an artificial image, an artifice, one that does not exist in "reality." Nonetheless, these images are useful aids for getting a handle on the murky issue of self. As E. M. Forster said, "Everything must be like something, so what is this like?" Metaphors allow us to think by analogy; they help us find common ground through the alikeness of separate things.

Aristotle, in the third century B.C., recognized the power of visual word-images (in his unfinished *The Poetics*) and counsels us across the centuries that

> The greatest thing, by far, is to be a master of metaphor. It is the one thing that cannot be learnt from others; and it is also a sign of genius since a good metaphor implies an intuitive perception of the similarity of dissimilars. Through resemblance, metaphor makes things clearer.

In her scholarly study of metaphors, Eva Feder Kittay (1987) explains that Aristotle most valued metaphoric, analogic thinking because he regarded this approach as important for reasoning. Reasoning by analogy has been discredited by many 20th-century scholars. "You can't prove anything by analogy," we learn as university sophomores, for just because things are alike in some respects, we can't conclude they are alike in *all* respects. Metaphors "tell the truth but not the whole truth" (Owens, 1969). True, but we are not trying to "prove" that we are a metaphor. Rather, we are courting insight into complex wholes. We are trying to describe our feelings about our multicultural selves; we are trying to describe persons who as yet have no commonly agreed upon descriptors, and metaphors are handy ways to do this. Metaphors are especially apt in descriptions of oneself within the larger context of culture (Knowles and Sibicky, 1990). In an especially pertinent discussion of identity formation ("self-in-context"), Thomas Fitzgerald (1993), in his scholarly book on the impact of social and cultural factors on communication, *Metaphors of Identity: A Culture-Communication Dialogue,* argues that the concept of identity is crucial in situations of interpersonal and cross-cultural communication. Moreover, Fitzgerald says, "metaphoric ambiguity" is "heightened in cross-cultural comparisons" (223). Metaphors, Fitzgerald says, "can link multifaceted domains of human experience, providing quick visual images of these realities" (12).

Generating metaphors to get a handle on something as germane as a sense of self is not a trivial pursuit. Gareth Morgan (1986), in his book *Images of Organization,* emphasizes not only the power of metaphors but their hidden assumptions as well. Do we think of ourselves as like some kind of machine, as the center of a web-like social system, as an entire organism, or as just a single organ such as a brain, or a heart? Do we see ourselves in a psychological system at the mercy of unconscious drives? Or do we see ourselves as some sort of political system composed of competing interests? Perhaps we perceive our self to be totally idiosyncratic, an entity that is all flux and transformation. Maybe we think of ourselves as some sort of divine cosmic breath. And—importantly—what assumptions underlie our metaphoric images of ourselves?

In Robert Sternberg's (1990) outstanding book on the nature of intelligence, he constructed seven categories of metaphors, each corresponding to a mindset. Each of his metaphor-mindsets identifies an approach to conceptualizing the components of intelligence (geographic, computational, biological, epistemological, anthropological, sociological, and the systems approach). Sternberg maintains that it is only when you make explicit the metaphor that you use to think about something that you can analyze the strengths and weaknesses of your construct. When we think about ourselves, does the metaphor we use to describe our multicultural identity provide a good fit? Does it embrace the complexity of our lives? (See also: Dufault, 1991; Fitzgerald, 1993; Lakoff and Johnson, 1980; Valle and Von Eckartsberg, 1980.)

The metaphors we examine are from different mindsets than those that Morgan or Sternberg use, because constructs of organizations or of intelligence have different dynamics from those of self-identity. How do we find metaphors that are sufficiently descriptive, metaphors with which we feel comfortable, metaphors that effectively communicate our reality to others? Almost anywhere. The arts and sciences and humanities, as well as to traditions of spirituality, for starters.

References and Further Reading

Adler, Nancy J. "Cultural Synergy: The Management of Cross-Cultural Organizations," in W. W. Burke and L. D. Goodstein, eds., *Trends and Issues in OD: Current Theory and Practice.* San Diego, CA: University Associates, 1980.

Adler, Peter S. "Beyond Cultural Identity: Reflections Upon Cultural and Multicultural Man," in Larry A. Samovar and Richard E. Porter, eds., *Intercultural Communication: A Reader,* 2nd ed. Belmont, CA: Wadsworth, 1976.

Aguirre Beltrán, Gonzalo. *La Población negra de México: estudio etnohistórico,* 2a. ed. México, DF: Fondo de Cultura Económico, 1972.

Alba, Richard D. *Ethnic Identity: The Transformation of Ethnicity in the Lives of Americans of European Ancestry.* New Haven, CT: Yale University Press, 1990.

Anderson, Benedict. *Imagined Communities: Reflections on the Origin and Spread of Nationalism,* rev. ed. New York: Verso, 1991.

Axtell, Roger E. *Gestures: The Do's and Taboos of Body Language Around the World.* New York: Wiley, 1991.

Bachnik, Jane, and Charles J. Quinn, Jr. *Situational Meaning: Inside and Outside in Japanese Self, Society, and Language.* Princeton, NJ: Princeton University Press, 1994.

Balibar, Etienne, and Immanuel Wallerstein. *Race, Nation, Class: Ambiguous Identities.* London: Verso, 1991.

Barkow, Jerome H., Leda Cosmides, and John Tooby. *The Adapted Mind: Evolutionary Psychology and the Generation of Culture.* New York: Oxford University Press, 1992.

Barth, John. *Once Upon a Time: A Floating Opera.* Boston: Little, Brown, 1994.

Bateson, Gregory. *Steps to an Ecology of the Mind.* New York: Ballantine, 1972.

Bean, Frank D., and Marta Tienda. *The Hispanic Population of the United States.* New York: Russell Sage Foundation, 1987.

Becker, Howard S. *Outsiders: Studies in the Sociology of Deviance.* New York: Free Press, 1963.

Ben-Zeev, Sandra. "Bilingualism and Cognitive Development," in Niklas Miller, ed., *Bilingualism and Language Disability: Assessment and Remediation.* London: Croom Helm, and San Diego, CA: College-Hill Press, 1984, pp. 55–80.

——————. "Mechanisms by Which Childhood Bilingualism Affects Understanding of Language and Cognitive Structure," in Peter A. Hornby, ed., *Bilingualism: Psychological, Social, and Educational Implications.* New York: Academic Press, 1977a: 29–55.

——————. "The Influence of Bilingualism on Cognitive Strategy and Cognitive Development." *Child Development* 48 (1977b): 1009–1018.

——————. *The Influence of Bilingualism on Cognitive Development and Cognitive Strategy.* Ph.D. diss. University of Chicago, 1972.

Bennett, Janet M. "Cultural Marginality: Identity Issues in Intercultural Training," in R. Michael Paige, ed., *Education for the Intercultural Experience,* 2nd ed. Yarmouth, ME: Intercultural Press, 1993, 109–135.

Bennett, Milton. Lecture on the major paradigms of marginality in the social science literature, Cross-cultural Training Services Seminar, International House, Tokyo, 1992.

Bentley, Jerry H. *Old World Encounters: Cross-Cultural Contacts and Exchanges in Pre-Modern Times.* New York: Oxford University Press, 1993.

Berger, Bennett M. "The Identity Myth." Lecture delivered at Forest Hospital, Des Plaines, Illinois, January 1968.

Berger, P., B. Berger, and H. Kellner. *The Homeless Mind: Modernization and Consciousness.* New York: Random House, 1973.

Bernal, Martha E., and George P. Knight, eds. *Ethnic Identity: Formation and Transmission among Hispanics and Other Minorities.* Albany, NY: State University of New York Press, 1993.

Bitterli, Urs. *Cultures in Conflict: Encounters Between European and Non-European Cultures, 1492–1800.* Cambridge: Polity, 1989. (English translation of *Alte Welt, neue Welt*)

Black, Max. *Models and Metaphors: Studies in Language and Philosophy.* Ithaca, NY: Cornell University Press, 1962.

Boas, Franz. "The Growth of Indian Mythologies: A Study Based upon the Growth of the Mythologies of the North Pacific Coast." *Journal of American Folklore* 9 (1896): 1–11.

Bolen, Jean Shinoda. *Gods in Everyman: A New Psychology of Men's Lives and Loves.* New York: HarperCollins, 1990.

——————. *Goddesses in Everywoman: A New Psychology of Women.* New York: Harper & Row, 1984.

Boucher, Jerry, Dan Landis, and Karen Arnold Clark, eds. *Ethnic Conflict: International Perspectives.* Newbury Park, CA: Sage, 1987.

Bowen, Murray. *Family Therapy in Clinical Practice.* Northvale, NJ: Aronson, 1978.

Brah, Artar. "South Asian Teenagers in Southhall." *New Community* 6, no. 3 (1978): 197–206.

Brazelton, T. Berry. *Neonatal Behavioral Assessment Scale,* 2nd. ed. Philadelphia: Spastics International Medical Publishing, J. B. Lippincott, 1984.

——————. *Infants and Mothers: Differences in Development,* rev. ed. New York: Merloyde Lawrence Book, Dell Publishing, 1983.

Brewer, Marilynn B. "The Social Self: On Being the Same and Different at the Same Time." *Personality and Social Psychology Bulletin,* 17, 1991: 475–482.

Brislin, Richard. *Understanding Culture's Influence on Behavior.* New York: Harcourt Brace, 1993.

Brooks, Linda Marie. *Alternative Identities: The Self in Literature, History, Theory*. New York: Garland, 1995.

Brown, Donald E. *Human Universals*. Philadelphia: Temple University Press, 1991.

Buijs, Gina. *Migrant Women: Crossing Boundaries and Changing Identities*. Oxford [England] and Providence, RI [USA]: Berg, 1993.

Calderón de la Barca, Pedro. *La Vida es sueño*. 1635. Published in English as *Life Is a Dream*, trans. by William-Alan Landes. Studio City, CA: Players Press, 1992.

Carbaugh, D. *Talking American: Cultural Discourses on Donahue*. Norwood, NJ: Ablex, 1989.

Carpenter, Edmund. *They Became What They Beheld*. New York: Outerbridge and Dienstfrey/Ballantine, 1970.

Carroll, John B., ed. *Language, Thought, and Reality: Selected Writings of Benjamin Lee Whorf*. Cambridge, MA: MIT Press, 1956.

Carvalho, José Jorge de. *Nietzsche e Xango: dois mitos do ceticismo e do desmascaramento*. Brasilia, DF: Universidade de Brasilia, Instituto de Ciencias Humanas, Departamento de Antropologia, 1989.

Cavalli-Sforza, Luca, Paolo Menozzi, and Alberto Piazza. *The History and Geography of Human Genes*. Princeton, NJ: Princeton University Press, 1994.

Cernic, David, and Linda Longmire, eds. *Know Thyself: Collected Readings on Identity*. Mahwah, NJ: Paulist Press, 1987.

Chan, Ronnie C. Quoted in *Business Week*, December 6, 1993, p. 64.

Christakis, Alexander N. "Cosmology of Design." Paper presented at the Annual Meeting of the American Society for Cybernetics, Virginia Beach, VA, February 19–23, 1986.

——————. "An Overview of Interactive Management." Fairfax, VA: The Center for Interactive Management, George Mason University, October 1984.

Cisneros, Sandra. *Woman Hollering Creek and Other Stories*. New York: Random House, 1991.

Coelho, George V., David A. Hamburg, and John E. Adams, eds. *Coping and Adaptation*. New York: Basic Books, 1974.

Coleman, Richard P., and Lee Rainwater. *Social Standing in America: New Dimensions of Class*. New York: Basic Books, 1978.

Connor, Walker. *Ethnonationalism: The Quest for Understanding.* Princeton, NJ: Princeton University Press, 1994.

Counts, David R., and Dorothy Ayers Counts. *Coping with the Final Tragedy: Cultural Variation in Dying and Grieving.* Amityville, NY: Baywood, 1991.

Crawford, James, ed. *Language Loyalties: A Source Book on the Official English Controversy.* University of Chicago Press, 1992.

Crick, Francis. *The Astonishing Hypothesis: The Scientific Search for the Soul.* New York: Macmillan, 1994.

Culkin, John. Quoted in Edmund Carpenter, *They Became What They Beheld.* New York: Outerbridge and Dienstfrey/Ballantine, 1970.

Dawkins, Richard. *River Out of Eden: A Darwinian View of Life.* New York: Basic Books, 1995.

Deikman, Arthur. *The Observing Self: Mysticism and Psychotherapy.* Boston, MA: Beacon Press, 1982.

Dennett, Daniel. *Consciousness Explained.* Boston: Little, Brown, 1991.

Díaz del Castillo, Bernal. *Historia verdadera de la conquista de la Nueva España.* 3 vols. México, DF: Porrua, 1955. [Editions in English are available.]

Dillard, Annie. *Living by Fiction.* New York: HarperCollins, 1982.

Doi, Takeo. *The Anatomy of Self: The Individual versus Society.* Tokyo and New York: Kodansha International, 1986.

Dufault, Roseanna Lewis. *Metaphors of Identity: The Treatment of Childhood in Selected Quebecois Novels.* Rutherford, NJ: Fairleigh Dickinson University Press; London: Associated University Presses, 1991.

Durant, Will. *The Story of Civilization. Volume 2: The Life of Greece.* New York, Simon & Schuster, 1939.

Durham, William H. *Coevolution: Genes, Culture, and Human Diversity.* Stanford, CA: Stanford University Press, 1991.

Eddington, Arthur Stanley. *The Nature of the Physical World.* New York: Macmillan, 1933.

Edmondson, Munro S. "Neolithic Diffusion Rates." *Current Anthropology* 2 (1961): 71–102.

Eldredge, Niles, and Marjorie Glicksman Grene. *Interactions: The Biological Context of Social Systems.* New York: Columbia University Press, 1992.

Ellis, Lee. *Social Stratification and Socioeconomic Inequality.* Westport, CT: Praeger, 1993.

Emerson, Ralph Waldo. "Self-Reliance," in Carl Bode and Malcolm Cowley, eds., *The Portable Emerson.* New York: Penguin Books, 1981, 138–164.

Erchak, Gerald Michael. *The Anthropology of Self and Behavior.* New Brunswick, NJ: Rutgers University Press, 1992.

Erez, Miriam, and Christopher P. Earley. *Culture, Self-Identity, and Work.* New York: Oxford University Press, 1993.

Fantini, Alvino. "Intercultural Education—Becoming Better Global Citizens: The Promise of Intercultural Competence." *Adult Learning* (February 1991): 15–19.

Farella, John R. *The Main Stalk: A Synthesis of Navajo Philosophy.* Tucson: University of Arizona Press, 1990.

Farley, Reynolds, and Walter R. Allen. *The Color Line and the Quality of Life in America.* New York: Russell Sage Foundation, 1987.

Ferguson, Russell, et al. *Out There: Marginalization and Contemporary Cultures.* New York: New Museum of Contemporary Art, 1990.

Fischer, David Hackett. *Albion's Seed: Four British Folkways in America.* New York: Oxford University Press, 1989.

Fitzgerald, Thomas K. *Metaphors of Identity: A Culture-Communication Dialogue.* Albany: State University of New York Press, 1993.

Fleischacker, Samuel. *The Ethics of Culture.* Ithaca: Cornell University Press, 1994.

Flemons, Douglas A. *Completing Distinctions: Interweaving the Ideas of Gregory Bateson and Taoism into a Unique Approach to Therapy.* Boston and London: Shambhala, 1991.

Forster, E. M. *Abinger Harvest.* London: E. Arnold, 1936.

Freud, Anna, and Sophie Dann. "Experiment in Group Up-Bringing." *Psychoanalytic Study of the Child* 6 (1951): 127–168.

Freud, Anna. *The Ego and the Mechanism of Defense.* New York: International Universities Press, 1946.

Friedan, Betty. *The Fountain of Age.* New York: Simon & Schuster, 1993.

Furnham, Adrian, and Stephen Bochner. *Culture Shock: Psychological Reactions to Unfamiliar Environments.* London; New York: Methuen, 1986.

Gamble, Clive. *Timewalkers: The Prehistory of Global Colonization.* Stroud, Gloustershire: A. Sutton, 1993.

Garmezy, N. "Vulnerable and Invulnerable Children: Theory, Research and Intervention." Master lecture on developmental psychology. Washington, DC: American Psychological Association, 1976.

Gazzaniga, Michael S. *Nature's Mind: The Biological Roots of Thinking, Emotions, Sexuality, Language, and Intelligence.* New York: Basic Books, 1992.

Geertz, Clifford. *After the Fact: Two Countries, Four Decades, One Anthropologist.* Cambridge, MA: Harvard University Press, 1995.

——. *The Interpretation of Cultures.* New York: Basic Books, 1972.

Gellner, Ernest. *Conditions of Liberty: Civil Society and Its Rivals.* New York: Allen Lane, Penguin Press, 1994.

——, John A. Hall, and I. C. Jarvie. *Transition to Modernity: Essays on Power, Wealth, and Belief.* New York: Cambridge University Press, 1992.

——. *Culture, Identity, and Politics.* Cambridge and New York: Cambridge University Press, 1987.

Gergen, Kenneth J. *The Saturated Self: Dilemmas of Identity in Contemporary Life.* New York: Basic Books, 1991.

——, and K. Davis. *The Social Construction of the Person.* New York: Springer-Verlag, 1985.

Glazer, Nathan, and Daniel Patrick Moynihan, eds. *Ethnicity: Theory and Experience.* Cambridge, MA: Harvard University Press, 1975.

——. *Beyond the Melting Pot: The Negroes, Puerto Ricans, Jews, Italians and Irish of New York City.* Cambridge, MA: MIT Press, 1963.

Goffman, Erving G. *Behavior in Public Places.* Westport, CT: Greenwood, 1980.

——. *Interaction Ritual.* New York: Pantheon, 1982.

——. *Encounters.* Indianapolis: Bobbs-Merrill, 1961.

——. *The Presentation of Self in Everyday Life.* New York: Doubleday, 1959.

Goodenough, Ward H. "Multiculturalism as the Normal Human Experience." *Anthropology and Education Quarterly* 7, no. 4, (November 1976): 4–7.

——. *Cooperation in Change.* New York: Russell Sage Foundation, 1963.

Goonetilleke, D. C. R. A. *Developing Countries in British Fiction.* London: Macmillan, 1977.

Gorden, Raymond L. *Living in Latin America: A Case Study in Cross-Cultural Communication.* Lincolnwood, IL: National Textbook Company, 1974.

Gordon, Edmund. Quoted in *Time,* July 8, 1991, 19.

Gordon, Milton M. *Assimilation in American Life: The Role of Race, Religion and National Origins.* New York: Oxford University Press, 1964.

Gouchenour, T., and A. Janeway. "Seven Concepts in Cross-Cultural Interaction: A Training Design," in *Beyond Experience: The Experiential Approach to Cross-Cultural Education.* Brattleboro, VT: Experiment in International Living, 1978.

Greenfield, Patricia Marks, and Rodney R. Cocking. *Cross-Cultural Roots of Minority Child Development.* Hillsdale, NJ: L. Erlbaum Associates, 1994.

Group for the Advancement of Psychiatry. Committee on International Relations. *Us and Them: The Psychology of Ethnonationalism.* New York: Brunner/Mazel, 1987.

Gudykunst, William B., and Stella Ting-Toomey. *Culture and Interpersonal Communication.* Newbury Park, CA: Sage, 1988.

Gussow, Mel. " 'A Moralist Possessed by Humor': A Conversation with Robertson Davies." *New York Times Book Review,* February 5, 1995, 24–25.

Haeberlé, Daniel. "Meta-Intercultural Communication: Intercultural Communication about Intercultural Communication Training." Paper presented at SIETAR Europa's Third Annual Symposium, March 11–14, 1993, Bad Nauheim, Germany, and at SIETAR International's XIX Congress, June 8–12, 1993, Washington, DC.

Hage, Jerald, and Charles H. Powers. P*ost Industrial Lives: Roles and Relationships in the 21st Century.* Newbury Park, CA: Sage, 1992.

Hall, Edward T. *The Dance of Life: The Other Dimension of Time.* New York: Anchor Press/Doubleday, 1983.

———. *Beyond Culture.* New York: Anchor Press/Doubleday, 1976.

———. *The Silent Language.* New York: Fawcett, 1961.

Hamaguchi, Eshun, et al. *Japanese Systems: An Alternative Civilization?* Yokohama: Matsuda Foundation/Sekotac, 1992.

———. "The 'Japanese Disease' or Japanization?" *Japan Echo* 8, no. 2, (1981): 53–55.

Hammonds, Beryl. *I Am Not a Dark-Skinned White-Girl!!: My Human "Self" Being a Journal for a Black Woman.* Vancouver, WA 98668: Distinct Production, P.O. Box 1764, 1993.

Harris, G. G. "Individual, Self, and Person in Description and Analysis." *American Anthropologist* 91, no. 3, (September 1989): 599–612.

Harris, LaDonna. Personal communication, 1990.

Harrison, G. Ainsworth. *Human Adaptation*. Oxford [England] and New York: Oxford University Press, 1993.

Haverson, Claire B. "Cultural-Context Inventory: The Effects of Culture on Behavior and Work Style," in J. William Pfeiffer, ed., *The 1993 Annual: Developing Human Resources*. San Diego, CA: Pfeiffer, 1993, 131–145.

Heath, D. H. *Maturity and Competence*. New York: Garner Press, 1977.

Hecht, Michael L., Sidney Ribeau, and Michael V. Sedano. "A Mexican American Perspective on Interethnic Communication." *International Journal of Intercultural Relations* 14 (1990): 31–55.

Heelas, Paul, and Andrew Lock, eds. *Indigenous Psychologies: The Anthropology of the Self*. London: Academic Press, 1987.

Hein, Piet. *Grooks I*. Garden City, NY: Doubleday, 1969.

Helms, J. A. *Black and White Racial Identity: Theory, Research and Practice*. Westport, CT: Greenwood Press, 1990.

Hendershott, Carmen. *Stranger than Paradise: Hosts and Guests in a New Age Community*. Ph.D. diss. New York: New School for Social Research, May 1989.

Henderson, Mae. *Borders, Boundaries, and Frames: Essays in Cultural Criticism and Cultural Studies*. New York: Routledge, 1995.

Henry III, William A. *Time. Special Issue: The New Face of America*, Fall 1993, 75.

Hillerman, Tony. *Sacred Clowns*. New York: HarperCollins, 1993. (Page citation from 1994 paperback edition.)

Hobson, J. Allan. *The Chemistry of Conscious States: How the Brain Changes Its Mind*. Boston: Little, Brown, 1994.

Hofstede, Geert. *Cultures and Organizations: Software of the Mind*. New York: McGraw-Hill, 1991.

Honig, Emily. *Creating Chinese Ethnicity: Subei People in Shanghai, 1850–1980*. New Haven, CT: Yale University Press, 1992.

Hooks, Bell. *Teaching to Transgress: Education as the Practice of Freedom*. New York: Routledge, 1994.

Horowitz, Donald L. *Ethnic Groups in Conflict*. Berkeley: University of California Press, 1985.

Houston, Jean. *The Possible Human: A Course in Extending Your Physical, Mental, and Creative Abilities*. Los Angeles: Jeremy P. Tarcher, 1982.

Hsu, Francis L. K. *Rugged Individualism Reconsidered: Essays in Psychological Anthropology.* Knoxville: University of Tennessee Press, 1983.

Hunt, Chester L., and Lewis Walker. *Ethnic Dynamics: Patterns of Intergroup Relations in Various Societies,* 2nd. ed. Holmes Beach, FL: Learning Publications, 1979.

Hutnik, Nimmi. *Ethnic Minority Identity: A Social Psychological Perspective.* Oxford: Clarendon Press; New York: Oxford University Press, 1991.

Inkeles, Alex, and David H. Smith. *Becoming Modern: Individual Change in Six Developing Countries.* Cambridge, MA: Harvard University Press, 1974.

—————. "The Fate of Personal Adjustment in the Process of Modernization." *International Journal of Comparative Sociology* 11 (1970): 81–114.

—————, and Daniel J. Levinson. "National Character: The Study of Modal Personality and Sociocultural Systems," in *Handbook of Social Psychology,* 2nd ed., vol. 4, G. Lindzey and E. Aronson, eds. Reading, MA: Addison-Wesley, 1969, 418–506.

Isaacs, Harold R. *Idols of the Tribe: Group Identity and Political Change.* New York: Harper & Row, 1975.

Iyer, Pico. *Time. Special Issue: The New Face of America,* Fall 1993, 86.

Janis, Irving L. *Groupthink: Psychological Studies of Policy Decisions and Fiascoes.* Boston, MA: Houghton Mifflin, 1983.

—————, and Leon Mann. *Design-Making: A Psychological Analysis of Conflict, Choice, and Commitment.* New York: Free Press, 1977.

—————. *Psychological Stress.* New York: Wiley, 1958.

Jeans, James. *The Mysterious Universe.* New York: Macmillan, 1931.

Johansen, Bruce E. *The Forgotten Founders: Benjamin Franklin, the Iroquois and the Rationale for the American Revolution.* Ipswich, MA: Gambit, 1982.

Josephy, Jr., Alvin M. *The Patriot Chiefs: A Chronicle of American Indian Resistance,* rev. ed. New York: Penguin Books, 1993.

Josselson, R. *Finding Herself: Pathways to Identity Development in Women.* San Francisco, CA: Jossey-Bass, 1987.

Kaminer, Wendy. *I'm Dysfunctional You're Dysfunctional.* New York: Addison-Wesley, 1992.

Kareem, Jafar, and Roland Littlewood. *Intercultural Therapy: Themes, Interpretations and Practice.* Oxford, England: Blackwell Scientific Publications, 1992.

Karttunen, Frances. *Between Worlds: Interpreters, Guides, and Survivors.* New Brunswick, NJ: Rutgers University Press, 1994.

Kass, Leon R. *The Hungry Soul: Eating and the Perfecting of Our Culture.* New York: Free Press, 1994.

Kavolis, Vytautas, ed. *Designs of Selfhood.* Rutherford, NJ: Fairleigh Dickenson University Press, 1984.

——————. "Civilizational Forms in Life Histories: Rousseau and Gandhi," in E. Leites, ed., *Life Histories as Civilizational Texts: Occasional Papers, No. 1.* Carlisle, PA: Dickinson College, 1977.

Kealey, Daniel J. "A Study of Cross-Cultural Effectiveness: Theoretical Issues, Practical Applications." *International Journal of Intercultural Relations* 13, no. 3 (1989): 387–428.

Kelly, George A. *The Psychology of Personal Constructs.* New York: Norton, 1955.

Kennedy, Morehead. *The Ayatollah in the Cathedral: Reflections of a Hostage.* New York: Hill & Wang, 1986.

Kerr, Michael E., and Murray Bowen. *Family Evaluation: An Approach Based on Bower Theory.* New York: Norton, 1988.

Keyes, Ken Jr. *The Hundredth Monkey.* Coos Bay, OR: Vision Books, 1986.

Kiernan, V. G. "Britons Old and New," in Colin Holmes, ed., *Immigrants and Minorities in British Society.* London: George Allen & Unwin, 1978, 23–27.

Kingston, Maxine Hong. *The Woman Warrior: Memoirs of a Girlhood among Ghosts.* New York: Knopf, 1976.

Kishima, Takako. *Political Life in Japan: Democracy in a Reversible World.* Princeton, NJ: Princeton University Press, 1992.

Kitahara, Michio. *The Tragedy of Evolution: The Human Animal Confronts Modern Society.* New York: Praeger, 1991.

Kitano, Harry H. L. *Japanese Americans: The Evolution of a Subculture.* Englewood Cliffs, NJ: Prentice-Hall, 1969.

Kittay, Eva Feder. *Metaphor: Its Cognitive Force and Linguistic Form.* New York: Oxford University Press, 1987.

Klineberg, O., and M. Zavallone. *Nationalism and Tribalism among African Students: Study of Social Identity.* Hague: Mouton, 1969.

Knowles, Eric S., and Mark E. Sibicky. "Continuities and Diversity in the Stream of Selves: Metaphorical Resolutions of William James' One-in-

Many-Selves Paradox." *Personality and Social Psychology* 16, no. 4 (1990): 676–687.

Kolve, V. A. *The Play Called Corpus Christi*. Stanford, CA: Stanford University Press, 1966.

Kondo, Dorinne K. *Crafting Selves: Power, Gender, and Discourses of Identity in a Japanese Workplace*. Chicago: University of Chicago Press, 1990.

Kotkin, Joel. *Tribes: How Race, Religion, and Identity Determine Success in the New Global Economy*. New York: Random House, 1992.

Kundera, Milan. *Jacques and His Master: A Homage to Diderot in Three Acts*. New York: Harper & Row, 1985.

Kurzweil, Arthur. *From Generation to Generation: How to Trace Your Jewish Family History and Genealogy*. New York: Morrow, 1980.

Lado, Robert. *Linguistics across Cultures: Applied Linguistics for Language Teachers*. Ann Arbor: University of Michigan Press, 1957.

Laing, R. D. *The Divided Self: An Existential Study in Sanity and Madness*. London and New York: Penguin Books, 1969.

Lakoff, George, and Mark Johnson. *Metaphors We Live By*. Chicago: University of Chicago Press, 1980.

Lavrijsen, Ria, ed. *Cultural Diversity in the Arts: Art, Art Policies and the Facelift of Europe*. Amsterdam: Royal Tropical Institute, 1993.

Lawrence, T. E. *The Seven Pillars of Wisdom*. New York: Doubleday, 1966.

Lazarus, Richard S., James R. Averill, and Edward M. Opton, Jr. "The Psychology of Coping: Issues of Research and Assessment," in G. V. Coelho, D. A. Hamburg, and J. E. Adams, eds., *Coping and Adaptation*. New York: Basic Books, 1974, 249–315.

——————. *Psychological Stress and Coping Process*. New York: McGraw-Hill, 1966.

Leakey, Richard. *The Origin of Humankind*. New York: Basic Books/HarperCollins, 1994.

Lear, Edward. *The Scroobious Pip*. New York: Harper & Row Junior Books, 1968.

Lee, Dorothy. *Freedom and Culture*. Prospect Heights, IL: Waveland Press, 1987.

——————. *Valuing the Self: What We Can Learn from Other Cultures*. Prospect Heights, IL: Waveland Press, 1986.

Lenski, Gerard, and Jean Lenski. *Human Societies: An Introduction to Macrosociology,* 5th ed. New York: McGraw-Hill, 1987.

LeVine, Robert A., and Donald T. Campbell. *Ethnocentrism: Theories of Conflict, Ethnic Attitudes and Group Behavior.* New York: Wiley, 1972.

Lieberson, Stanley, and Mary C. Waters. *From Many Strands: Ethnic and Racial Groups in Contemporary America.* New York: Russell Sage Foundation, 1988.

Liebline, A. J. "The Islander," in Edmund Carpenter, ed., *They Became What They Beheld.* New York: Outerbridge and Dienstfrey/Ballantine, 1970.

Lifton, Robert Jay. *The Protean Self: Human Resilience in an Age of Fragmentation.* New York: Basic Books, HarperCollins, 1993.

"The Living Tree: The Changing Meaning of Being Chinese Today." *Daedalus: Journal of the American Academy of Arts and Sciences* 120, no. 2 (Spring 1991).

Locher, J. L., ed. *The World of M. C. Escher.* New York: Abradale Press, Harry N. Abrams, 1988.

Lockland, George T. *Grow or Die: The Unifying Principle of Transformation.* New York: Random House, 1973.

Lorenz, Konrad. *Civilized Man's Eight Deadly Sins.* New York: Harcourt Brace Jovanovich, 1973.

Louden, D. "Self–Esteem and Locus of Control." *New Community* 6, no. 3 (1978): 218–234.

Lu Chi. *Lu Chi's Wen Fu: The Art of Writing,* rev. ed. Trans. Sam Hamill. Minneapolis, MN.: Milkweed Editions, 1991.

Lummis, C. Douglas. *Boundaries on the Land, Boundaries in the Mind.* Tokyo: Hokuseido Press, 1982.

Ma, Suk Yee. Identity Among Hong Kong Student Returnees. Tokyo: International Christian University Senior Thesis, Languages Division 1993.

Malraux, André. *Man's Hope.* New York: Modern Language, 1983. [Originally published in 1938 by Random House.]

Mancuso, James C., ed. *Readings for a Cognitive Theory of Personality.* New York: Holt, Rinehart, and Winston, 1970.

Maraini, Fosco. *Japan: Patterns of Continuity.* Tokyo: Kodansha International, 1971.

Marsella, Anthony J., George A. De Vos, and Francis L. K. Hsu. *Culture and Self: Asian and Western Perspectives.* New York: Tavistock, 1985.

──────────. "Depressive Experience and Disorder Across Cultures," in H. Triandis and J. Draguns, eds., *Handbook of Cross-Cultural Psychology. Volume 6: Psychopathology*. Boston: Allyn and Bacon, 1980, 237–289.

──────────, and Kenneth O. Sanborn. "The Modernization of Traditional Cultures: Consequences for the Individual." Working paper, Third Annual SIETAR Conference, Chicago, February 1977.

Martin, Judith N., ed. *Intercultural Competence*. A special issue of *International Journal of Intercultural Relations* 13, no. 3 (1989).

──────────, and Mitchell R. Hammer. "Behavioral Categories of Intercultural Communication Competence: Everyday Communicators' Perceptions." *International Journal of Intercultural Relations* 13, no. 3 (1989): 303–332.

Martínez, Oscar J. *Border People: Life and Society in the U.S.-Mexico Borderlands*. Tucson, AZ: University of Arizona Press, 1994.

Mascie-Taylor, C. G. N., and Gabriel Ward Lasker. *Biological Aspects of Human Migration*. Cambridge [England] and New York: Cambridge University Press, 1988.

Masuda, Yoneji. *The Information Society in the Year 2000*. Bethesda, MD: Futures Society, 1980.

McCulloch, Warren S. *Embodiments of Mind*. Cambridge: MIT, 1965.

McGrath, Joseph E., ed. *Social and Psychological Factors in Stress*. New York: Holt, Rinehart & Winston, 1970.

McNeill, W. H. *The Rise of the West*. New York: Mentor, 1965.

McNickle, D'Arcy. *Native American Tribalism: Indian Survivals and Renewals*. New York: Oxford University Press, 1973.

Mead, Margaret, and T. G. Harris. "A Conversation with Margaret Mead and T. George Harris on the Anthropological Age." *The Bridge* (Spring 1977): 22–25, 48–51.

Mischler, E., and N. Scotch. "Sociocultural Factors in the Epidemiology of Schizophrenia." *International Journal of Psychiatry* 1 (1965): 258–295.

Miyanaga, Kuniko. *The Creative Edge: Emerging Individualism in Japan*. New Brunswick, NJ: Transaction Press, 1991.

Mol, Hans. *Identity and Religion: International, Cross-Cultural Approaches*. London and Beverly Hills, CA: Sage, 1978.

Montagu, Ashley. *Man's Most Dangerous Myth: The Fallacy of Race*. New York: Columbia University Press, 1942.

Morgan, Gareth. *Images of Organization.* London: Sage, 1986.

Morris Brian. *Anthropology of the Self: The Individual in Cultural Perspective.* London and Boulder, CO: Pluto Press, 1994.

Moustakas, C. E., ed. *The Self.* New York: Harper Colophon, 1956.

Murdock, George P., et al. *Outline of World Cultures,* 5th ed. New Haven, CT: Human Relations Area File, 1983.

—————. "The Common Denominator of Cultures," in George P. Murdock, ed., *Culture and Society.* Pittsburgh: Pittsburgh University Press, 1965, 88–110.

Murphy, H. "Social Change and Mental Health," in *Causes of Mental Disorders: A Review of Epidomiological Knowledge, 1959: Proceedings.* New York: Milbank Memorial Fund, 1961.

Murphy, Jane. "Sociocultural Change and Psychiatric Disorder among Rural Yorubas in Nigeria." *Ethos* 1 (1973): 239–262.

Nakashima, C. "An Invisible Monster: The Creation and Denial of Multiracial People," in M. Root, ed., *Mixed Race People Coming of Age in America.* Newbury Park, CA: Sage, 1991.

Nash, Manning. *The Cauldron of Ethnicity in the Modern World.* Chicago: University of Chicago Press, 1989.

Ní Dhomhnaill, Nuala. "Why I Choose to Write in Irish, The Corpse That Sits Up and Talks Back." *New York Times Book Review,* January 8, 1995, 3, 27–28.

Okimoto, Daniel. *American in Disguise.* New York: John Weatherhill, 1971.

Olebe, Margaret, and Jolene Koster, "Exploring the Cross-Cultural Equivalence of the Behavioral Assessment Scale for Intercultural Communication." *International Journal of Intercultural Relations* 13, no. 3 (1989): 333–347.

Owens, Thomas. *Metaphor and Related Subjects.* New York: Random House, 1969.

Paige, R. Michael, ed. *Education for the Intercultural Experience,* 2nd ed. Yarmouth, ME: Intercultural Press, 1993.

Papastergiadis, Nikos. "The South in the North." *Third Text* 14 (Spring 1991).

Park, Robert E. *Race and Culture.* New York: Free Press, 1950.

—————. "Human Migration and the Marginal Man." *American Journal of Sociology* 33 (1926): 881–893.

——————, and Herbert Miller. *Old World Traits Transplanted.* Chicago: University of Chicago Press, 1925.

Peckham, Morse. *Beyond the Tragic Vision: The Quest for Identity in the 19th Century.* New York: Braziller, 1962.

Peele, Stanton. *The Diseasing of America.* Lexington, MA: Lexington Books, 1989.

Penrose, Roger. *Shadows of the Mind: A Search for the Missing Science of Consciousness.* New York: Oxford University Press, 1994.

Pereda, Victor. *The Cross and the Pear Tree: A Sephardic Journey.* New York: Alfred A. Knopf, 1995.

Pickens, Stuart. Personal communication, 1992.

Pike, Kenneth L. *Stir, Change, Create.* Grand Rapids, MI: William B. Eerdmans, 1967.

Pinker, Steven. *The Language Instinct: How the Mind Creates Language.* New York: William Morrow, 1994. (HarperPerennial paperback edition, 1995.)

Platt, Larry A., and V. Richard Persico. *Grief in Cross-Cultural Perspective: A Casebook.* New York: Garland, 1992.

Price, Reynolds. *A Whole New Life.* New York: Atheneum, 1994.

Quinn, Arthur. *A New World: An Epic of Colonial America from the Founding of Jamestown to the Fall of Quebec.* Boston: Faber & Faber, 1994.

Rawlinson, A. "Yoga Psychology," in Paul L. Heelas and Andrew Lock, eds., *Indigenous Psychologies: The Anthropology of the Self.* New York: Academic Press, 1981, 247–264.

Reddy, Maureen T. *Crossing the Color Line: Race, Parenting, and Culture.* New Brunswick, NJ: Rutgers University Press, 1994.

Redfield, Robert. *Outline of the Study of Acculturation.* Social Science Research Council, 1935.

Reed, Robert D. *How and Where to Research Your Ethnic-American Cultural Heritage: Black Americans.* Saratoga, CA: Reed, 1979.

——————. *How and Where to Research Your Ethnic-American Cultural Heritage: Chinese Americans.* Saratoga, CA: Reed, 1979.

——————. *How and Where to Research Your Ethnic-American Cultural Heritage: Irish Americans.* Saratoga, CA: Reed, 1979.

——————. *How and Where to Research Your Ethnic-American Cultural Heritage: Japanese Americans.* Saratoga, CA: Reed, 1979.

—————. *How and Where to Research Your Ethnic-American Cultural Heritage: Native Americans.* Saratoga, CA: Reed, 1979.

Rhinesmith, Stephen H. *A Manager's Guide to Globalizing: Six Keys to Success in a Changing World.* Homewood, IL: Business One Irwin, 1993.

Rich, Frank. "On Broadway, American History Cracks Open," *International Herald Tribune,* May 7, 1993, 9.

Ricoeur, Paul. *Hermeneutics and the Human Sciences: Essays on Language, Action and Interpretation.* Ed. and trans. John B. Thompson. New York: Cambridge University Press, 1981.

Roland, Alan. *In Search of Self in India and Japan: Toward a Cross-Cultural Psychology.* Princeton, NJ: Princeton University Press, 1988.

Root, Maria P. *Racially Mixed People in America.* Newbury Park, CA: Sage, 1992.

Rosenwald, George C., and Richard L. Ochberg. *Storied Lives: The Cultural Politics of Self-Understanding.* New Haven, CT: Yale University Press, 1992.

Ross, Marc Howard. *The Culture of Conflict: Interpretations and Interests in Comparative Perspective.* New Haven, CT: Yale University Press, 1993a.

—————. *The Management of Conflict: Interpretations and Interests in Comparative Perspective.* New Haven, CT: Yale University Press, 1993b.

Rottenberg, Dan. *Finding Our Fathers: A Guidebook to Jewish Genealogy.* New York: Random House, 1977.

Rouse, Irving. *Migrations in Prehistory: Inferring Population Movement from Cultural Remains.* New Haven, CT: Yale University Press, 1986.

Ruben, B. D., and Dan Kealey. "Behavioral Assessment of Communication Competency and the Prediction of Cross-Cultural Adaptation." *International Journal of Intercultural Relations* 3 (Spring 1979): 15–47.

Rushdie, Salman. *East, West: Stories.* New York: Pantheon, 1994.

—————. *Imaginary Homelands: Essays and Criticism, 1981–1991.* London: Granta Books (Penguin), 1992.

—————. *Grimus.* New York: Viking, 1991.

Russell, Bertrand. *The Autobiography of Bertrand Russell, 1872–1914.* Toronto: McClelland and Stewart, 1967.

Rutherford, Jonathan, ed. *Identity, Community, Culture, Difference.* London: Lawrence & Wishart, 1990.

Ryan, Paul. *Birth and Death and Cybernation: Cybernetics of the Sacred.* New York: Interface, Gordon and Breach, Science Publishers, 1973.

Sagan, Carl, and Ann Druyan. *Shadows of Forgotten Ancestors: A Search for Who We Are.* New York: Random House, 1992.

Salett, Elizabeth Patty, and Diane R. Koslow, eds. *Race, Ethnicity, and Self: Identity in Multicultural Perspective.* Washington, DC: National Multicultural Institute, 1994.

Sapir, Edward. *Culture, Language and Personality: Selected Essays.* Berkeley: University of California Press, 1949.

Sarans, Gopala. *The Methodology of Anthropological Comparisons: An Analysis of Comparative Methods in Social and Cultural Anthropology.* Tucson, AZ: University of Arizona Press, 1975.

Scheick, William J. *The Half-Blood: A Cultural Symbol in 19th Century American Fiction.* Lexington, KY: University Press of Kentucky, 1979.

Schroder, Harold M., and Julian B. Rotter. "Rigidity As a Learned Behavior," in J. C. Mancuso, ed., *Readings for a Cognitive Theory of Personality.* New York: Holt, Rinehart and Winston, 1970, 510–525.

Schweder, Richard A., ed. *Thinking Through Cultures: Expeditions in Cultural Psychology.* Cambridge, MA: Harvard University Press, 1991.

Seelye, H. Ned, and Alan Seelye-James. *Culture Clash: Managing in a Multicultural World.* Lincolnwood, IL: NTC Business Books, 1995.

——————. *Teaching Culture: Strategies for Intercultural Communication,* 3rd ed. Lincolnwood, IL: National Textbook Company, 1993.

——————. "Self Identity and the Bicultural Classroom," in H. LaFontaine, B. Persky, and L. Golobshick, eds., *Perspectives in Bilingual Education.* Wayne, NJ: Avery Pub. Group, 1978, 290–298.

——————, and Marilyn B. Brewer. "Ethnocentrism and Acculturation of North Americans in Guatemala." *Journal of Social Psychology* 80 (April 1970): 147–155.

——————. "An Objective Measure of Biculturation: Americans in Guatemala, A Case Study." *Modern Language Journal* 53, no. 7 (November 1969): 503–514.

Sheed, Wilfrid. *In Love with Daylight: A Memoir of Recovery.* New York: Simon & Schuster, 1995.

Shipman, Pat. *The Evolution of Racism: Human Differences and the Use and Abuse of Science.* New York: Simon & Schuster, 1994.

Singer, Marshall. *Intercultural Communication: A Perceptual Approach.* Englewood Cliffs, NJ: Prentice Hall, 1987.

Skårdal, Dorothy Burton. *The Divided Heart: Scandinavian Immigrant Experience through Literary Sources.* Lincoln: University of Nebraska Press, 1974.

Slonim, Maureen. *Children, Culture, and Ethnicity: Evaluating and Understanding the Impact.* New York: Garland, 1991.

Smith, Jessie Carney. *Ethnic Genealogy: A Research Guide.* Westport, CT: Greenwood Press, 1983.

Soddy, Kenneth, ed. *Identity, Mental Health and Value Systems.* London: Tavistock, 1961.

—————, ed. *Mental Health and Infant Development.* London: Routledge & Kegan Paul, 1955.

Sparrow, Lise. "Beyond Multicultural Man: Complexities of Identity." A paper read at SIETAR International Congress, Ottawa, Canada, June 17, 1994.

Stavans, Ilan. *The Hispanic Condition: Reflections on Culture and Identity in America.* New York: HarperCollins, 1995.

Steinberg, Stephan. *The Ethnic Myth: Race, Ethnicity, and Class in America.* Boston: Beacon Press, 1989.

Steiner, Ivan D. "Personality and the Resolution of Interpersonal Disagreements," in B. A. Maher, ed., *Progress in Experimental Personality Research,* Volume 3. New York: Academic Press, 1966, 195–239.

Stepan, Nancy Leys. "Race and Gender: The Role of Analogy in Science," in David Theo Goldberg, ed., *Anatomy of Racism.* Minneapolis: University of Minnesota Press, 1990, 38–57.

Sternberg, Robert J. *Metaphors of Mind: Conceptions of the Nature of Intelligence.* New York: Cambridge University Press, 1990.

Stevens, Wallace. "The Man with the Blue Guitar," in *The Collected Poems of Wallace Stevens.* New York: Knopf, 1968.

Stevenson, Robert Louis. *The Strange Case of Dr. Jekyll and Mr. Hyde.* (Reprint of 1886 book.) Lincoln: University of Nebraska Press, 1990.

Stewart, Edward C., and Milton J. Bennett. *American Cultural Patterns: A Cross-Cultural Perspective,* rev. ed. Yarmouth, ME: Intercultural Press, 1991.

Stonequist, Everett V. *The Marginal Man: A Study in Personality and Culture Conflict.* New York: Charles Scribner's, 1937.

——————. "The Problem of a Marginal Man." *American Journal of Sociology* 41 (1935): 1–12.

Sumner, William Graham, and Albert Galloway Keller. *The Science of Society.* 4 vols. New Haven, CT: 1927.

Swiderski, Richard M. *Lives Between Cultures: A Study of Human Nature, Identity and Culture.* Juneau, Alaska: The Denali Press, 1991.

Sykes, Charles J. *A Nation of Victims: The Decay of the American Character.* New York: St. Martin's Press, 1992.

Szasz, Margaret. *Between Indian and White Worlds.* Norman: University of Oklahoma Press, 1994.

Takaki, Ronald. *From Different Shores: Perspectives on Race and Ethnicity in America.* New York: Oxford University Press, 1987.

Takamatsu, Kuniko. *Like Dust I Rise . . .* Senior thesis, Languages Division. Tokyo: International Christian University, June 1994.

Taylor, Charles, and Amy Gutmann. *Multiculturalism and the Politics of Recognition.* Princeton, NJ: Princeton University Press, 1992.

Taylor, T. W. *The Bureau of Indian Affairs.* Boulder, CO: Westview, 1984.

Teilhard de Chardin, Pierre. *Le Phenomene humain.* Paris: Editions du Seuil, 1955.

Thoits, P. "Multiple Identities and Psychological Well-Being: A Reformulation and Test of the Social Isolation Hypothesis." *American Sociological Review* 48 (1983): 174–187.

Ting-Toomey, Stella. *The Challenge of Facework: Cross-Cultural and Interpersonal Issues.* Albany: State University of New York Press, 1994.

Tobias, Phillip V. *The Meaning of Race,* 2nd ed. Johannesburg: South African Institute of Race Relations, 1972.

Třeštik, Dušan. "Věrnym Cechům." *Lidové Noviny,* March 7, 1995, 5.

Triandis, Harry C., Richard Brislin, and C. Harry Hui. "Cross-Cultural Training across the Individualism-Collectivism Divide." *International Journal of Intercultural Relations* 12, no. 3 (1988): 269–289.

——————. *Interpersonal Behavior.* Belmont, CA: Wadsworth, 1977.

——————, et al. *The Analysis of Subjective Culture.* New York: Wiley-Interscience, 1972.

Trompenaars, Fons. *Riding the Waves of Culture.* Burr Ridge, IL: Irwin Professional Publishing, 1994.

Tuan, Yi-Fu. *Passing Strange and Wonderful: Aesthetics, Nature and Culture.* Washington, DC: Island Press, Sherwater Books, 1993.

——————. *Segmented Worlds and Self: Group Life and Individual Consciousness.* Minneapolis: University of Minnesota Press, 1982.

Underwood [Spenser], Paula. *The Walking People: Native American Oral History.* San Anselmo, CA: A Tribe of Two Press, 1993a.

——————. "Rule of Six." Occasional paper. Georgetown, TX: A Tribe of Two Press, 1993b.

Useem, John, and Ruth Hill Useem. "The Interfaces of a Binational Third Culture: A Study of the American Community in India." *Journal of Social Issues* 23, no. 1 (1967): 130–143.

Useem, Ruth Hill, and Richard D. Downie, "Third Culture Kids," in *Today's Education* (September–October 1967): 103–105.

——————, ed. *The Third Culture Children: An Annotated Bibliography.* East Lansing, MI: Institute for International Studies in Education, Michigan State University, 1975.

Valle, Ronald S., and Rolf Von Eckartsberg. *The Metaphors of Consciousness.* New York: Plenum Press, 1980.

Van Wolferen, Karel. *The Enigma of Japanese Power: People and Politics in a Stateless Nation.* London: Macmillan, 1989.

Vasconcelos, José. *La Raza cósmica: Misión de la raza iberoamericana, Argentina y Brasil,* 5th ed. México: Espasa-Calpe Mexicana, 1977.

Veloz, Josefina Estrada. *Chicana Identity: Gender and Ethnicity.* Ph.D. diss. New Mexico State University, 1981.

Vonnegut, Jr., Kurt. "Afterword," in Marlo Thomas, *Free to Be . . . You and Me.* New York: McGraw-Hill, 1974, p. 139.

Wagner, Roy. "Culture and Communication," in Michael Prosser, ed., *USIA Intercultural Communication Course: 1977 Proceedings.* Washington, DC: International Communication Agency of the United States of America, 1977.

Wallace, Anthony C. *Culture and Personality.* New York: Random House, 1963.

Wallace, Ronald L. *The Tribal Self: An Anthropologist Reflects on Hunting, Brain, and Behavior.* Lanham: University Press of America, 1991.

Warfield, J. "Fundamentals of Complexity." Draft paper. Fairfax, VA: Institute for Advanced Study in the Integrative Sciences, 219 Thompson Hall, George Mason University, 1987.

Warner, Marina. *Six Myths of Our Time: Little Angels, Little Monsters, Beautiful Beasts, and More.* New York: Vintage Books, 1995.

Wasilewski, Jacqueline Howell. *Roots of Resilience: Sources of Minority Energy and Power.* In preparation.

——————. *Effective Coping and Adaptation in Multiple Cultural Environments in the United States by Native, Hispanic, Black, and Asian Americans.* Ph.D. diss., University of Southern California, Los Angeles, 1982.

Waters, Mary C. *Ethnic Options: Choosing Identities in America.* Berkeley and Los Angeles: University of California Press, 1990.

Watts, Alan W. *The Book: On the Taboo Against Knowing Who You Are.* New York: Random House, 1989.

Weatherford, Jack. *Native Roots: How the Indians Enriched America.* New York: Ballantine Books, 1991.

——————. *Indian Givers: How the Indians of the Americas Transformed the World.* New York: Fawcett Columbine, 1988.

Wenders, Wim, with Yohji Yamamoto. *Notebook on Cities and Clothes.* Berlin: Road Movies Filmproduktion GmBH, 1989. Videocassette (80 min.), sd., col., c 1/2 in. English, with occasional subtitles for Japanese. Distributor: Connoisseur Video Collection, Santa Monica, CA.

Whitman, Walt. "Song of Myself," in *Leaves of Grass.* (Reprint of 1891–1892 version.) Mount Vernon, NY: Peter Pauper Press, 1944. See also Mitchell Stevens, ed. *Song of Myself.* Boston, MA: Shambhala, 1993.

Whorf, Benjamin Lee. *Language, Thought and Reality: Selected Writings of Benjamin Lee Whorf.* Ed. J. B. Carroll. Cambridge: MIT, 1964.

Wildavsky, Aaron. Cited in Charles J. Sykes, above.

Williams, John E., and Deborah L. Best. *Sex and Psyche: Gender and Self Viewed Cross-Culturally.* Newbury Park, CA: Sage, 1990.

Wilson, Anne. *Mixed Race Children: A Study of Identity.* London and Boston: Allen & Unwin, 1987.

Wolin, Steven, and Sybil Wolin. *The Resilient Self: How Survivors of Troubled Families Rise above Adversity.* New York: Villard, 1993.

Wright, Robert. *The Moral Animal: The New Science of Evolutionary Psychology.* New York: Pantheon Books, 1994.

Yamada, Nancy. *Between Parenting and Husband's Retirement: An In-Depth Study of Post-War Tokyo Housewives.* Master's thesis, Division of Comparative Culture. Tokyo: International Christian University, 1992.

Yankelovich, Daniel. *New Rules: Searching for Self-Fulfillment in a World Turned Upside Down.* New York: Random House, 1981.

Yetman, Norman R. *Majority and Minority: The Dynamics of Race and Ethnicity in American Life.* Newton, MA: Allyn & Bacon, 1985.

Yinger, J. Milton. *Ethnicity: Source of Strength? Source of Conflict?* Albany: State University of New York Press, 1994.

Yoshikawa, Muneo J. "The Double-Swing Model of Intercultural Communication between East and West," in D. Lawrence Kincaid, ed., *Communication Theory: Eastern and Western Perspectives.* San Diego, CA: Academic Press, 1987, 319–329.

Zack, Naomi. *Race and Mixed Race.* Philadelphia: Temple University Press, 1993.

Zaman, Kaiser. "In Search of Home," *Washington Post,* August 4, 1974, CI.

Index

A

Acculturation, 78–80
Actors. *See* Role playing
Adaptation, cultural, 67–68
Adler, Nancy, 141
Aesthetics, morals and, 170. *See also*
    Art; Beauty
African Americans. *See also* Race
    classification as, 40
    physical characteristics of, 42
Aguilar, Jerónimo de, 4, 30
America *See also* Art; Beauty
African Americans. *See also* Race
    classification as, 40
    physical characteristics of, 42
Aguilar, Jerónimo de, 4, 30
America. *See* United States
Americans, hyphenated, 56–57
Ancestors, 19
Ancestry, multicultural, 12
Anderson, Benedict, 26–27
Anglo culture, 75, 138–139
Animals, breeding of, 16
Anthropology
    multicultural studies by, 78–80
    societal comparisons and, 63–64
Appearance, and race, 42–43
Archetypes, 123
Aristotle, 198

Art, 165–166. *See also* Beauty
Aryan race, 43
Assigned roles, 99–100
Assumed roles, 99–100
Australian aboriginal groups, 98
Aztecs, 5–6

B

Bands, 13
Barth, John, 101
Bateson, Gregory, 62
Beauty
    blending with truth, 167–171
    as cultural mission, 164–167
    and race, 42–43
Beauty Way, 164–166
Behavior(s), 1–2
    eliciting changes in, 111–112
    language and, 45–46
    roles and, 96
    shared, 64
    social validation of, 45–46
    unusual, 84–87
Belongingness, multi-, 143–144
Bennett, Janet, 83
Bennett, Milton, 83, 176
Ben-Zeev, Sandra, 51–52
Beyond Culture (Hall), 129–130

Biases, cultural, 80
Biculturalism, consequences of, 73–74
Bicultural space, 79
Bilingual education, 48, 81–82
Bilingualism, 18, 49–51
  advantages of, 51–52
Biological diversity, 15–16
Biological self, 105
Biology
  adaptation and, 67–68
  race and, 42–43
  self and, 104
Blacks. *See* African-Americans
Blood types, and race, 41
Boas, Franz, 78
Body, self-image and, 37–43
Borderlanders (fronterizos), 75
Borman, Randy, 66–67
Borrowing, cultural, 63
Boundaries, 25–34
  body and, 37–43
  culture as, 61–70
  ethnicity as, 30–32
  kinship and, 14
  language and, 45–57
  nationality and, 26–30
  pressures on, 73–87
  village/city as, 32–34
Brazelton, T. Berry, 104
Breeding, animal, 16. *See also* Inter-
  breeding
British, as mixture of peoples, 12
Brooke, Peter, 119
Buber, Martin, 110

C

Campbell, Donald T., 81
Caucasians, physical characteristics of,
  42
Cisneros, Sandra, 131–132
Cities, multicultural nature of, 139.
  See also Village/city
City-states, 33

Clans, 13
Classical science cosmologies, 130–
  133
Clown, as self, 155
Cognitive complexity, 151–152
Communication, intercultural, 65,
  176
Community, nationality as, 28
Complex self, 114–115, 120–121,
  123
Confederation, as political form, 27
Conformity, multicultural attitudes
  and, 18–19
Consciousness, 104
Conscious self, 105
Constructive cultural marginality, 83
Contact cycle, 78–79, 80
Context, of language, 53–54
Coping strategies, 80–81
Cortés, Hernando, 4
Cosmic race, 38
Cosmologies, 125–135
  classical science, 130–133
  set spirituality systems and, 127–
    130
  spiritual and religious, 126–127
Cultural diversity, 16–17, 84
Cultural marginality, 83
Cultural relativism, 84
Culture(s). *See also* Monoculturalism;
    Multiculturalism; Society
  accommodating, 7–8
  as boundary, 61–70
  comparing societies and, 63–66
  in-between, 140–141
  language and, 5, 46
  movement of, 3–8
  multifaceted, 139
  perspectives on, 62
  pull of, 6
  role of, 67–70
  shared language and, 48
  traditions of expression and,
    132–133

D

Davies, Robertson, 132
Developing world, Western World and, 154
Diaspora, 12
Dictionary, multicultural people described in, 54–55
Dillard, Annie, 150, 163
Disease metaphors, 78, 80–81
Diversity
  biological, 15–16
  cultural, 16–17, 84
Dominant self, 114–115
Doña Marina. *See* Malinche
Drama, in life, 150
Dream, life as, 152
Drives, 68
Dynamic constructs, 154–155
Dynasties, 26, 27
Dysfunctional behavior, 85

E

Education, bilingual, 48, 81–82. *See also* Foreign language instruction
Eisley, Loren, 151
Empire, 26
Encapsulated cultural marginality, 83
Endangered species, 16
English language, 48
Epistemology. *See* Truth
Ethics. *See also* Values
  beauty and, 164–167
  truth and, 162–164
Ethnicity, 30–32
  conflict and, 31–32
  nationality and, 28
Experience, shared, 64

F

Families, 13–14
Family names, 14

Fantini, Alvino, 19
Findhorn, community at, 128–129
Firmat, Gustavo Pérez, 57
Fitzgerald, Thomas, 198–199
Fletcher, James, 112
Foreign language instruction, 47
Freud, Anna, 78

G

Game, life as, 155–156
Geertz, Clifford, 46
Gender, 191
Generations, multicultural attitudes and, 17
Genetics, 15–16
  animal breeding and, 16
  and blood types, 41
Globalization, diversity and, 19
God, search for, 126–127
Goffman, Erving, 113–114
Gordon, Edmund, 19
Grooks I (Hein), 164
Group identity, 26
Grow or Die (Lockland), 131
Guerrero, Gonzalo, 4–5

H

Hage, Jerald, 114, 120, 123
Half-bloods, 101
Hamaguchi, Eshun, 169
Hamill, Sam, 166
Hammonds, Beryl, 100
Harris, G. G., 104, 105
Harris, LaDonna, 133
Hein, Piet, 164
Hendershott, Carmen, 128–129
Henry, William A., III, 7
Hillerman, Tony, 164–165
Hindu psychology, 170–171
Holonic Paradigm Research Institute, 110
Honda, 142
Honne, 113–114

Hopi people, 97
Hundertwasser, F., 19
Hyphenated Americans, 56–57
Hysteria, 85

I

Identification, and shared language,
    48
Identities
    culture and, 69–70
    ethnic, 30–32
    formation of, 198–199
    group, 26
    hyphenated Americans and, 56–57
    "in-between," 111
    kinship and, 14
    language and, 55
    multiple, 143–144
    nationality and, 26–30
    personal metaphors and, 177–182
    roles and, 101–104
    village/city and, 32–34
Images
    body and, 37–43
    novel, 150–151
Images of Organization (Morgan), 199
Imagination, 151–153
    exotic visions and, 149
    of self, 134–135
"In-between" cultures, 140–141
"In-between" identity, 111
India, movement from, 12
Indians, Mexican, 6. See also Native
    Americans
Individuals, multifaceted, 138. See also
    Self
Innovation, cultural, 63
Intelligence
    bilingualism and, 50
    Sternberg on, 199
Interbreeding, 11–14
Intercultural communication, 65, 176
Intermarriage, 12–13, 143
    Indian-white, 102–103
    in New World, 39–40

Iroquois League, 27
Iyer, Pico, 29

J

Janssen-Matthes, Mieke, 65
Japan, 98
    kejime in, 113
    liminal being in, 141–144
    metaphors from, 183–189
    music in, 167–168
    roles in, 117
    self in, 106
    social systems in, 169–170
Japanese people, roles of, 99
Jekyll-Hyde phenomenon, 97
Jews, movement of, 12

K

Kawai, Yoshiko, 114
Kejime, 113
Kelly, George, 151
Kiernan, V. G., 12
Kingston, Maxine Hong, 126
Kinship, 13–14
Kishima, Takako, 141
Kittay, Eva Feder, 198
Knowledge, search for, 153–156
Koster, Jolene, 140–141
Kunugi, Tatsuro, 170
Kurds (Turkey), 29

L

Labels, 14, 18
    culture and, 69–70. See also
        Metaphors
Lado, Robert, 49
Language(s), 5, 45–57. See also
        Bilingualism; Metaphors
    and identity, 55
    obscure, 8–9
    shred, 48
    thinking in, 52–53

Lawrence, T. E. (Lawrence of Arabia), 73–74
Liebline, A. J., 20, 33–34
Life, as game, 155–156
Liminal being, 141–144
Living by Fiction (Dillard), 163
Lockland, George, 131
Lone Ranger attitude, 106
Lorenz, Konrad, 85
Lummis, C. Douglas, 25n, 84

M

Malinche, 5–6
Maori, 75–76
Marginal man, 83, 141
Marriages, mixed-race. *See* Intermarriage
Martínez, Oscar, 75
Masuda, Yoneji, 143
Mayans, 4–5, 6
McNeill, W. H., 170
"Me." *See* Self
Mechanical/structural metaphors, 130–131
Metaphors
  disease, 78, 80–81
  exotic visions and, 149–151
  of imagination, 151–153
  from Japan, 183–189
  mechanical/structural, 130–131
  for multifaceted self, 123–124
  personal, 175–182
  personal uniqueness as, 137–139
  of pure process, 133–134
  use of, 197–199
  "You Tonto, me Lone Ranger," 78–79
Metaphors of Identity: A Culture-Communication Dialogue (Fitzgerald), 199
Mexican Americans, 75
Mexican Indians, 6. *See also* Native Americans

Mexico, 4–7
  culture of, 138–139
  languages in, 4–6, 8–9
Migration, stress and, 76–77
Minority groups, 31
Missions, truth and beauty as, 161–167
Mixed-bloods, 101
Mixed-race marriages, 12–13. *See also* Intermarriage
Miyanaga, Kuniko, 191
Modernization, 78
Monoculturalism, limitations of, 20, 86
Morals, aesthetics and, 170. *See also* Ethics; Values
Morgan, Gareth, 199
Movement of peoples, 3–8, 11–12
  traditions of, 132–133
Multicultural ancestry, 12
Multiculturalism. *See also* Mexico; United States
  conformity and, 18–19
  dictionary descriptions of, 54–55
  education and, 81–82
  generational attitudes and, 17
  role playing and, 93–106
  stress of, 75–82
  in Timbuktu, 6–7
  urbanization and, 76–77
  valuing, 17–20
Multicultural people
  cognitive complexity and, 151–152
  reality and, 151
Multicultural space, 79
Multifaceted cultures, 139
  intercultural space and, 140–141
Multifaceted individuals, 138
Multilingualism, 47–48
Multiple socialization, 66–67
Murdock, George, 64
Music, 167–169
Mutations, 15–16
Mysterious, need for, 150
Mythology, 125–126

N

Names, family, 14
Nationality, identity and, 26–30
Nation of Victims, A (Sykes), 100
Nation-states, 26, 27
  ethnic lines and, 30
  modern, 27
Native Americans, 27
  ancestry from, 40
  classification as, 40–41
  intermarriage of, 102–103
  stress of, 76
Navajo, Beauty Way of, 164–165
Needs, behavior and, 64–65
Negro. *See* African-Americans
New Age community, 128–129
New World
  intermarriage in, 39–40
  Spaniards in, 4–6
New York City, 139
New Zealand, 75–76
Ní Dhomhnaill, Nuala, 53
Nonverbal language, 45–46

O

Objective truth, 162–164
Obligatory self, 114
Official languages, 48
Oguss, Karl, 86
Olebe, Margaret, 140–141
"One-drop" rule, 40
Organic systems, 131–133
Organization, political, 26–28
Ortega y Gasset, José, 138
Outline of the Study of Acculturation
  (Redfield), 79
Outsiders, 144

P

Paradigms, 176
Park, Robert, 78
Patriotism, 28

Perception, 159–171
  assumptions about, 182–183
Pereda, Victor, 12
Personae, 116–117
Personality
  consistency of, and roles, 94–95
  personae and, 116–117
Personal metaphors, 175–182
Perspectives
  multicultural, 19, 20
  perception and, 161
Physical characteristics, and race, 42
Physical features, 32
Pickens, Stuart, 162–163, 165
Pike, Kenneth, 82
Pluralism. *See* Multiculturalism
Polite fiction (*tatemae*), 114
Political organization, 26–28
Polyphony. *See* Beauty; Music
Powers, Charles H., 114, 120, 123
Presentation of Self in Everyday Life,
  The (Goffman), 113–114
Price, Reynolds, 100
"Primitive" peoples, and urbanized
  people, 78–79
Process, metaphors of, 133–134
Psychology, Hindu, 170–171
Pueblo Indian culture, 138–139

Q

Quests. *See* Missions

R

Race. *See also* Intermarriage; Labels
  as biological construct, 42–43
  blood types and, 41
  classifications by, 40
  concept of, 38–43
  mixing of, 12–13
  selective nature of, 39–41
  as social construct, 38–39
Rat colony, at Findhorn, 128–129

Reality
    language and, 53–54
    nature of, 164
Redfield, Robert, 78, 79
Relationships. *See* Kinship
Relativity, cultural, 68–69
Religious cosmologies, 126–127
Rhinesmith, Stephen, 67
Role playing, 93–106
Roles, 1–2
    assigned vs. assumed, 99–100
    "authentic self" and, 109–121
    behaviors and, 96
    daily, 95–100
    identity and, 101–104
    Jekyll-Hyde phenomenon and, 97
    new, 115–116
    personae and, 116–117
    redefinition and negotiation in,
        114
    scripts for, 115–116
    set design and, 117
    social vs. self, 112–115
    subtleties of, 97–98
    switching among multiple, 96–97
Rural life, vs. urban life, 76–77
Rushdie, Salman, 193
Ryan, Paul, 153

S

Sapir, Edward, 53
Schizophrenia, 86–87
Schools. *See* Education
Science, and truth, 163
Scripts. *See* Roles
Second language, 9. *See also* Bilingual-
    ism
Secular practices, religious values and,
    129
Seelye, H. Ned, 49, 192–193
Self
    authentic, 93–95, 109–121
    biological, 105
    conscious, 105

culture and, 69–70
defined, 103–104
kinds of, 114–115
nationality and, 29
personal metaphors and, 177–182
personal uniqueness and, 137–139
roles, identity, and, 101–104
search for, 153–156
social, 105–106
Self-image, body and, 37–43
Sheed, Wilfred, 100
Singer, Marshall, 142
Situational self, 114–115
Slaves. *See* African-Americans
Social dynamics, shared, 64–65
Socialization
    drives and, 68
    multicultural, 138–139
    multiple, 66–67, 75–82
Social self, 105–106
Social systems, in Japan, 169–170
Society. *See also* Race
    comparing, 63–66
    context of language and, 53–54
    language and, 45–46
    mental aberration and, 87
    roles in, 112–113
Sound systems, 49
Space, of multicultural people, 78–79
Spaniards, conquests of, 4–7
Speech. *See* Language(s)
Spiritual cosmologies, 126–127
Spirituality, values and, 127–128
Split personality, 101–102
Spoken language, 45, 46–54. *See also*
    Language(s)
Steinmetz, Charles Proteus, 151
Sternberg, Robert, 199
Stonequist, Everett V., 83, 141
Stress, of multiculturalism, 82. *See also*
    Multiculturalism
Subcultural groups, 69
Subjective truth, 164
Survival, culture and, 68
Sykes, Charles, 100

T

T'ai chi ch'uan, 133
Taita people (Kenya), 154
Takamatsu, Kuniko, 142
Tatemae, 113–114
Terminology, dictionary definitions
  and, 54–55
Theater, traditions of, 118–120
Thinking, languages and, 52–53
Timbuktu, 6–7
Travel, 7
Třeštik, Dušan, 27–28
Tribes, 27
True feeling (*honne*), 114
Truth
  blending with beauty, 167–171
  as cultural mission, 162–164
  subjective vs. objective, 162–164
Tuan, Yi-Fu, 94–95
Turtle Clan, 13

U

Uniqueness, personal, 137–139
United States. *See also* New World
  borderlanders and, 75
  as confederation, 27
  culture of, 7
  hyphenated Americans in, 56–57
  multicultural ancestry in, 12–13
  official language in, 48
Urbanization
  multiculturalism and, 139
  stress of, 76–77
Useem, Ruth, 140

V

Values, 69. *See also* Culture; Ethics;
  Morals
  spirituality and, 127–128

Verbal language, 45, 46–54. *See also*
  Language(s)
Victims, roles and, 99–100
Village/city, identity and, 32–34
Virtual reality, and self, 156
Vocabulary, bilingualism and, 51
Vonnegut, Kurt, Jr., 68–69

W

Wasilewski, Jacqueline Howell, 116,
  167, 191–192
Wenders, Wim, 119
Western world
  developing world and, 154
  truth in, 165
White people, 42. *See also* Anglo
  culture
Whorf, Benjamin, 53, 87
Wildavsky, Aaron, 99
*Woman Warrior, The: Memoirs of a
  Girlhood among Ghosts*
  (Kingston), 126
World War II
  as liminal event, 142
  migration and, 76, 77–78
Wright, Robert, 63–64, 65

Y

Yamada, Nancy, 191
Yoshikawa, Muneo, 110–111
"You Tonto, me Lone Ranger"
  metaphor, 78–79
Yucatán, 4–5

About the Authors

H. Ned Seelye has lived, studied, and worked for some 20 years outside the country of his birth. His master's degree thesis for la Universidad de San Carlos de Guatemala centered on U.S. citizens' acculturation in that country. In the United States, he worked for the Illinois Department of Public Instruction, first as a state foreign language supervisor and subsequently as the agency's first state director of bilingual education. He was associate professor of anthropology and sociology at George Williams College (Downers Grove, IL), executive director of the Spanish Education Development Center (Washington, DC), and president of International Resource Development, Inc. (LaGrange, IL). Seelye has been elected twice to the governing board of the Society for International Education, Training, and Research. He has taught in universities in seven countries and is listed in *Who's Who in International Education.*

Seelye's cultural antecedents are Celtic-Anglo: his mother was Welsh (the granddaughter of Welsh immigrants to Pennsylvania), and his father was Anglo with, over the previous nine generations, some Scots and Irish mixed in for spice. The first Seeley in North America, Robert, arrived from England

233

in 1630. (The spelling was changed several generations later to Seelye by an ancestor of the author.) The Briton paternal line, prior to moving to America, is descended from 10th century Normans (themselves a mixture of Scandinavian and Frank), a descendant of whom accompanied William the Conqueror on his conquest of England in 1066. Over the next five centuries, his paternal line mixed with an amalgamation of Anglo-Saxon, Danish, and Celtic stocks. Long before, his ancestors were successful nomadic hunters and gatherers on several continents.

Seelye was socialized as a child and early adolescent in Pennsylvania German country while it was still under Puritan influences (no movies on Sunday, for example). His socialization continued as a mid-adolescent and young man in Hispanic traditions, in places such as Mexico, Cuba, Dominican Republic, Puerto Rico, and Guatemala, in Anglo-Saxon traditions in places such as Utah, California, and Pennsylvania, and in Cajan French-Hispanic-Anglo-Scots-Irish-Black traditions in Louisiana. He lived for several years in Italy. He currently resides in Albuquerque, New Mexico. He is bilingual in English and Spanish and sometimes functional in Portuguese and Italian.

Jacqueline Howell Wasilewski is associate professor of international communication, International Christian University (Tokyo, Japan), a position she has held since 1990. Her doctoral dissertation for the University of Southern California focused on coping strategies that minority people in U.S. society (Native Americans, Hispanic, Black, and Asian) use to manage their multiculturalism. She speaks French, German, some Spanish, a little New Guinea Tok Pisin, and is learning Japanese.

Her multicultural experience began in an Irish, French-Canadian, English, Welsh, Cherokee, Danish, Swiss family growing up between Anglo, Hispanic, and Indian cultures in the Southwestern United States. It continued as a student in Austria, as the daughter-in-law in a Polish-Lithuanian family from Pennsylvania whose son received his doctorate in geophysics from the University of Tokyo, and as a consultant on intercultural relations and multicultural education projects in the United States, Ecuador, and Papua New Guinea. She has worked for many organizations, including the Spanish Education Development Center, the World Bank, the Ministry of Education of Papua New Guinea, and Americans for Indian Opportunity. After eight years in "Indian Country, USA" she accepted her present post in Japan.

Wasilewski is currently President of the Society for Intercultural Education, Training and Research (SIETAR International).

TITLES OF INTEREST IN
BUSINESS AND INTERNATIONAL BUSINESS

HOW TO CREATE HIGH-IMPACT BUSINESS PRESENTATIONS, by Joyce Kupsh and Pat Graves
EFFECTIVE BUSINESS DECISION MAKING, by William F. O'Dell
HOW TO GET PEOPLE TO DO THINGS YOUR WAY, by J. Robert Parkinson
HANDBOOK FOR MEMO WRITING, by L. Sue Baugh
HANDBOOK FOR BUSINESS WRITING, by L. Sue Baugh, Maridell Fryar, and David A. Thomas
HANDBOOK FOR PROOFREADING, by Laura Killen Anderson
HANDBOOK FOR TECHNICAL WRITING, James Shelton
HOW TO BE AN EFFECTIVE SPEAKER, by Christina Stuart
FORMAL MEETINGS, by Alice N. Pohl
COMMITTEES AND BOARDS, by Alice N. Pohl
MEETINGS: RULES AND PROCEDURES, by Alice N. Pohl
BIG MEETINGS, BIG RESULTS, by Tom McMahon
HOW TO GET THE MOST OUT OF TRADE SHOWS, by Steve Miller
HOW TO GET THE MOST OUT OF SALES MEETINGS, by James Dance
A BASIC GUIDE TO EXPORTING, by U.S. Department of Commerce
A BASIC GUIDE TO IMPORTING, by U.S. Customs Service
CULTURE CLASH, by Ned Seelye and Alan Seelye-James
DOING BUSINESS IN RUSSIA, by ALM Consulting, Frere Chomeley Bischoff, and KPMG Peat Marwick
THE GLOBAL MARKETING IMPERATIVE, by Michael Czinkota, Ilkka Ronkainen and John Tarrant
THE INTERNATIONAL BUSINESS BOOK, by Vincent Guy and John Matlock
INTERNATIONAL BUSINESS CULTURE SERIES, by Peggy Kenna and Sondra Lacy
INTERNATIONAL HERALD TRIBUNE: DOING BUSINESS IN TODAY'S WESTERN EUROPE, by Alan Tillier
INTERNATIONAL HERALD TRIBUNE: GUIDE TO EUROPE, by Alan Tillier and Roger Beardwood
INTERNATIONAL HERALD TRIBUNE: GUIDE TO BUSINESS TRAVEL IN ASIA, by Robert K. McCabe
DOING BUSINESS WITH CHINA
MARKETING TO CHINA, by Xu Bai-Yi
THE JAPANESE INFLUENCE ON AMERICA, by Boye De Mente
JAPANESE ETIQUETTE & ETHICS IN BUSINESS, by Boye De Mente
CHINESE ETIQUETTE & ETHICS IN BUSINESS, by Boye De Mente
KOREAN ETIQUETTE & ETHICS IN BUSINESS, by Boye De Mente

For further information or a current catalog, write:
NTC Business Books
a division of NTC *Publishing Group*
4255 West Touhy Avenue
Lincolnwood, Illinois 60646–1975